Dec 17/04
Sharon

INSTRUMENTS OF MURDER

Also by Max Haines

Bothersome Bodies

Calendar of Criminal Capers

Crime Flashback #1

Crime Flashback #2

Crime Flashback #3

The Murderous Kind

Murder & Mayhem

The Collected Works of Max Haines Vol. 1

That's Life

True Crime Stories

True Crime Stories Book II

True Crime Stories Book III

True Crime Stories Book IV

The Collected Works of Max Haines Vol. 2

True Crime Stories Book V

Doctors Who Kill

Multiple Murderers

Multiple Murderers II

Celebrity Murders

The Collected Works of Max Haines Vol. 3

Murders Strange But True

Canadian Crimes

Murder Most Foul

The Collected Works of Max Haines Vol. 4

Unnatural Causes

INSTRUMENTS OF MURDER

MAX HAINES

VIKING
CANADA

VIKING CANADA

Published by the Penguin Group

Penguin Group (Canada), 10 Alcorn Avenue, Toronto, Ontario, Canada M4V 3B2
(a division of Pearson Penguin Canada Inc.)

Penguin Group (USA) Inc., 375 Hudson Street, New York, New York 10014, U.S.A.
Penguin Books Ltd, 80 Strand, London WC2R 0RL, England
Penguin Ireland, 25 St Stephen's Green, Dublin 2, Ireland (a division of Penguin Books Ltd)
Penguin Group (Australia), 250 Camberwell Road, Camberwell, Victoria 3124, Australia
(a division of Pearson Australia Group Pty Ltd)
Penguin Books India Pvt Ltd, 11 Community Centre, Panchsheel Park, New Delhi – 110 017, India
Penguin Group (NZ), Cnr Airborne and Rosedale Roads, Albany, Auckland, New Zealand
(a division of Pearson New Zealand Ltd)
Penguin Books (South Africa) (Pty) Ltd, 24 Sturdee Avenue, Rosebank, Johannesburg 2196, South Africa

Penguin Books Ltd, Registered Offices: 80 Strand, London WC2R 0RL, England

First published 2004

1 2 3 4 5 6 7 8 9 10 (FR)

Publisher's note: This book is a work of fiction. Names, characters, places and incidents either are the product of the author's imagination or are used fictitiously, and any resemblance to actual persons living or dead, events, or locales is entirely coincidental.

Manufactured in Canada.

LIBRARY AND ARCHIVES CANADA CATALOGUING IN PUBLICATION

Haines, Max
Instruments of murder / Max Haines.

ISBN 0-670-04480-6

1. Murder. 2. Weapons. I. Title.

HV6515.H3565 2004 364.152'3 C2004-904579-2

For Carley Star

Acknowledgments

Many individuals and organizations have contributed greatly to this book. I am particularly indebted to the Ontario Provincial Police, Scotland Yard and the FBI. I am also grateful to the wardens and other officials of several prisons who gave of their time and insight.

My thanks to the following people whose contributions to this effort are incalculable: Irv Borchiver, John Clark, Marshall Cohen, Susan Dugas, Clarissa Feliprada, Dr. Al Gold, Jillian Goddard, Dr. Jack Holtzman, Julie Hornby, Dr. Elliot Hudes, Bob Johnson, Julie Kirsch, Selena Ladd, Mel Lefton, Bob Levy, Bill Mausser, Jerry Mortfield, Phil Myerson, John Newsom, Jack Pinkus, Ted Richmond, Nathan Rosenberg, Al Shukster, Ubby Spiegel, Glenna Tapscott, Joyce Wagler, Gerry Waldston and Kathy Webb Nelson.

This book would not have been possible without the dedication of co-editors Glenn Garnett and Liba Berry.

My gratitude to my daughters, Susan, Maureen and Eleanor, whose years of encouragement have kept me focused. A special thanks to my wife, Marilyn, whose contributions have been immeasurable.

CONTENTS

Kurt & Ursula Adomeit

(AXE)

GEORG RICHER, 19, made a big play for the most attractive girl in the village. Thirteen-year-old Ursula was one of those blond, blue-eyed German girls who caused pulses to race and heads to turn. The little village of Emslage-Ruehlerfeld, located near the German–Holland border, was home to other pretty girls, but Ursula was different. She looked 21 and had the figure of a silicone-enhanced movie star.

Once Georg was successful in seducing Ursula, she took to sex like Moll Flanders took to haymows. Ursula soon found herself checking and rechecking the calendar. There was no doubt about it—she was more than somewhat pregnant.

Little Anja came into the world only a few months after her parents married. Within the next four years, three more daughters blessed the union. Anja was followed by Kathi, Alexandra and Petra. The expanding family did not come about by accident, nor was Georg the instigator. No, Ursula was the aggressive lovemaking partner of the pair. In fact, Georg was tired most of the time. The poor man hardly got any sleep.

While having a schnapps in a bar one night, Georg met 19-year-old Kurt Adomeit. We will never know what Georg had in mind when he invited Kurt, a truck driver by profession, to move in to the Richer home. Now, it would be remiss of me not to point out that Kurt had the looks of a Greek god, complete with muscles and, we can only assume, the necessary auxiliary equipment.

Georg may have invited the new roomer into his home for financial reasons, but it isn't a stretch to imagine that he welcomed what he suspected would inevitably happen. Sure as God made little green apples, Ursula and Kurt commenced doing it at every opportunity. And tongues wagged in the village.

You can just imagine the gossip when, on June 6, 1972, Ursula travelled to Meppen, the closest town, and reported her loving husband missing. The local police didn't have to be staffed with a Hercule Poirot to come to several conclusions. Ursula and Kurt were lovers. Georg Richer loved his four daughters and would never desert them. Once their little grey cells started percolating, police felt that it was quite possible that murder most foul had taken place, but, darn it all, they had no proof that any crime had been committed.

Two days after the missing persons report was filed, Meppen police received word that a vehicle belonging to Georg Richer had been found submerged in a pond in the village of Neuringe, right on the Dutch border. Was it possible that he was alive and had attempted to get rid of his car before crossing the border into Holland? On the other hand, it was always possible that his killer had planted the car to make it appear that Georg had fled the country. The vehicle was returned to Meppen, but the only other information garnered from the auto was that Georg hadn't been submerged with it.

Months passed. Police explored every lead that could connect Ursula and Kurt to the missing Georg Richer. Despite their strong suspicions, they could find nothing concrete connecting the pair to the missing man. A year passed before Ursula filed for divorce on the grounds of desertion. The divorce was granted without delay.

The lovers used discretion in public. It was rumoured that Ursula's four young daughters had accepted Kurt as their father. A year after the divorce and two years after Georg's disappearance, Kurt and Ursula officially tied the knot. The four Richer children, ranging in age from four to nine, were bridesmaids at the wedding.

Another year passed. The police had made a habit of keeping tabs on the two suspects. Rumours reached them that Ursula was stepping out at night when her truck-driver husband was out of town. While on one of his trips, Kurt was arrested in Osnabrueck for peddling drugs. He confessed to selling the drugs in several judicial districts and was brought back to Meppen, where he was put in jail.

Detectives, who well remembered the disappearance of Georg Richer, decided to take advantage of Kurt's one weakness. Unlike husband number one, Kurt was extremely jealous of his overactive wife. The police decided to plant a detective, posing as a drunk, in Kurt's cell. The imposter would attempt to elicit incriminating information from the suspect.

It didn't take long. The detective bragged that he had met one of the sexiest women in the country in the village of Emslage-Ruehlerfeld at a bar named the Black Lamb. Kurt asked about the woman's name. The detective said he didn't know her last name, but was sure her first name was Ursula. Kurt saw red. He became violent and had to be restrained by guards. Then he blurted out the entire story of his unfaithful wife. He told the police that he shouldn't have expected anything better, because Ursula had cheated on her first husband so that she could bed down with him.

The time was ripe. His interrogators told Kurt that they knew he and Ursula had killed Georg and buried his body. They urged him to unburden his guilty conscience. Kurt turned pale. He didn't realize that the police had nothing on him. All he had to do was keep quiet and Georg's murder would remain unsolved forever. Kurt slumped into a chair and exclaimed, "I'll show you where the body is buried."

On July 1, 1975, Kurt led police to the skeletal remains of Georg Richer. He told investigators that Georg had not been a jealous man and had probably known that he and Ursula were having a prolonged affair. Perhaps he had even been relieved that someone else was helping out in the lovemaking department.

Kurt told police that Ursula had put sleeping tablets in Georg's tea. Unfortunately, for the collaborators, the drug didn't even make the intended victim sleepy. Frustrated, Ursula put a whole jar of tablets in Georg's tea. Again, they had absolutely no effect. Undaunted, Ursula purchased rat poison. She put large quantities of poison in Georg's food, only to be told that her cooking had greatly improved. Kurt claimed that he had told Ursula to give up; Georg was proving to be too difficult to kill. Besides, he thought she should attempt to obtain a divorce, but Ursula was adamant—Georg had to go.

On May 13, 1972, Kurt had returned home around 10 P.M. The girls were already in bed. She gave the hatchet to Kurt with the pointed suggestion, "Now is the time to do it. He's asleep." Kurt did as he was told. He struck the sleeping man with all his might. "His head sort of exploded," Kurt told the police.

Ursula cleaned the blood from the bedclothes and the floor of the bedroom. Together, she and Kurt drove to the forest and buried poor Georg. Kurt admitted that he had driven Georg's car to the Dutch border and into a pond to lead police to believe that Georg had left the country. He had then caught a bus back to Meppen.

Ursula was advised of Kurt's confession. Initially she denied any involvement, but soon broke down and told all. She added that lust and sin had not been the motive behind the crime and was able to prove that Georg had often beaten her severely.

The evidence of wife beating had some effect on the German court. In 1973, Ursula and Kurt Adomeit were found guilty of second-degree murder and were sentenced to the relatively light term of ten years each in prison.

Lee Andrews

(GUN)

NO ONE HAD A BAD WORD to say about Lee Andrews. Why should they? After all, around Grandview, Kansas, he was reputedly a bright boy with an even brighter future.

Lee graduated from high school with the highest marks ever achieved by a Kansas student. His IQ was in the near-genius category. After entering the University of Kansas, Lee became an honours student. For relaxation, he played the bassoon in the university band.

Like many big men, Lee was kind and gentle. At over 6 feet and 260 pounds, he was an imposing figure in the tiny community. He regularly accompanied his parents and his sister, Jenny, to the Grandview Baptist Church. Lee often had long chats with his minister, the Reverend V.D. Dameron. They discussed religion and world events. Reverend Dameron, who was Lee's father's best friend, often remarked that everyone should be blessed with a son like Lee Andrews.

Who knows when Lee Andrews first decided that there were pursuits in life other than scholastic ones. In hindsight, the germ of the idea was probably planted in his mind when his parents' home was burglarized. Big Lee figured that with brains and imagination he could plan and carry out the perfect crime. Why wander further afield than his own family? His parents always had a couple of thousand dollars in their bank account. Then there was the 250-acre spread his father owned. Lee figured it had to be worth $50,000. If his parents were to die suddenly, he and Jenny would inherit their entire estate. Of course, if Jenny were to die at the same time, Lee would be sole heir.

For months, the ideal son fantasized about killing his family, inheriting their worldly goods and leading the good life. Right off, he would purchase a car and clothing; not jeans or T-shirts, but made-to-measure suits. He would quit university and travel the world. There would be no clues. This would be the perfect murder.

Lee considered poisoning his family but dismissed the idea as too risky. No, he would shoot them and fake a robbery. The police would be no match for him. As the only surviving member of the family, not counting the family dog, he would be the recipient of much sympathy. It was ironic. His parents had given him a .22 repeater rifle last Christmas to go with his German Luger. He would snuff out their lives with their Christmas present. Lee figured the very best time to kill his family would be during the Thanksgiving break, when he would be home from school.

On Friday, November 28, 1958, Lee prepared to commit the triple murder. As he talked to his father that afternoon, he idly glanced out the living-room window. He noticed that the bread man had made a delivery to a neighbour and was slowly making his way to the Andrews home to deliver the usual weekend supply. How silly, thought Lee. There would be no one alive to eat the bread. He ran outside and told the bread man that they wouldn't be requiring their usual delivery that weekend.

Thanksgiving dinner went off without a hitch. Lee's dad made a mini speech, saying how happy he was to have his family together for Thanksgiving. Lee kept waiting for an excuse to leave the room. Just as he was about to leave, his mother started to clear the dishes. This was no good at all. For his particular purposes, Lee wanted all the members of his family to be together. At last, his mother and Jenny joined him and his father in the living room.

Lee got up, excused himself and went to his bedroom. He loaded his .22 rifle and silently placed the Luger in his pocket. His plan was now in motion. To simulate a burglary, he pushed out his screen and opened the window. Then he opened the drawers of his dresser. The young boy with the bright future proceeded to the living room, his purpose clear, his mind unclouded. The killings were well planned.

In the living room, Jenny watched as her mother adjusted the controls of the TV. Mr. Andrews was engrossed in the daily paper. No one paid attention to Lee. He stood in the doorway and calmly slammed four slugs into his mother. She died instantly. Jenny turned. Lee fired three times. One of the slugs smashed into Jenny's brain, killing her before she crumpled to the floor. Mr. Andrews managed to rise and move into the kitchen before bullets entered his back. He staggered. Lee followed, firing as he went until his father sprawled dead on the floor. Standing over his father, Lee fired into his body again and again. An autopsy later revealed that the dead man had been shot seventeen times. The house became deadly quiet.

Calmly following his plan, Lee drove his father's car to the Kaw River and threw his two guns into the water. He smiled as he heard the splash. So much for incriminating weapons.

Lee continued to his room at the University of Kansas in Lawrence. He spoke to his landlady, being careful to mention that he was there to pick up his typewriter and that it had taken him a long time to get there due to icy road conditions. That took care of one witness who would place him in Lawrence at the time of the murders, but you couldn't be too sure in this business. Lee took in a movie called *Mardi Gras* and talked for some time to a girl behind the confectionery counter. On the way home, he purchased gasoline, making sure to get a receipt. That should do it for alibi witnesses.

Lee arrived home about 1 A.M. He called police, who arrived at the house about ten minutes later. They found Lee sitting in the sunroom, petting the family dog. When the police inquired as to the nature of the emergency call, Lee didn't say anything. He just nodded toward the living room. Inside the house were the bodies of the Andrews family.

Police turned to Lee. The bright boy with the bright future didn't realize that most people who stumble on the bodies of their sister and parents are usually upset. Lee was as cool as a cucumber. He related his story without shedding a tear: he had had Thanksgiving dinner with his family, had gone to Lawrence to pick up a typewriter, had taken in a movie and had filled the family car with gas on his way home. He volunteered that burglars must have entered the house through his bedroom window.

Investigators followed Lee to his bedroom. They expected to find the room in shambles. Instead, they noticed that while Lee's dresser drawers were pulled out, nothing had been scattered about the room. This was the tidiest burglary the police had ever encountered. They were also surprised to learn that nothing had been stolen from the house.

The big lumbering boy didn't seem to care that his entire family had been murdered. It wasn't natural. The police questioned Lee in detail about his activities. He told them that he had been to Lawrence—his landlady would verify that. He had taken in a movie—the girl at the confectionery counter would verify that. He had purchased gas on the way home. Sure, he had a receipt.

It was all too much. The boy had left so many tracks a Boy Scout could have traced his movements. Lee was informed that he was a prime suspect in the triple murder. When he was taken to jail, he asked to speak to his father's best friend, Reverend Dameron. In minutes, the minister was brought up to date on the crime. Like police, he was amazed at Lee's nonchalant demeanour.

Lee had not planned it this way, not at all. Reverend Dameron seemed to be as suspicious as the police. It was obvious that he believed that Lee had committed the murders. When the reverend asked, "You didn't do it, did you?" Lee replied in his usual calm manner, "Yes, I did." Now that Lee had confessed to the murders, his minister pressed him for his motive until the boy admitted that he had wanted his family's money.

The entire town of Grandview attended the Andrews funeral. Lee wasn't one of their number. Throughout his incarceration and trial, he remained calm and collected. His lawyers attempted to prove that he was insane at the time he committed the murders and that he had acted impulsively. The State produced the bread man, who testified that Lee had cancelled the usual weekend bread delivery on the afternoon of the murders. Only Lee knew there would be no one alive at the Andrews home after the Thanksgiving Day meal.

Lee was convicted of the murders of his family and was sentenced to death. He never displayed any remorse for what he had done. On November 30, 1962, 22-year-old Lee Andrews was hanged at Lansing Prison.

William Dale Archerd

(INSULIN)

WILLIAM DALE ARCHERD WAS BORN IN ARKANSAS. He left his father's ranch at the age of 15 to wander the Midwest, taking odd jobs to keep body and soul together. By the time he was 17, he had gravitated to hospital work, obtaining employment as a hospital attendant. At that early age, he married the first of his seven wives. The marriage lasted four years. His second marriage was even less successful and ended after two years.

While employed in Oakland in the 1940s, Archerd met yet another young lady, who quickly became wife number three. Unfortunately, he and his new bride encountered some difficulty when they were apprehended with heroin in their possession. This little caper resulted in Archerd spending three years in San Quentin after his good wife testified against him.

Upon his release from prison, Archerd drifted from job to job. It is believed that for the next twenty years this tall, handsome man with the shock of thick white hair became a killing machine. His implements of death were insulin and a hypodermic needle. Archerd had become something of an expert on the effects of insulin while employed as a hospital attendant.

In 1947, Archerd was employed at the Kaiser Hospital in Fontana, California, when a friend of his, 34-year-old William Jones, was rushed to hospital in a coma. Ten hours later, Jones died of insulin shock, although insulin had not been prescribed for him. At the time, the death was considered puzzling, but no official action was taken. It would be twenty years before authorities would delve into Jones's death and discover that Archerd had profited by $10,000 from his friend's demise.

On May 14, 1956, Archerd's marriage to wife number three was annulled. The very next day he married Zella Winders. Within a week, he was looting his new wife's bank account. It took only a few days for the well to run dry. Archerd called police and told them a fantastic story. He claimed that two robbers had entered his home and injected him and Zella with a hypodermic needle, after which they took off with about $500 in cash.

Police investigated but could find no evidence that intruders had been in the home. Archerd insisted that he and his wife had been bound and injected with some mysterious substance. Next day, Zella fell into a coma and died before she could be removed to hospital. Official cause of death was listed as pneumonia. Archerd collected $619 in life insurance. The marriage had lasted only twelve days. Zella had over $10,000 in the bank the day she married. The day she died, her account was down to a few hundred dollars.

Soon after Zella's death, Archerd married again. If you are keeping track, we are now up to wife number five. It would be another brief liaison. Juanita Plum had recently divorced. Under the terms of her divorce, she came into possession of property that included a $40,000 home. In addition, she received $500 a month in alimony payments. No question about it: Juanita was a fine catch. On March 10, 1958, the happy pair was married in Las Vegas. Two days later, Juanita fell into a coma and died. Death was attributed to cardiac arrest.

One can only imagine Archerd's surprise when Juanita's will was read. She left her lady-killing husband exactly one dollar. The balance of her estate was bequeathed to members of her family.

Wife number six was something of a novelty. She survived and lived on to testify at her former husband's trial. Not all of Archerd's wives were as fortunate.

In 1960, Archerd and a friend, Frank Stewart, flew to Las Vegas. Just before boarding, Frank took out an insurance policy for $80,000. It covered any accident that might occur on the plane or in the two airports involved. Once in Las Vegas, Frank supposedly fell in the men's room and struck his head. He was rushed to Southern Nevada Hospital, but doctors there could find no physical evidence that a fall had taken place. Next day, Frank's buddy, William Dale Archerd, visited him in hospital. That night, Frank died.

Archerd attempted to collect the insurance money, but the insurance boys balked, and with good reason. They produced a young lady who had visited Frank in hospital and witnessed Archerd open a parcel containing a hypodermic needle and insulin. Archerd had told the girl he was going to inject Frank with the insulin so he would display the symptoms of a bad fall. Archerd had assured her that, other than rendering Frank unconscious for a short while, there would be no lasting effects from the injection. Archerd didn't collect the insurance, and although he was questioned by the police, no charges were laid against the suave charmer.

The year 1960 proved to be a busy one for the angel of death. His divorced brother, Everett, was killed in an industrial accident. Archerd was granted custody of Everett's 15-year-old son, Burney. As official guardian, he was issued a workman's compensation insurance cheque in the amount of $7,000 to be held in trust until Burney reached the age of majority. That cheque was tantamount to a death sentence.

On the day Archerd cashed the cheque, his nephew was admitted to Long Beach Memorial Hospital. The boy had supposedly been struck by a hit-and-run driver. Three hours later, after a visit from Uncle William, Burney's left eye dilated. He lapsed into a coma and was taken to an operating room. The dilated eye indicated pressure on the brain or intercranial bleeding. Surgeons drilled burr holes into the boy's skull to relieve the pressure. They were surprised to see no evidence of bleeding or damage of any kind. Thirteen days after being admitted to hospital, the boy died. Death was listed as terminal bronchopneumonia.

In February 1965, Archerd met 60-year-old Mary Brinker Post. Miss Post was assistant director of publicity for Claremont College and author of the bestselling novel *Annie Jordan*. Two months later, on April 18, they were married. It took our boy eighteen months to spend the $21,000 his wife had brought to the marriage, as well as $14,000 she didn't have. On October 15, Mrs. Archerd the seventh filed for bankruptcy.

Toward the end of the month, Mrs. Archerd was involved in a minor traffic accident as she drove to the college from her home. Archerd was in San Francisco at the time but returned to Los Angeles as soon as he received the news. On the day after the accident, he had photos taken of the vehicle and his wife's minor injuries. He put in a claim that same day to the college's insurance company.

On October 30, two days after the accident, Archerd knocked on his neighbour's door and told them that his wife wouldn't wake up. An ambulance was summoned and the stricken woman was taken to Pomona Valley Hospital. The next afternoon she died without regaining consciousness. Although no insulin had been prescribed, an autopsy indicated she had died from bronchopneumonia secondary to hypoglycemia.

Seven was not a lucky number for Archerd. Maybe it was because of the prominence of his victim or because the death was so obviously the result of an insulin injection that authorities decided to put William Dale Archerd's life under a microscope. It didn't take long for detectives to uncover Archerd's past, including the fact that not only had he worked as a hospital attendant, he had been employed in an insulin-shock ward for more than a year.

A team of eight detectives sifted through the killer's life for the previous twenty years. They believed that he had murdered two friends, a nephew and three wives. Authorities decided to prosecute on the three strongest cases, those of Zella, Burley and Mary Archerd.

William Archerd was found guilty of murdering all three. It was the first time anyone in the United States was convicted of using insulin as a murder weapon.

On March 6, 1968, Supreme Court Judge Adolph Alexander sentenced Archerd to death in California's gas chamber. For nine years he resided on death row at San Quentin, but in the end he cheated the gas chamber. William Dale Archerd died of natural causes while still in prison.

Mary Aylward

(SCYTHE)

MURDER HAS NO RESPECT for location. The evil that permeates the murderer's mind is released in urban and rural areas with equal ferocity. Neither has it any respect for time. Let's travel back to 1862 and visit the rural surroundings of Hastings County, about a hundred miles north of Belleville, Ontario.

Two families, the Munros and the Aylwards, lived across a dirt road from each other. William Munro, his wife, and 14-year-old son Alec worked hard. The result of their labours was a crude but comfortable home etched out of the wilderness. Richard and Mary Aylward were much younger than the Munros. They had moved to their home opposite to the Munros shortly after their marriage a year before. Richard was 24; Mary, 22.

Initially, the Munros and Aylwards were friendly enough, as were most pioneer neighbours. Old records do not indicate what sowed the seed of discontent between the two families. Maybe a wife was insulted, perhaps one family's crop failed while the other's flourished. Whatever the reason, the two families became bitter enemies.

On May 16, 1862, the feud was to erupt into bloody murder. William Munro and his son were working the fields when they heard the loud report of a shotgun blast coming from the Aylward farm. William immediately figured that the hated Aylward was taking potshots at some of the Munro hens that might have strayed onto his property. Accompanied by Alec, he ran over to the Aylward farm. Once there he encountered Richard Aylward. Mary Aylward was not to be seen and was apparently inside her home.

"Did you shoot my hens?" asked Munro.

"I didn't shoot them, but I wish I had," was Aylward's curt reply.

"Are my hens in the wheat field?" queried Munro.

Instead of replying, Aylward went into his house and reappeared with a shotgun. Munro, Alec and Aylward walked into the wheat field. Suddenly the two older men began to scuffle. Somehow the shotgun was fired. Young Alec was hit by pellets in the arm, back and legs, but was able to run to his home. His mother bandaged his wounds, which were painful but not extremely serious.

Moments later, William Munro staggered home. He was in terrible shape, with a deep, hideous gash on his head. His left arm was also badly cut. Mrs. Munro did the best she could. There was no doctor available. Alec recovered, but William lay silent on his straw pallet, growing weaker with each passing day. Twelve days later, on May 28, he lapsed into unconsciousness and died.

While William Munro was still alive, word of the terrible attack reached Belleville. On May 31, unaware that Munro had expired, Constable E.D. Edis left Belleville by horse and wagon, bound for the Munro farm. He picked up Dr. Augustus A. Yeomans in Madoc. Two days later they arrived at their destination only to learn that Munro was dead.

Richard and Mary Aylward were arrested, charged with murder and taken south to be lodged in the Belleville jail. All that summer they remained behind bars until their trial for the murder of William Munro began in October.

The Aylward trial dwarfed all other news in Ontario and even drifted to the far corners of the land soon to be known as the

Dominion of Canada. It wasn't often in pioneer days that a woman of the soil stood accused of murdering a fellow pioneer.

The first witness for the prosecution, young Alec Munro, reiterated the story of how he'd sustained his own wounds. He told how Aylward had pointed his shotgun at his father. William had grabbed at the barrel of the gun. As he did so, Aylward pulled out a pistol from his pocket. William was able to knock the pistol from Aylward's hand. As it fell to the ground, William shouted to Alec to pick it up. Alec instinctively obeyed his father.

As Alec rose, he was looking directly into Richard Aylward's eyes peering down the sight of his shotgun, taking direct aim at Alec's head. Alec dived to the ground as the shotgun roared. He managed to avoid the main blast of pellets, but twenty-six pieces of lead were later extracted from his arm, back and legs. He completely recovered from his wounds. The boy's recitation raised eyebrows in the court. It was obvious that young Alec had not seen the attack that had taken his father's life. Why was Mary Aylward on trial? It appeared she had nothing to do with the murder.

Mrs. Mary Ann McCrae, nearest neighbour of the Munros and Aylwards, took the stand. She informed the court that a few days before the assault, the two defendants had visited her home and while there had sharpened their scythe. Mrs. McCrae was mildly curious about the sharpening of the scythe as the haying season was still months in the future. The Aylwards left her farm without incident.

However, on the day of the attack, they once again showed up at her farm. This time they were carrying a shotgun as well as the scythe. Mary Aylward said, "I cut the head off the old man and Richard shot Alec." Mrs. McCrae was horrified at this confession, but there was more to come. As if possessed, Mary Aylward held the scythe high over her head and boasted how she had struck down William Munro. That's when Mrs. McCrae saw the blood-smeared blade of the scythe. She firmly ordered the Aylwards off her property.

The court buzzed as Mrs. McCrae finished giving her evidence. Now there was little doubt in anyone's mind why Mary Aylward stood beside her husband in the prisoner's box.

Next, William Johnston, who lived a quarter of a mile down the road from the two quarrelling families, took the stand. He told of meeting the Aylwards along the road after Munro's death. Richard was carrying his shotgun, Mary her friendly scythe. She even pointed out that she'd intended to decapitate her victim but hadn't the strength to do a proper job. Mary demonstrated how she wielded her deadly farm implement, adding that she had prayed to God to increase the dying man's pain as he lay near death.

Evidently, Mary had no compunction about telling the world of her evil deed. The prosecution paraded Margaret Glen, Theophilus Golder and George Selby to the stand. Mary had boasted to them that she had swung her scythe with poor aim but with desired results.

It is important to note that a hundred years ago there was a kinship amongst pioneer farmers. They stuck together to brave the elements, to hunt and to erect buildings. To turn against one's neighbour was a rare occurrence. I point this out because, in this case, while the evidence against Mary Aylward was conclusive, the same cannot be said about Richard Aylward. Certainly he had wounded Alec Munro, but he had not struck the fatal blow to William Munro. In fact, there is no evidence that he ever handled the scythe at all. However, such was the mood at the time that both Aylwards were found guilty and sentenced to death.

The obscure murder in the remote rural area gained prominence across the land as the execution date of December 8, 1862, approached. Would the couple's sentence be commuted, as the jury must have anticipated when they'd added their recommendation of mercy?

Such was not to be the case. Public opinion against the Aylwards was so strong that politicians of the time would not attempt to save the accused pair.

Six thousand spectators gathered in front of the Belleville Jail as the priest accompanied Mary and Richard Aylward to the gallows. Trembling and weak-kneed, they had to be assisted to the proper locations before taking their plunge to eternity.

Blodwen Bayle

(pillow)

THOSE WHO KNEW Blodwen Morgan had only sympathy for the Welsh beauty. It seemed that one day Blodwen had everything a woman could ask for and the next day nothing but disaster.

At the time of the tragedy, Blodwen was a sparkling 22-year-old. She and her husband, John, had three lovely daughters: Susan, 2, Sarah, 1, and the baby, Sheila. One sunny day John left for work in Swansea and returned home in a pine box. An industrial accident had claimed the head of the young family.

The wake was understandably a sad affair, if a bit noisy, with the baby crying and the two older girls running about. Blodwen, with the help of her parents, served dainty Scotch squares and tea to those paying their last respects. Some of the men quietly sipped whisky and were heard to remark that the late John had been a fine fellow, which seemed only appropriate under the circumstances.

What was a girl with three young daughters to do? This burning question was answered by Blodwen's parents, who insisted that the family move in with them.

Frank Bayle, a good friend of Blodwen's parents, met the now-unattached beauty and fell hard. Blodwen, ever the lady, kept the hot-to-trot Frank at arm's length. After all, she was in mourning. Of course, it occurred to her that a widow with three daughters might not be considered a great catch by too many eligible bachelors.

But Frank was different. He was tall, handsome and rich, all attributes noted by Blodwen's parents. To be brief, they said, "Go for it." Blodwen and Frank tied the knot a year after hubby number one went to his great reward.

As the years passed, Frank became a father to the girls in every sense of the word. He treated them extremely well, seeing to it that they received a fine education. All three grew up to be beauties just like their mother. For almost twenty years, all was harmonious in the Bayle household.

Who knows why Frank began running around with 20-year-old girls? We do know that he became a regular old stud, going through a series of mistresses, some of whom were no older than his daughters. Just like in the movies, however, word of Frank's peccadilloes eventually drifted back to Blodwen. Sure, she was hurt, but after considerable thought she decided to do absolutely nothing. After all, things could be worse. She had a very comfortable life as the wife of a well-to-do businessman. Her daughters were beautiful, well-educated young women. She decided to let Frank have his fun.

Then Frank went too far. His latest conquest was his secretary, 24-year-old Doreen Soupton. All of a sudden, Frank and Doreen simply disappeared. Was there no shame to the man, running off and leaving his wife and stepdaughters? Blodwen was disturbed, annoyed even, but she didn't burst into tears, nor did she have a nervous breakdown.

Financially, Blodwen was well fixed. All of Frank's wealth was jointly owned. When he took off with Doreen, he left everything behind. For Blowden, there was the indignity of it all, but the cash and property helped soothe her injured pride.

Three years passed. Blodwen got along just fine. Her lifestyle, if you discount the absence of a husband, hadn't changed an iota. She and her daughters had every material advantage. Still, something started to bother Blodwen. She became so disturbed that she sought solace in religion, attending church services regularly. She grew very close to her vicar, who would later reveal that he always felt that Blodwen was carrying a heavy burden on her shoulders.

One day, Blodwen could keep her secret no longer. She confessed to her vicar, starting at the beginning when she had first met Frank. The man could think of only one thing and that was sex. He had pursued Blodwen from the very first day he'd met her at her parents' house. About nine months after her husband's death, he seduced her in her own room. No, Blodwen wouldn't go as far as to say rape, but close. From that moment on she had sex with Frank on command.

To give Frank his due, right from the beginning he wanted to marry Blodwen, but she held out until the time-honoured year of mourning had passed before she consented to marriage. Frank's wealth and the welfare of her three young daughters had been of prime importance in making up the widow's mind.

When Frank reached the age of 40, he had the first of his many affairs. Blodwen was hurt, but the woman didn't have a jealous bone in her body. She could live with the knowledge that her husband preferred younger women.

Then the incident occurred that proved to be the dealbreaker. In 1975, Blodwen's youngest daughter Sheila celebrated her eighteenth birthday. A few months later she confided to her mother that she thought she was pregnant. Blodwen was shocked when she heard her daughter's story.

The girl told her mother that one day shortly after her birthday she had been in the house and had decided to take a shower. She and Frank were the only ones at home. He strolled into the bathroom to wash his hands, which wasn't that unusual. In a playful manner, he squirted cold water at her. She instinctively jumped out of the shower. Frank grabbed the startled girl and right there on the bathroom floor, they had intercourse.

Sheila had been a virgin, but didn't resist Frank's advances. Rape, in the strictest sense, had not taken place. The cunning rascal had waited until Sheila was 18 and no longer a minor. As Frank was not her biological father, incest had not taken place. In fact, no law had been broken.

Blodwen was beside herself. She was living with a monster. When Susan and Sarah told their mother that they too had been seduced by Frank when they had turned 18, she knew she had to do something drastic. Blodwen thought of going to the police but couldn't figure out if any crime had been committed. Besides, she didn't want to publicly humiliate her three daughters. She knew she had to do something. Frank was still having intercourse with her daughters.

Blodwen bided her time. When Doreen Soupton went away to accept another job without telling anyone, she knew it was the opportune moment to strike. She told everyone that Doreen had run away with Frank. It didn't take long for the rumour to spread.

On September 8, 1975, Blodwen dissolved a quantity of sleeping pills in a bottle of her husband's wine. When Frank fell into a deep sleep, she placed a pillow over his face until he stopped breathing. It was tough going, but she managed to lug the body out of the house and lift it into the trunk of her car. She drove to the cliffs south of Swansea. Once there, she lugged the body across a field to the edge of the cliffs. She then pushed her husband's body over the edge and into the briny.

Blodwen had unknowingly entered a unique club whose members consist of those rare individuals who have committed the perfect murder. The murder weapon, the pillow, was used continually after the murder. There was no body. No one had reported Frank missing because everyone knew that he had run away with that hussy, Doreen Soupton. No one was aware that murder had taken place.

The stunned vicar recommended that Blodwen tell her story to the police. They in turn checked out the unusual yarn. The three daughters verified that they had been seduced by their stepfather. Doreen Soupton was located. She admitted to her affair with Frank but had assumed that he was living back in Swansea with his family.

Blodwen stood trial for the murder of her husband. All the details of her confession were verified. She was found guilty of murder with extreme extenuating circumstances and was given a two-year suspended sentence. She left the courtroom with her three happy daughters.

Oh, yes, Sheila wasn't pregnant after all. It had been one of those cruel lunar tricks that nature sometimes likes to play on young, inexperienced girls.

Herbie Bennett

(BOOTLACE)

HERBERT JOHN BENNETT was one of those English youngsters who aspired to a station in life denied to him by the accident of birth.

Herbie had an elementary-school education but talked as if he had just sailed through Oxford. The rascal was a charmer who felt that his smooth patter could lift him to the genteel life he so desired.

When Herbie was 17, he fell in love with Mary, a winsome young girl two years his senior. The object of Herbie's affection was a piano teacher. It is believed he was attracted to her because he felt piano playing was an upper-class art.

The young people became husband and wife in 1897. Soon a child blessed the union, but the bloom quickly cascaded from the rose. The gift of gab that had flowed from Herbie's lips promising his bride a life of stability and luxury was quickly replaced by the reality of an unstable income and the insecurity accompanying the lack of coin.

Fortunately, Mrs. Bennett had a grandmother who took them into her home, where they stayed until her death. Before the elderly lady died, she presented her granddaughter with a distinctive gold chain. Understandably, the gift held great sentimental value for the youthful Mary Bennett. She wore it constantly.

Meanwhile, Herbie worked at various menial tasks. Often he was out of work. At other times, he sold fake violins. Always, Herbie operated amidst a web of lies and subterfuge. By 1900, at the ripe old age of 20, he succeeded in obtaining employment some distance from his lodgings at Bexley Heath. To be closer to work and to put some distance between himself and his wife and child, Herbie moved to Woolwich, where he went under the name Hood.

Herbie met Alice Meadows in the summer of 1900. She was enraptured by the polite, worldly Herbie. He told her of his many adventures throughout the world. He also insinuated that he was expecting a substantial inheritance. Alice took Herbie home to Mummy and Daddy. They, too, were impressed by the knowledgeable young man.

When the subject of summer vacations came up, Alice was delighted to spend a long weekend with Herbie at the seaside in Yarmouth. Herbie made reservations at the Crown and Anchor, a conservative rooming house. Strictly legit. Herbie and Alice had separate bedrooms. They talked of marriage and their future life together as they strolled along the Yarmouth beach. When they returned to London, our hero presented Alice with an engagement ring.

Wouldn't you just know it—back at Bexley Heath, the neglected Mrs. Bennett, who by this time only received rare visits from Herbie, suggested a summer vacation. Herbie thought that Yarmouth would be a pleasant spot for her and their child. He would make all the arrangements, which wasn't that difficult. After all, he had spent a weekend there only a month earlier with Alice Meadows.

Herbie gave his wife the name of a boarding house run by a Mrs. Rudrum. The idea of murder was planted in his mind. Herbie, sly devil that he was, then told his wife to use the name

Mrs. Hood while in Yarmouth. Mrs. Bennett had often used the alias before and thought to herself that Herbie must be mixed up in another one of his get-rich-quick schemes. She checked into the boarding house and was known only as Mrs. Hood for the few days she and her daughter lived there. Later, Mrs. Rudrum would remember Mrs. Hood as a quiet woman who took good care of her little girl. She also remembered the distinctive gold chain Mrs. Hood habitually wore around her neck.

A day after her arrival in Yarmouth, while walking on the beach, Mrs. Bennett had her photograph taken by a beach photographer. That same day, she placed the photograph on her night table in Mrs. Rudrum's boarding house.

One day during her stay, a letter arrived from Woolwich addressed to Mrs. Hood. The letter was noted by Mrs. Rudrum, but, of course, she had no idea what it contained. Only Mary Bennett saw what was in that letter. Later, it was theorized that Herbie made an appointment to meet his wife that Saturday night at a certain location in town. He most probably made some excuse as to why he could not be seen in Yarmouth and no doubt told his wife not to mention his visit to anyone. He also must have advised her to destroy the letter. Poor Mary. In her three years of marriage to Herbie, she had become accustomed to his schemes and subterfuge. So, she did what she was told to do.

Saturday night arrived. Mary put her daughter to bed and left her lodgings. She was seen in front of the town hall, a popular meeting place in Yarmouth. Significantly, the town hall is near the railway station. A few minutes later, Mary was seen accompanied by a young man in a nearby inn. Later, the pair was observed walking toward South Beach, a favourite location for lovers. The shore had several hollows or indentations that afforded some measure of privacy.

That night, another pair of lovers were lying in one of those hollows when they observed another couple walk onto the beach and lie down. They heard groans, which they later said were pleas for mercy. At the time, the young lovers were too busy to take much notice. A few yards away, Herbie Bennett had taken a bootlace from his pocket and twisted it around his wife's neck. Seconds later she was dead.

Herbie had gall. Around midnight he showed up at the Crown and Anchor, where he had previously stayed with Alice Meadows. At that time of night he was met by the night porter. Herbie explained that he had arrived on the late train and had to leave first thing in the morning. The porter, who knew him as the man who had recently visited with his fiancée, put him up in a room. Next morning, the porter called Bennett, who caught the train back to London.

That same morning, Mary Bennett's body was found on the beach. Initially, police found nothing on the body to identify the victim. However, when Mrs. Rudrum heard of the murder and realized that one of her roomers had been out all night, she visited the mortuary to view the body. She immediately identified the dead woman as her lodger, Mrs. Hood.

Mrs. Rudrum told police that all the woman's rings were accounted for, but a gold chain was missing. She told police that Mrs. Hood had been wearing the distinctive chain when she had gone out the night before. As a matter of fact, there was a picture of Mrs. Hood wearing the chain on the night table in her room.

A search of the dead woman's room recovered not only the photograph but also some linen marked with the code number 599. When Mrs. Rudrum told police of the letter with the Woolwich postal mark, they decided to canvas every laundry in Woolwich. Nothing turned up, but six weeks later a laundry manager in Bexley Heath saw a photograph of the laundry mark in the newspapers. She recognized it as the handiwork of her own establishment. Number 599 was the number given to Mrs. Bennett.

It didn't take long to trace Herbie Bennett. He attempted to weasel out of his insidious lies, but everywhere he turned, he faced a stone wall. He said he had never been to Yarmouth in his life. Police produced several witnesses who had seen him there during his weekend with Alice Meadows. That poor girl was devastated at the turn of events. She told police Herbie had been with her over the bank holiday.

The one piece of evidence that cooked Herbie's goose was the gold chain. A search of his lodgings produced the incriminating chain and sealed his fate. One wonders why Herbie took the chain and why he didn't dispose of it. Many believe that Mary Bennett prized the chain to such an extent that when she was invited to lie on the sand, she took off the chain and gave it to her husband for safekeeping. When police didn't seem to be close to solving the case after weeks had passed, Herbie figured he was in the clear and simply didn't bother to get rid of the chain.

Herbie Bennett proclaimed his innocence to the very end. On March 21, 1901, he was hanged at Norwich Jail.

Two strange footnotes are worth mentioning. First, at the time of his execution, while the traditional black flag was being hoisted, the flagstaff broke. To some, this was an indication that Bennett was innocent. Second, on July 14, 1912, at precisely the same spot where Mary Bennett's body was found, another murder victim, Dora May Gray, was found dead. She had been strangled with a bootlace.

Dr. Bob Buchanan

(MORPHINE)

Doctors should really stay out of the murder business and stick to healing. Don't get me wrong; as a class of killer, men of medicine can be extremely adept at sending the unsuspecting to the great hereafter, but for some reason, at the conclusion of the dastardly deed, they are prone to act in a downright stupid manner.

Dr. Robert Buchanan left Halifax, Nova Scotia, to set up his office in New York City. He and wife, Helen, settled at 267 West 11th Street, where he gradually built up a lucrative practice.

Bob was not the robust, swashbuckling type. He was a short man with a rather sad countenance set off by a scraggly moustache. He did have two outstanding traits. He loved the ladies and had a thirst that could only be quenched in the many saloons that dotted his neighbourhood.

After living in New York for four years, Doc Bob was a regular patron at a saloon owned by Richard Macomber. He got to know Macomber and another regular, William Doria, extremely well. The three men downed many a slug of rotgut during the cold New York nights. Boys will be boys. One night in 1890 the three friends ventured to Newark, New Jersey, to visit a house of ill fame owned and operated by the partnership of madam Anna Sutherland and elderly janitor James Smith.

Can we take a moment here to describe Anna Sutherland? Just as the doctor's wife, Helen, was an attractive woman, Anna was not. She was fat, I mean really big. She wore excessive makeup and dyed her hair a hideous shade of red. Unfortunately, she had a distinctive and prominent wart on her nose. Doc Bob was not yet 30; Anna was twice the good doctor's age.

When Doc Bob's two buddies tired of their periodic junkets to Newark, the doctor continued to visit Anna. Soon he was taking care of her minor medical ills. Quite unexpectedly, Doc Bob informed his friends that he was divorcing Helen. He swore he was through with marriage. The divorce was granted on November 12, 1891. Exactly fourteen days later, Anna Sutherland made out a will, leaving everything she owned to her husband or, if she died single, to her dear friend, Dr. Bob Buchanan. Three days after she made out her will, Anna married Bob. Helen moved back to Halifax. Bob relocated his practice in Anna's brothel on Halsey Street in Newark.

As a rule, medicine and prostitution do not mix. Male patients would often be accosted by Anna at the doctor's front door. She would inquire as to their preferences in a sex partner. This did nothing to enhance Doc Bob's medical practice. To make matters worse, James Smith, Anna's partner in the prostitution business, was extremely jealous of the doctor, whom he considered an interloper. After all, James had proposed more than once to Anna and had been turned down every time.

Folks, the marriage didn't work, but Doc Bob hung on until well into 1892. There is little doubt that the doctor put his plan into action in March of that year when he purchased a single ticket to Edinburgh to further his medical studies. The ticket was for travel on April 25. When Anna heard that she wasn't included in the trip, she threatened to cut him out of her will. On April 21, Doc Bob told his buddies down at the saloon that dear Anna had become too ill to travel and that he had cancelled the trip.

On April 22, Dr. B.C. McIntyre was called in to minister to the ailing Anna. The doctor found Mrs. Buchanan raving and near hysteria. She complained that her throat was contracting. When his patient lapsed into a coma, Dr. McIntyre called in Dr. H.P. Watson for a second opinion. Next day, after an illness of only twenty-six hours, Anna died with both doctors in attendance. Death was attributed to a cerebral hemorrhage.

Doc Bob displayed no sorrow at the loss of his wife. In fact, he was elated. Anna had left him a cool $50,000, an absolute fortune before the turn of the century. Bob took off for Halifax, but, for some reason known only to himself, before he left he hired a private detective to guard his late wife's grave. That was a stupid thing to do.

Lurking in the reeds, observing everything through his beady eyes, was Anna's old partner, James Smith. That sterling gentleman smelled a rat and hightailed it to the coroner's office with his suspicions. The coroner listened, but upon learning that two reputable doctors had been at Anna's bedside throughout her illness, dismissed Smith as a troublemaker.

A reporter for the *New York World* overheard the conversation and decided to look into Anna's untimely death. He dropped into Doc Bob's favourite watering hole and learned of the doctor's aborted trip to Scotland. He checked with the steamship company and learned that Bob had cancelled his passage and had obtained a refund on April 11, more than a week before his wife had taken ill.

The reporter, now hot to trot, also learned that Doc Bob and his cronies had often discussed a current New York murder case that involved morphine. Doc Bob had expressed the opinion that he could administer a lethal dose of morphine that would never be detected. When the reporter learned that the doctor had remarried his first wife, Helen, in Halifax, he knew he was tracking down a diabolical killer.

The *New York World* put its case to the coroner, who agreed to exhume Mrs. Buchanan's body. An autopsy revealed the presence of a residue of morphine, indicating that Anna had been given enough morphine to kill her. When the dead woman's eyes were checked for telltale contractions of the pupils—even after death an obvious symptom of morphine poisoning—doctors were shocked to note that there was no contraction of the pupils.

The district attorney's office was convinced that Doc Bob had found a method of concealing this symptom. Someone in the DA's office remembered that, as a little boy, he had been given drops of belladonna to enlarge his pupils for an eye examination. Anna's eyeballs were tested for belladonna. Sure enough, they tested positive. When a nurse who had attended Anna before the two physicians arrived at the house recalled that Doc Bob had given his wife eyedrops for no apparent reason, the doctor was arrested and taken into custody.

On March 20, 1893, Doc Bob stood trial for the murder of his second wife. The evidence against him was entirely circumstantial. A strange demonstration took place in the courtroom. A cat was poisoned with morphine. Belladonna was dropped into the cat's eyes, which served to disguise the contraction of its pupils.

On April 26, the New York jury deliberated for twenty-eight hours before returning a verdict of guilty of murder in the first degree. Dr. Robert Buchanan lingered on Sing Sing's death row for two years. On July 2, 1895, he was executed in the electric chair.

Edith Carew

(Arsenic)

REMEMBER WHEN BRITANNIA ruled the waves? In those long-ago days, selected British ladies and gentlemen had the cushy assignments of being posted to foreign climes to represent their government. In those countries, the Brits did much to popularize cricket and, when not thus engaged, a number of them passed the time of day guzzling gin and tonic. Sometimes, when things got really boring, they killed each other.

Edith and Walter Carew were members of the tight little English community that took care of England's interests in Yokohama, Japan, way back in 1896. The Carews had two children, a daughter, 6, and a son, 5, as well as an English governess, Mary Dobson. The family was young, healthy and good looking. But, alas, in that summer of '96 Walter complained of severe pains in his tummy. The family physician, Dr. Wheeler, prescribed nothing more drastic than Vichy water.

Initially, Walter seemed to respond to this most plain of all remedies, but a few days later the pains returned with a vengeance. Dr. Wheeler called in a colleague. Both doctors were puzzled at the symptoms and departed the Carews' residence somewhat concerned. When Dr. Wheeler reached his home, a servant handed him a cryptic note. It read, "Three bottles arsenic in one week. Maruya."

The light went on in Dr. Wheeler's brain. Of course, that was it. Carew was being poisoned with arsenic. All his symptoms pointed to that very thing. Within an hour, the good doctor had his patient removed to the British Royal Naval Hospital. It was too late. Two hours after being admitted, Walter passed away.

A post-mortem indicated that Walter Carew had died from several large doses of arsenic. The inquest into his death revealed that a chemist named Maruya had supplied Mrs. Carew with several bottles of arsenic in liquid form in the week prior to Walter's demise. Written orders had been hand delivered to Maruya by the Carews' governess, Mary Dobson.

Edith Carew informed the inquest jury that her husband had often taken small quantities of arsenic, which seemed to relieve his minor aches and pains. She also related a rather strange tale, which was to have far-reaching consequences. She said that after she and Walter had been married for only four months, he confided to her that he had been on intimate terms with one Annie Luke. She and Walter had discussed this topic that one time only.

Now, after all that time, Edith claimed that a strange lady had called on her two weeks earlier. The stranger wouldn't talk to her and had insisted on seeing Walter. At the time seeing him was impossible, but the woman had given Edith her card. On it were the initials A.L. Edith had passed the card along to her husband. Their friends had teased him about the mysterious A.L.

After her husband's death, Edith had found a note written to her husband and signed simply "Annie." The note read:

I must see you. Why have you done nothing since you got my card? Or, perhaps she never let you have it. I cannot meet her again; she makes me mad when I think of all I might have done for you. I cannot give you any address. I am living wherever I can find shelter; but you can find and help me if you will, as I know you will, for the sake of old times.

Another letter had been found, obviously undelivered, from Walter Carew to Miss A. Luke, Post Office Yokohama:

I feel greatly distressed about you, and ever since I got your card last Saturday I have been endeavouring to find you. I wish to and will help you if I can only find you. Meet me this evening at 5:30 on the Bund.

Well, it never rains but it pours. Edith's lawyer produced a letter from the mysterious Annie Luke. So did the coroner. Both letters hinted that the writer was going to commit suicide. Both were written in the same handwriting as the letter Edith had produced.

The next startling revelation was provided by bank employee Fred James, a friend of Mr. and Mrs. Carew. He stated that he had seen a heavily veiled woman near "the club" on the same day as Mrs. Carew swore the strange woman had called on her. An immediate search was conducted to find the woman, who presumably was Annie Luke. She was not located.

The inquest jury ruled that Walter had died from the effects of arsenic—"but by whom the poison was administered there is no direct evidence to show." Five days later, Edith Carew was arrested and charged with her husband's murder. On January 5, 1897, Edith's murder trial began, which tended to break up the rather disappointing social calendar that season. The little courthouse was crammed full. After each day's proceedings, the English would belly up to the bar at The Club and discuss the pros and cons of the trial.

The trial rehashed all the inquest's findings, but there was more. The Carews' governess, Mary Dobson, did not get along well with Edith. Their relationship had deteriorated to the point where Mary believed Edith was intercepting her mail from England. Mary searched Edith's scrap baskets. She didn't find letters addressed to her, but she did come across torn-up letters written to Edith by none other than bank teller Fred James. Mary meticulously sewed the pieces of the letters together. They caused a sensation when read in court.

Fred James took the witness stand. He admitted that he had written passionate love letters to Edith. She, in turn, wrote him sizzling letters, but darn it all, their relationship was a platonic one. Fred James stated that he had been deeply in love with Edith. She, however, was on the best of terms with her husband while professing undying love for Freddy by mail. In her letters to Freddy, she wrote that her husband was a brute who often beat her.

Edith was either playing a dangerous game with a young suitor or was indeed in the midst of an unhappy, violent marriage. Most believed she had been toying with Fred James's affections, while he was seriously in love with her. His love grew while he was being fed terrible stories about Walter's cruelties to his wife. Otherwise, James stated he had "no dislike of Mr. Carew."

Handwriting experts were called by the prosecution. These gentlemen stated that the letters purportedly written by Annie Luke had been written by Edith Carew. Defence attorneys summoned their own experts, who refuted the prosecution's witnesses.

The trial lasted fourteen sensational days. The defence summed up by stating that there was no evidence that Edith Carew had administered poison to her husband, nor was there an iota of a motive for killing a man she obviously loved dearly.

The prosecutor didn't dwell on whatever game Edith was playing with Fred James. Instead, he pointed out that Edith was the only possible killer—the one who had given orders to purchase the arsenic and the one who had had the opportunity to administer the poison.

The jury deliberated only a half hour before bringing in a verdict of guilty. Edith Carew was sentenced to be executed, but this sentence was later commuted to life imprisonment.

Styllou Christofi

(PLATE & SCARF)

IT IS MY OPINION that sons should treat their mothers with respect, no matter what the circumstances. This is especially true if you happen to have a mean mummy who doesn't like your wife. Sound like the beginning of a Greek tragedy? Well, that's exactly how it turned out. Allow me to introduce you to Mrs. Styllou Christofi, mean mummy extraordinaire.

Mrs. Christofi hailed from Cyprus. The 53-year-old peasant woman had been born to poverty and remained illiterate all her life. She had never left her home village until she travelled to London, England, to visit her son, Stavros.

Rather than being proud of her son's accomplishments, Mrs. Christofi was furious that he had abandoned the way of life she cherished back in Cyprus. The truth of the matter was that Stavros had carved out a new and comfortable life since emigrating to England in 1937. He was a wine waiter in a fashionable restaurant in London's West End. Along the way he had married Hella, a pretty German girl whom he loved dearly. The Christofis had three young children and a comfortable home. All in all, the ambitious Greek boy had done very well for himself and his family.

Stavros's mother simply didn't see it that way. She watched with steely eyes, hatred oozing out of every pore. How dare this interloper Hella poison her son's mind so that he had become more English than Greek? Each evening he went off to his soft job, a far cry from the sun-drenched days in the fields back home. And the children? Were they to grow up in this prosperous society, never understanding the work ethic that was such an important part of their heritage? Mrs. Christofi was further frustrated by not being able to speak English. She was effectively cut off from conversing with her daughter-in-law and grandchildren.

On July 29, 1954, at precisely 8 P.M., Stavros left for work as he did every evening. His mother had been living with him now for the better part of a year. The arrangement just hadn't worked out. On three different occasions, his mother had moved out but had always returned. The incessant insinuations about his casting aside his roots had started all over again.

Mrs. Christofi blamed Hella for all the discord in the family. The venomous feeling directed toward Hella didn't go unnoticed. Hella often became depressed because of the obvious animosity displayed by the older woman. Finally, it was unofficially agreed that Hella would take the children and visit her family in Germany. When she returned, Mrs. Christofi would leave for Cyprus. In Mrs. Christofi's mind, she was being tossed out of her own son's home. What's more, in her mind, the expulsion was tantamount to being removed from his life.

This night would be different. Stavros kissed Hella goodbye, unaware that he would never see his wife again. Once he was out of the house, Hella put the children to bed. The two women busied themselves cleaning the kitchen. Without warning, Mrs. Christofi picked up a heavy metal plate used to collect ashes from the stove and struck Hella on the back of the head. The unconscious woman fell to the floor. Mrs. Christofi proceeded to strangle Hella with a scarf belonging to one of the children.

The house was deathly quiet. For the next few hours, Mrs. Christofi was a busy mummy, but her deeds were performed with a singleness of purpose.

At 11:30 P.M., John Young, the Christofis' next-door neighbour, took his dog for a run in the backyard. He noticed a bonfire in the adjoining yard. John shouted but received no response. He peered over the brick wall separating the two properties and observed what he thought was a mannikin burning in the fire. As he turned to go back into his home, he saw someone leave the Christofi house and walk toward the fire. Young later stated, "I left when I saw someone I recognized. I thought all was in order." John Young was wrong. Mummy dearest had just come out to stoke the fire. She was burning her daughter-in-law.

At about 1 A.M., Mr. and Mrs. Burstoff were driving to their home in Hampstead when they were hailed down by Mrs. Christofi. In broken English, she said over and over, "Fire. Burning. Children sleeping." The Burstoffs accompanied Mrs. Christofi to her home and discovered the badly burned body in the backyard. They called police. While they waited, Mrs. Christofi told the Burstoffs, "My son marry Germany girl he like. Plenty clothes, plenty shoes."

Police were quickly on the scene. They found bloodstains on the kitchen floor, which had been partially cleaned. Beside Hella's body they found paper that had been soaked in paraffin. Hella's wedding ring was not on her finger but was recovered from Mrs. Christofi's room. In a dustbin were three portions of a child's scarf. The scarf had been cut into pieces in order to remove it from Hella's neck.

Police questioned Mrs. Christofi. She told them, "I wake up, smell burning, go downstairs. Hella burning. Throw water, touch her face. Not move. Run out, get help." Through an interpreter, Mrs. Christofi claimed that she and her daughter-in-law had been on perfect terms. She had gone to bed that night, leaving Hella in a good mood doing household chores.

In due course, Mrs. Christofi was arrested and charged with Hella's murder. Her trial was unique in that every word was translated into Greek. The English jury took only a matter of hours to find Mrs. Christofi guilty of murder. She was sentenced to death. All appeals failed. The execution was to proceed as scheduled.

On the day before the execution, it was revealed, via the British press, that the chief medical officer at Holloway Prison had filed a report before the trial, stating, "The clinical picture is that of a nonsystemized delusional mental disorder." The doctor had insinuated that Mrs. Christofi was incapable of realizing that what she had done was wrong.

This caused quite a disturbance and great efforts were made to commute the condemned woman's sentence at the last minute. All these efforts were doomed to failure and Mrs. Christofi was hanged as scheduled.

Only after her execution was it revealed that Mrs. Christofi was no amateur in the gentle art of murder. Back in 1925, in Cyprus, she had killed her mother-in-law by ramming a burning torch down her throat. The crime had been one of hate and jealousy involving her husband and his mother. Inexplicably, on that occasion, she had been acquitted. As I said, Mrs. Christofi was one mean mummy.

Adolfo Constanzo

(MACHETE)

ADOLFO CONSTANZO could easily have passed for a youthful executive who had made it to the top rung of the corporate ladder. Tall, good-looking Constanzo excelled in his chosen professions of witchcraft, smuggling and murder.

Born in Miami on November 1, 1962, to a Cuban immigrant mother, he was raised in Puerto Rico, where his mother married for the second time. When his stepfather died, Adolfo and his mother returned to Miami.

The attractive youngster left school after completing grade nine and took odd jobs to help support his mother and his four brothers and sisters. Drawn to the big money being made in the drug trade, Constanzo left Florida in 1984 for Mexico. Here, the charismatic Constanzo earned his spurs in the drug business. Before long, he was the leader of a gang of smugglers based in Matamoros. It is believed that Constanzo's take was 50 percent of everything the Hernandez gang took in from their illegal operations.

Geographically, the gang's base of operations couldn't have been located more advantageously. Matamoros is situated on the U.S.–Mexican border. The International Gateway Bridge across the Rio Grande separates Brownsville, Texas, and Matamoros, Mexico.

Despite his youth, Constanzo demanded respect, and with good reason. He mixed fear with cold hard cash. His followers soon had more money and a better life than they ever had before their young leader came on the scene. He organized the marijuana trade, shipping it from distant farms to where it was stored in a barn on the Rancho Santa Elena near Matamoros. From there, it was smuggled across the river into the United States, eventually reaching Miami and Houston.

Followers of Constanzo practised a form of witchcraft in which animals and human parts were used to ward off evil spirits. In time, they believed that Constanzo could foretell the future and was a kind of devil. He was called El Padrino, the Godfather. Constanzo told his close cult followers that the police would never harm or harass them, and they never did. It wasn't really witchcraft; Constanzo was paying off the officials.

Constanzo often ordered his followers to pick up a human to be sacrificed to the gods. There, in a tiny shack on the farm, the blindfolded victim, in many cases unknown to the abductors, would be killed. Often, the person's heart and brains would be removed and placed in a cauldron with spices. By candlelight, strange rituals were enacted.

Mark Kilroy lived in a different world than Adolfo Constanzo. Mark was a junior at the University of Texas in Austin. He dated girls, cheered for the Longhorns and studied hard, with the intention of becoming a doctor. He was looking forward to March break when he and buddies Bradley Moore, Bill Huddleston and Brent Martin planned on travelling down to South Padre Island near Brownsville. Over a quarter of a million young people had the same idea.

Mark and his friends made the trip. After two days of ogling girls and drinking beer in South Padre, the boys crossed the bridge to Matamoros. They were enveloped by wall-to-wall pedestrians, mostly American students like themselves. The boys had beer at several of the inviting pubs. They met other students and had fun swapping stories until it was time to return to the other side of the Rio Grande. At 2 A.M., the crowds had thinned out. The four boys made their way toward the International Gateway Bridge. Sometimes one or two strolled ahead of the others, sometimes one lagged behind. Mark Kilroy lagged behind the other three as they passed Garcia's restaurant. Then he was gone—vanished. The three boys retraced their steps, thinking that Mark might have turned around for some reason. Eventually, they returned to their car and drove around looking for their friend. The streets were deserted when they reported Mark missing to the Mexican police. Next morning, in Matamoros, the boys advised the American consulate of their missing friend, after which they called Mark's parents in Santa Fe and told them their son was missing in Mexico.

Unknown to all, Mark Kilroy had been hustled away in a truck and taken to the Rancho Santa Elena. His head was split open with a machete. His brains and heart were extracted and used in Satanic rituals by Adolfo Constanzo and his followers. Then he was buried. Authorities on both sides of the border were soon conducting a massive search for the missing American student.

Sara Aldrete, 24, was an honours student at Texas Southmost College in Brownsville. A dark beauty, she stood six feet one inch tall. Sara was also El Padrino's girlfriend and constant companion, even though she knew he was a homosexual and had two male lovers. She willingly took part in the Satanic rituals.

Rumours concerning the Rancho Santa Elena as the drug dropoff point had come to the attention of the police on several occasions. But nothing was ever done. It is alleged that those in authority accepted bribes totalling millions of dollars in return for allowing the drugs to flow.

Now, a new officer, Juan Benitez, headed the Matamoros police. The honest, 35-year-old policeman swept clean. He had a drug shipment traced to Rancho Santa Elena. On April 9, 1989, the police swooped down and took into custody Serafin Hernandez, a courier and cult member. In quick succession, Elio Hernandez, David Serna and Sergio Martinez were arrested.

Benitez was cracking down on the drug trade, but he also had a photo of Mark Kilroy, the missing American student, which he showed to everyone during the course of his drug investigations. Always, he received the same answer. No one had seen Mark Kilroy. That is, until he showed the photo to a farmhand at Rancho Santa Elena. His name was Domingo Reyes. Without hesitation, Domingo told the officer, "Yes, I remember, I gave him a drink of water. Later they took him down to the shack and after that I never saw him anymore."

Police, accompanied by Domingo, went to the shack. A lock was broken, revealing the horror of what had gone on in that shack. There, in three pots, was a stew containing a human brain. An iron cauldron held dried blood, a roasted turtle and another human brain. In the general area of the cauldron were melted candles, a goat's head and part of a chicken.

The police now knew that the infamous drug-smuggling activities of El Padrino included murder, but even with the evidence of stark horror, they had no idea of the scope of the killings they were about to uncover. The four men lodged in jail were questioned regarding murder. All confessed, adding horror upon horror to the unbelieving police. Eventually, the accused men directed police to gravesites on the ranch and close by, where a total of fifteen bodies were brought to the surface. One body was that of Mark Kilroy.

The hunt was on for Constanzo, Sara Aldrete and other cult members. They were traced to Mexico City, holed up in an apartment. A veritable army of 80 plainclothesmen and 110 uniformed police officers surrounded the building. Inside were Constanzo,

Sara, Alvara de Leon, Omar Orea and Martin Quintana. A shootout ensued. Realizing the futility of his situation, Constanzo entered a tiny closet with his lover, Martin Quintana. He ordered Alvara de Leon to shoot them both through the flimsy closet doors. Alvara sprayed the closet with machine-gun fire.

El Padrino, the Satanic drug king, was no more. The rest of his drug-smuggling Satanic worshippers were taken into custody.

James Cook

(IRON BAR)

SOME WOMEN ARE DRAWN to vile murderers. Henri Landru, who burned his lovers in his furnace, received more than a hundred proposals of marriage while awaiting the placement of his neck on Dr. Guillotine's infernal machine. In more modern times, convicted murderer Dr. Sam Sheppard had an attractive divorcée waiting for him when he was released from prison.

Not all women attracted to prisoners have romance on their minds. Many simply become enthralled with the excitement of being in proximity to someone who has committed murder. They visit their selected prisoner and attempt to make his lot behind bars as pleasant as possible.

Back in 1832, when Merrie England didn't treat its criminals with undue kindness, one killer, James Cook, was the recipient of one lady's genteel attentions.

James was a bookbinder who carried on business on Wellington Street, Leicester. From all reports he was a rather handsome 19-year-old when he established his enterprise and could have gone on to bigger and better things had he continued to apply himself. But the hard work and discipline wore James down. By the time he was 22, he was neglecting his business. Sometimes he would close up shop for days on end. When he did work, it was usually at night in a desperate attempt to catch up. Naturally his bookbinding business floundered. Bills piled up until the threat of bankruptcy loomed like a cloud over James Cook.

Matters came to a head when a supplier, John Paas of High Holborn, London, informed James by mail that he would be arriving in one week's time to collect in cash the £8 owed to him. James knew Paas well. Not to pay him would mean ruin. There seemed no way out of his predicament. He thought of fleeing to America, but without funds this was no more than a passing idea.

No doubt Paas would be on an extensive collection trip. James knew his route and figured he would be one of the last businesses his supplier would call on. James was also well aware of Paas's insistence on payment in cash when he made one of his trips. He correctly surmised that his nemesis would have a sizeable amount of cash on him by the time he entered his shop.

James came to the not-so-unique solution to his problem. He would kill John Paas and burn his body in the furnace. With the money derived from Paas's purse, he would emigrate to America and start a new life. It seemed like a good idea and James prepared diligently for the great event.

John Paas showed up on May 30, 1832. James's one employee ushered Paas into the shop. The lad was then sent on an errand while the two men conducted their business. James crept up behind his unsuspecting victim and, with one blow of an iron bar, laid John Paas deader than a mackerel. James stripped the body of £60 and some jewellery, including a relatively expensive gold watch.

James cut the body into manageable sections and fed them to the fire already roaring in the furnace. It was no easy task. He worked most of that night before leaving the shop for a short nap. Next day the fire roared and Mr. Paas cooked. When James left the shop, several neighbouring businessmen became concerned that he would burn down his building and the entire street. They talked to him about the real danger of a fire, but James assured them that he had received a large order and had to work nonstop to fill it.

The men went along with that for a while, but the very next night when James left his shop with the fire still burning, the owner of an adjoining pub broke in and extinguished the flames. While he was on the premises, he found a few large portions of meat. Suspecting the worst, he contacted Constable Measures, who, it is unfortunate to report, was less than sober when he conducted the preliminary investigation into the Cook affair.

Measures checked the interior of James's shop, with special emphasis on the large portions of meat. He decided that the meat should be examined by a doctor and that James would have to appear the next morning to hear the results of the doctor's examination. To assure that he would show up, Measures would accompany him to jail. Before being escorted to jail, James received permission from Measures to pick up a few items of clothing from his father's house. While the not-too-bright Measures waited in the front room, James left via the back door.

James got as far as Liverpool and almost made it to a ship leaving for America when he was intercepted by police. He confessed to killing Mr. Paas but stated it was in self-defence. He claimed that he had struck Paas during a heated argument over the amount of debt he owed. Fearing that no one would believe him, he had burned the body in his furnace.

Like most murderers, James didn't look or behave like a man who would dissect a fellow human being and methodically go about burning the resultant parts. He was pleasant to look at, a delight to talk to and possessed a shyness that was most becoming.

Details of his gruesome crime received wide publicity and came to the attention of Annie Payne, a lady who was a virgin by bad luck, resolute by nature and religiously inclined. With all these attributes, it is no wonder that she was convinced she was ordained by a higher power to bring holiness and all that was good to murderer James Cook. Miss Payne wrote James, pleading with him to repent and fly straight from the scaffold to heaven.

James received her missive and saw in it many potential advantages. He invited Miss Payne over to the jail for a visit. Annie showed up with a basket of fruit, a tin of shortbread cookies, a stack of Bibles and a few placemats. James knew he was on to a good thing right from that very first visit. He made up his mind that if he had to hang, he would swing in style.

The accused man claimed to be indifferent to religious persuasion, but with humble and cunning delicacy, let himself gradually be led to the light. A few more visits by Miss Payne with quantities of selected jams and cakes and James became positively ecclesiastical. His conversion was astounding. His demeanour, always pleasant, was now practically papal in its reverence. Although he didn't share Jimmy Swaggart's propensity for visiting motels, our James became just as adept as that famed man of religion at quoting the scriptures.

James held some slight hope that this silly woman might sway public opinion, enabling him to gain a reprieve. But such was not to be the case. While everyone directly connected with the murder case learned of the accused man's startling conversion, the news never did filter down to the public. Meanwhile, Miss Payne and James concluded every visit with long sessions of hymn singing, which was most annoying to the jailers.

James played his part to the hilt. As he was led out of jail to stand trial, he told his jailers, no doubt sorry to see him, the jellies, jams and roast chickens depart the premises, not to mourn. If fate should decree that he arrive in heaven first, James said, he would patiently wait for them beyond the pearly gates.

Miss Payne no longer looked upon James as a murderer but rather as a saint. In court, James didn't disappoint. He mumbled prayers, looked skyward and in general acted like an all-round religious guy. Unfortunately for James, Mr. Justice Parker, probably an atheist, dismissed the geyser of religious enthusiasm displayed by the defendant and went directly to the meat of the diabolical murder. He described the killing in detail before finding James guilty and sentencing him to death.

James Cook lived better than any previous condemned man in all of England, but he failed to escape the death penalty. He was hanged on schedule. As an added touch, his body was gibbeted in Saffron Lane, where twenty thousand mortals held a party for several days until the body was removed.

Richard Dadd

(STRAIGHT RAZOR)

ROBERT DADD WAS A RETIRED APOTHECARY, as the English called those individuals who dispensed pills and potions in the 19th century. Upon retirement, he took up residence in London.

On Monday, August 28, 1843, Robert drove into the tiny village of Cobham with his son Richard in tow. There are two things you should know about Richard. First, he was not rowing with both oars in the agua. His father realized that Richard was extremely unstable. The boy had just returned from the Mediterranean. From all reports available to the elder Dadd, Richard had behaved irrationally and had caused several disturbances. The concerned father had English doctors examine Richard. They agreed that he was unstable and dangerous. Second, Richard was an artist of some renown and promise. His paintings featured fairies drawn from his imagination. They were a commercial success and had been the subject of several exclusive shows.

Robert Dadd was deeply involved with his son's well-being. He stayed with Richard most of the time. On this day late in August, he was accompanying Richard on the short trip to Cobham as a sort of vacation, which he felt his son needed. He had no way of knowing that his son was hallucinating. Richard was receiving messages from the ancient Egyptian god Osiris. In his hallucinatory state, he had come to regard his father as "the man who calls himself my father." Unknown to Robert, his son was stalking him under the direction of Osiris.

The Dadds pulled up to The Ship, a well-known watering hole in the village. Robert asked the publican, John Adams, if they could provide beds for the night. Adams, who knew Robert slightly, explained that they didn't have rooms, but because they received so many requests for accommodations, they had a working arrangement with locals who lived in cottages close to the pub. They could provide one double bed.

Before Adams could continue, Robert said that one double bed would do just fine. He introduced Adams to his son. Richard rather brusquely stated that he wanted his own bed. Adams explained that there would be no trouble providing single beds, but the two would have to sleep in separate cottages. Richard agreed to these arrangements.

Father and son had a beer and then went out for a walk to take in the pleasant summer evening. An hour later they returned and ordered supper. Richard behaved somewhat erratically. At one point during his meal, he dashed to another area of the pub and gulped down two glasses of water when all the while there was a tumbler of water within arm's reach at his table.

At about 8:45 P.M., Robert and Richard went for another walk in the fading light. Near a gravel pit beside a large tree whose branches almost touched the ground, Richard hit his father from behind. The blow to the head stunned the older man, who fell to the ground. Richard was on his father like a crazed animal, raining blows to the poor man's head and body. He pulled his half-conscious father under the branches of the tree. He then took a straight razor out of his pocket and relentlessly slashed at his helpless victim.

Because Robert's clothing was bunched up from being dragged under the bushes, the razor didn't inflict any real damage. Frustrated, Richard extracted a large new seaman's spring-bladed knife from his pocket. Well-directed blows with this formidable weapon ended his father's life. In Richard's warped mind, he had killed Satan, who had been posing as his father.

That evening, some villagers passed near the body. They paid scant attention, figuring that someone had had too much grog and was sleeping it off. The following morning, one of the villagers who had seen the still form the night before decided to investigate. It was he who raised the cry of bloody murder.

Richard had had a night's head start. He made his way to Dover, where he hired a small private boat to take him to France. From Calais, he travelled to Paris. Fellow passengers on the coach well remembered the wild-eyed Englishman who had been their travelling companion. After a shopping binge for a new wardrobe in Paris, Richard booked passage on a stage coach bound for Vienna, Austria.

Before Richard left French soil, Osiris once more spoke to him. Osiris told him that Satan was the lone fellow traveller sitting right beside him. Satan had to be annihilated. Again, with spring-bladed knife Richard slashed viciously at the man's throat, but the attack was far different from the one that had taken place on the deserted country road. The intended victim screamed and the coachman quickly came to his rescue, pulling Richard away.

Once overpowered, Richard settled down and was turned over to the authorities. He was sent to an asylum at Melun and later to Clermont-Ferrand, where he stayed ten months. Initially, the French were reluctant to allow Richard to be extradited, fearing that an English court would execute an insane man. However, once they received assurances from English authorities that he would be certified insane, they agreed to send him back.

It is interesting to note that, despite the murderous attack on his father, Richard's family considered the gifted painter to be a sick person rather than a criminal. This was certainly an enlightened view for those times.

Richard was sent to Bethlem Royal Hospital, an insane asylum in Beckenham, Kent, that is credited with giving us the word *bedlam*. Many believed that a masterful artist would be lost to the world, but such was not to be the case. Richard was transferred to Broadmoor when that infamous institution was opened. Here he painted diligently and produced some of his finest works, featuring fairies and fantasy scenes. He died of natural causes in the institution in 1887, at the age of 70.

In 1960, much of Richard's work was discovered by an archivist who had been left the old Bethlem Royal Hospital's records and files. Scholars have studied the paintings and believe them to be the work of a genius. In 1974, the prestigious Tate Gallery in London held an exhibition of his works.

Today, one of Richard's finest works, *The Fairy Feller's Master Stroke,* is permanently on display in the Tate Gallery. If you look closely enough at the obsessively detailed studies of gnomes and elves, you will find the likeness of Robert Dadd.

Somewhere along the line, Osiris decreed that the image of Richard's murdered father would live forever in the work of his son.

Jeffrey Dahmer

(DRUGS)

DURING THE DAY HE WORKED at the Ambrosia Chocolate Co. in Milwaukee. At night he killed people and cut up their bodies.

Jeffrey Dahmer had always been a bit different. As a kid in Akron, Ohio, he loved to dissect insects and small animals. When his middle-class parents divorced in 1978, Jeffrey was attending Ohio State University. He dropped out after only one semester. That same year, 18-year-old Jeffrey committed his first murder.

Stephen Hicks had hitchhiked to a rock music concert thirty miles from his home in Coventry, Ohio. Then he simply disappeared off the face of the earth. His parents offered a reward to anyone who could lead them to their son, but no one came forward with information. Stephen, one day a typical teenager, next day had ceased to exist.

It would be thirteen years before his parents would learn that Jeffrey Dahmer had given their son a lift after the concert. They drove to Jeffrey's house for a few beers, but when Stephen attempted to leave, Jeffrey struck him over the head with a barbell and proceeded to strangle him. Jeffrey had nothing against Stephen. He just didn't want him to leave.

Jeffrey dragged the body outdoors into a crawl space between the ground and the floor of the house. He cut the body into pieces and poured acid over the parts. It took a few weeks before he was able to remove excess flesh from the bones, which he then crushed with a sledgehammer. Once the bones were in tiny pieces, he scattered them over his backyard.

Out of sight, out of mind. Jeffrey joined the U.S. Army and served overseas in Germany for three years before being discharged for excessive drinking. In 1982, he moved in with his grandmother in West Allis, a suburb of Milwaukee.

For the next few years, Jeffrey drank heavily and was in and out of trouble with the law. He was given suspended sentences for his sex-related crimes. Once, he lowered his trousers in a crowd. On another occasion, he was accused of masturbating in public.

Almost ten years had passed since the murder of Stephen Hicks. That strange urge which he had managed to suppress for so long again had to be satisfied. It was 14-year-old James Doxtator's misfortune to cross Jeffrey Dahmer's path. Doxtator was accustomed to selling his body to weirdos for a price. Jeffrey picked him up with the promise that he would pay well if the boy would pose for nude pictures. At the diabolical hands of Jeffrey Dahmer, Doxtator was drugged, strangled and dismembered. Dahmer applied acid to his body, which was eventually pulverized with a sledgehammer.

Jeffrey Dahmer was now a killing machine. He frequented gay bars, where men were susceptible to being picked up. Richard Guerrero was one such man. He disappeared after falling into the deadly grasp of the man with the unnatural compulsion to kill and mutilate.

It became increasingly difficult and inconvenient to bring men to his grandmother's home. Jeffrey moved into the Oxford Apartments at 808 North 24th Street in Milwaukee. Later he would move into apartment 213, an address that one day would be flashed around the world.

Not everyone lured to Jeffrey's apartment was murdered. A few boys sensed that drugs had been placed in their beer or coffee and raced out of the apartment. One boy, a Laotian named Sinthasomphone, pressed charges. As a result, Jeffrey found himself convicted of sexual assault. He received a five-year jail sentence but was allowed out on day parole so that he could continue to work at the chocolate factory. Ten months later, he was given full parole.

The killings continued. Anthony Sears, Ray Smith, Edward Smith, Ernest Miller and David Thomas all were reported missing in the eighteen-month period between March 1989 and September 1990. Jeffrey would later claim that he had had sex with these men before strangling them.

By now, Jeffrey Dahmer had developed an extraordinary trait, one which places him in a unique category among serial killers who keep trophies of their kills. While trophy collecting is common amongst serial killers, most keep items such as a glove or wallet. Jeffrey kept heads and entire limbs. Anthony Sears's skull was painted and kept in a refrigerator. Other heads, limbs and organs were kept as mementos of sex and murder.

Months passed. Neighbours complained of the odour emanating from the Dahmer apartment. Jeffrey satisfied them with plausible excuses and promises that he would remedy the situation. No one took any concrete action. The killing spree went on unabated. Curtis Straughter, 18; Errol Lindsey, 19; and Tony Hughes, 31, all ended up as victims of the human monster who retained portions of their bodies for trophies.

Konerak Sinthasomphone, 14, coincidentally the younger brother of the boy responsible for Dahmer's earlier imprisonment for sexual assault, was a student at Pulaski High School. He was picked up by Jeffrey Dahmer and enticed into unit 213 at the Oxford Apartments. Konerak was given a beer laced with a knock-out drop. He lost consciousness and was subjected to a sexual assault. Noticing that he was out of beer, Jeffrey left to pick up a six-pack. While he was gone, Konerak regained consciousness and staggered, bleeding and naked, out of the apartment and down into the street, where he was spotted by Dahmer.

Others also witnessed the scene and called police. Three patrolmen, John Balcerzak, Joe Gabrish and Richard Porubcan, were soon at the scene of the incident. All three officers were experienced members of the Milwaukee Police Force, and throughout their careers had received several citations for heroism and acting beyond the call of duty.

Jeffrey had to talk fast. He assured the officers that his gay lover was a drunken adult and that there was really nothing amiss. The officers accompanied Jeffrey to his apartment, unaware that the body of Tony Hughes lay decaying in the bedroom at the time of their visit. Jeffrey showed the officers Polaroid pictures of Konerak posing in a skimpy bathing suit. The officers assumed they had been called to a domestic dispute between two consenting males. They were tragically wrong. After they left, Jeffrey strangled Konerak Sinthasomphone to death.

All three officers would later be suspended with pay for their actions that night. The three policemen maintained that there appeared to be a loving relationship between the two participants and that there were none of the usual warning signs that anything was drastically wrong.

His brief brush with the law didn't discourage Jeffrey. On June 30, 1991, Matt Turner was murdered in Dahmer's apartment. Jeremiah Weinberger, Oliver Lacy and Joseph Bradehoft met the same fate. All four heads were later found in the refrigerator.

On July 22, 1991, police officers Robert Rauth and Rolf Mueller were in their patrol car when they were flagged down by Tracy Edwards. Edwards wanted the cops to get him out of the handcuffs he was wearing. He told the officers a wild story of a man who had threatened to cut out his heart and eat it. The officers had the frightened man lead them to Jeffrey Dahmer's apartment.

The first thing to hit the officers was the vile odour of the apartment. They questioned Jeffrey and radioed headquarters to do a routine check on their suspect. Word came back that Dahmer had a felony conviction against him. The officers looked around the filthy apartment. One of them opened the refrigerator door and within hours the world was privy to the secret life of Jeffrey Dahmer.

Dahmer's trial in 1992 attracted worldwide attention. Security in the Milwaukee courtroom was unprecedented with police dogs used to sniff for explosives and an eight-foot-tall bullet-proof glass and steel wall erected to protect the accused from the gallery, which consisted largely of the families of his seventeen victims.

Casting aside his lawyer's advice, Dahmer changed his plea to guilty by reason of insanity. That put his lawyer, Gerald Boyle, in the position of having to prove that the vile acts of his client in torturing, dispatching and dismembering his seventeen victims could only have been performed by a madman. It became one of the most graphic and disturbing defences ever presented in an American courtroom. Ultimately Boyle failed—after five hours of deliberation, a jury found Dahmer both guilty and sane. He was sentenced to fifteen consecutive life terms, a total of 957 years in prison.

Two years later, Dahmer was attacked in the prison chapel by a prisoner he had never met before. In spite of this, he was later able to persuade authorities to grant him more access to the general prison population and was given janitorial duties. On November 28, 1994, guards found Dahmer dead, his head crushed by a fellow inmate and member of his work detail.

Pasquale Della Rose

(GUN)

THE EXPLOSION OCCURRED in New York City at 12:55 P.M. on Saturday, March 9, 1963. Twenty-seven-year-old Pasquale Della Rose stood beside his 1959 Ford screaming hysterically. He had good reason. Inside the vehicle, slumped over the steering wheel, was the body of his wife, Gloria. She was very dead.

Two minutes later, police officers were at the scene. They were greeted by a strange sight. There was Pasquale beside his car, shouting, "It's all my fault, it's all my fault."

Someone had wedged a double-barrel shotgun inside the back of the Ford. The sawed-off stock was on the floor against the rear seat and the barrels were firmly in place against the back of the front seat. The murderer had rigged up a pulley system, so that when the driver adjusted the seat forward, a Venetian-blind cord wrapped around the trigger would fire the shotgun. The infernal apparatus had been covered with a floor mat. Gloria had a hole in her back as big as a fist. She had died instantly.

Detectives examined the homemade killing machine and listened to Pasquale's story, particularly since he kept insisting that it was all his fault. He told them that he and Gloria had been married for a year and a half. She was only 19 years old. That morning, they had eaten breakfast at eight o'clock. At nine, his wife had gone shopping with a girlfriend, Sally Nunzio. Gloria had returned at around eleven.

Pasquale went on to tell police that he had had an industrial accident at the Bronx lamp factory where he worked. His doctor had recently died and he had been notified by the doctor's widow to pick up his medical records and take them to another doctor. That morning, he and Gloria attempted to pick up his records, but the doctor's wife had not been home. They told a maid that they would return later.

The pair proceeded to a market to shop for food. Pasquale had not had occasion to look in the back seat at any time that day until they went to park beside the market. As Gloria attempted to park the car, he turned around in the front seat to guide her into a parking space. As he did so, he noticed the bulge on the floor of the car behind the driver's seat. He reached down and pulled on the floor mat. The shotgun discharged and Gloria was dead in a flash of gunfire.

Pasquale had the sympathy of his interrogators. They asked him if he knew of anyone who would set such a booby trap. He told them he had no enemies.

Meanwhile, both Gloria's body and the Ford came under close examination. It was discovered that when Gloria had moved her seat forward earlier in the day, the shotgun had not been discharged because whoever rigged the apparatus left too much slack on the Venetian-blind cord. When Pasquale pulled on the floor mat, his action took up the slack and fired the weapon.

Police wanted to know who was aware that Gloria drove with the car seat in the forward position. Pasquale said he thought that anyone who was acquainted with her knew that she drove with her chest practically against the wheel. The first thing she did upon entering any vehicle was to adjust the seat forward.

Detectives had Pasquale repeat his story several times in case the emotional man would add some detail that would give them a clue to the killer's identity. As an afterthought, Pasquale mentioned that just before he married Gloria he had been beaten up by several men. He was sure it was the work of a disgruntled suitor, Santo Mordante. At the time, he had told police of his suspicions. They had questioned Mordante, but as there had been no proof, no charges were laid.

Mordante was located and questioned. He was upset at being interrogated about Gloria's death and stated that he hadn't seen the girl since her marriage to Pasquale. He also swore that he had had nothing to do with Pasquale's beating. Mordante was now a happily married man himself and resented being harassed.

Twelve hours had passed since the shotgun blast that had taken Gloria's life, and police still had no idea who had murdered her, nor did they know when the killer had placed the weapon in the vehicle. Now that the Ford had been examined by laboratory technicians, detectives decided to re-create the firing of the gun. Pasquale would go through his exact movements. A detective, the same size and weight as Gloria, took a position behind the steering wheel.

Pasquale sat beside the driver. When asked to turn around, he moved his body and head to the left, facing the detective. He continued to turn his body, lifting his left arm over the back seat. As he peered out the rear window, he said he saw the bulge on the floor. He then took hold of the floor mat with his left hand, pulling it up along with the concealed shotgun.

Pasquale smiled, glad that the demonstration was over. The experiment was repeated. This time a detective exactly the same height and weight as Pasquale was chosen to duplicate Pasquale's role. He sat in the passenger seat. Slowly he turned, moving his left arm across the back of the driver's seat. As he did so, he peered over his left shoulder out the back window. When asked to look down at the bulge on the floor, the detective couldn't do it. His line of vision from a seated position didn't allow him to view the rear floor. The only way he could see the bulge on the floor was to raise his body and crane his neck forward.

Pasquale observed the demonstration in shocked silence. His composure crumbled. He would answer no more questions until police allowed him to view his wife's body. Accompanied by officers, Pasquale was escorted to Jacobi Hospital Morgue, where he looked upon Gloria and burst into tears, moaning, "Oh God, forgive me! I loved her so much."

Now Pasquale told the true story. He said he was very much in love with his wife, but that she had insisted he was mentally ill and needed treatment. He claimed that she had threatened him with divorce if he didn't check himself into the hospital. Pasquale knew in his heart that he wasn't crazy, and he didn't want to be confined. He decided that the only way out of his predicament was to murder his wife. The shotgun had been purchased at Sears Roebuck in the Bronx. Sometime later he purchased shells but threw them all away except for the two used in the murder. Then he sawed away the stock of the shotgun so that the weapon would fit the back of his Ford. The booby trap was set, taking into account his wife's habit of adjusting her seat forward. The shotgun was placed in position in the middle of the night while Gloria slept. That morning, when his wife went shopping with Sally Nunzio, he watched from a window, fully expecting to see and hear the blast. He was amazed when nothing happened.

When Gloria returned with the car, he planned on checking out the contraption to find out what had gone wrong. Because she had insisted that they leave immediately to pick up his medical records, he didn't have an opportunity to check the weapon. As they were parking at the market, he decided to set off the shotgun himself, figuring it would go off if he applied more tension.

Pasquale was charged with his wife's murder. Ironically, at his trial, through questioning Gloria's family, it was established that she had had no intention of having him confined to a mental institution. She was merely following a doctor's advice to get her husband hospital treatment for the back injury he had suffered at his place of employment.

Pasquale Della Rose was found guilty of murder in the first degree. He was sentenced to life imprisonment.

Laura Doyle & Karen Severson

(WATER)

KAREN SEVERSON AND MISSY AVILA lived on the same street in Arleta, California, a suburban community located in the San Fernando Valley. They met when they were 8 years old and grew up together.

The two girls, who were such close friends, were different in many ways. Karen developed into an obese teenager, while Missy, who stood just under five feet tall, had a petite figure and a beautiful, wholesome face. Missy did well in school. Karen floundered. When it came to dates, Missy could pick and choose. Every boy at Mission High School vied for a date with her. She had several boyfriends by the time she was 17.

Karen had few boyfriends and envied Missy's popularity. When she managed to latch onto one of the local boys, she became pregnant. Karen dropped out of school and gave birth to a little girl. She decided to keep her child despite the fact that the baby's father denied all responsibility. Throughout this troubled time, Karen's good friend Missy was constantly at her side, offering her encouragement and companionship when others weren't as kind.

On October 1, 1985, Missy left her home with a friend, Laura Doyle. She told her mother that they were planning on driving to Stonehurst Park. The girls left the house in the best of spirits, laughing and joking. Irene Avila made a mental note to expect her daughter home at six that evening.

At around six, Laura called the Avila home, asking for Missy. She expressed surprise when she was told that Missy had not arrived home. In fact, Mrs. Avila thought that her daughter was still with Laura. Laura explained that they had driven to Stonehurst Park, where Missy had seen three boys she said she knew in a blue Camaro. Laura had dropped her off and had taken the opportunity to drive a short distance to purchase gas. When she returned, Missy was gone. Laura had been a bit disappointed, but figured that Missy had simply driven off with friends. She went on to tell Mrs. Avila that she didn't know the boys, but to have Missy call her when she got home.

Missy never returned home that evening or any other evening. After a sleepless night, Mrs. Avila reported her daughter missing to police. For three days Missy's friends and family frantically searched their minds for any clues that would assist police in their hunt for the missing girl. Laura had no idea what the boys looked like and, despite repeated questioning, could only state that their car was a blue Camaro. Understandably, she couldn't recall the licence number.

On October 4, two hikers trudging through the woods off Big Tujunga Road came across the body of tiny Missy Avila in a stream no more than eight inches deep. A large log had been placed over her back. Detectives ascertained from the condition of the victim's face that her head had been pushed into pebbles covering the bottom of the stream. The log was probably placed over the body to make death a certainty.

The hunt was on for the three boys in the blue Camaro. Laura was questioned again, but could add nothing to her original statement. Missy's good friend Karen took the murder particularly hard. As weeks turned into months, with no sign of the killer or killers being apprehended, Karen led discussion groups among Missy's family and friends in an attempt to jar their memories with some word or phrase Missy might have said that would help solve the riddle. On several occasions, she travelled up Big Tujunga Road to the scene of the crime to search for clues the police might have overlooked.

Karen was also a great comfort to the Avila family. She counselled Mrs. Avila and visited Missy's grave several times each week. For a while, Karen moved into the Avila home. Everyone was pleased that she was able to comfort Missy's mother.

Slowly, the individuals close to Missy put their lives back in order. Laura obtained a job as a clerk in a bakery. Karen took a beautician's course, but the memory of her friend's death was always in her mind. The tragedy became an obsession with Karen. Once she openly blamed the murder on a former boyfriend of hers and had him beaten up by a group of Missy's friends. The badly beaten youngster left the area for his own safety. Another friend of Missy's, Eva Chirumbolo, left Arleta for Las Vegas. She and her boyfriend obtained work and started life anew, far from the pall that had fallen over them back in California after Missy's death.

Eva was troubled by the unsolved murder. She often had nightmares about Missy. You see, Eva knew the details of Missy's death, but was fearful for her own life. The three years following the tragedy had not been easy for Eva. She was racked with guilt over the terrible secret she harboured. When she received word that her brother had committed suicide, the bad news seemed to act as a catalyst. Eva Chirumbolo went to the police with her fantastic story.

Eva told detectives that she, Laura Doyle, Karen Severson, and Missy had driven up Big Tujunga Road in two cars. She and Laura were in the lead car. Missy and Karen followed.

Once in the mountains, the girls got out of their cars. They approached Missy and all the pent-up venom came pouring out. Karen told Missy that she had been jealous of her all her life and, in fact, hated her. Eva looked on as Laura berated Missy for stealing her boyfriends. Missy cried, unable to comprehend how her friends had turned against her. Karen pushed Missy into the shallow stream. Eva couldn't stand it any longer. She ran back to the cars. As she ran, she heard a hideous, frantic scream. In a few moments, Karen joined her and told her to wait. She returned to the stream to help Laura cover Missy's body with the log. On the drive back down the mountain, Laura informed Eva that she and Karen had killed Missy. She laughed as she told Eva that she had taken her friend's life.

Karen and Laura were arrested and charged with Missy's murder. Missy's family and friends were incredulous. These girls had been her closest friends. Mrs. Avila fainted when she was told that Karen Severson, who had been such a pillar of strength over the years, was a suspect in her daughter's murder.

In custody, both girls admitted to killing Missy. Since each attempted to minimize her involvement, we can't be sure who actually held Missy's head down under the water. Photographs of the body indicate that both girls were involved, one holding Missy's feet, the other her head.

Laura Doyle and Karen Severson were found guilty of second-degree murder. Both were sentenced to fifteen years' to life imprisonment. The girls considered the verdict a victory. Had they been found guilty of murder in the first degree, they could have been sentenced to death in California's death chamber.

Frank Egan, Verne Doran & Alfred Tinnan

(AUTOMOBILE)

IT HAS BEEN SAID that the perfect crime is one in which a criminal act is never suspected. Dear old granny falls down the front stairs; a tragic accident, true enough, but the entire scenario lacks intrigue. Indeed, the diabolical details cannot be shared if murder is never suspected.

Law enforcement agencies, with their modern scientific equipment, are more than a match for most inept murderers. Occasionally, however, a bona fide intelligent member of society takes it upon himself to beat the system. That's exactly what happened on the evening of August 29, 1932, when someone ran over Mrs. Jessie Scott Hughes in San Francisco. Jessie's husband, Joe, had gone to his great reward some years previously, leaving her a wealthy woman. She aged gracefully, clipped coupons and lived alone in a small but comfortable home.

A young couple returning from an evening at the theatre sighted a body on the road. They rushed to the elderly woman's side and quickly ascertained that she was dead. Police were summoned. They confirmed that Jessie was beyond help, the apparent victim of a hit-and-run driver, and noted distinctive tire impressions on her red knitted sweater. Searching for a means of identifying the dead woman, police examined the inscription on her ring. It read, "From Joe to Jessie."

Next morning, Jessie's description was carried in the newspapers. An old acquaintance, John Kane, identified Jessie Hughes. That same evening, an array of the blue-rinse gang viewed the body. Tears flowed down wrinkled cheeks. Who would do such a thing to their dear friend? No one knew the answer to that one, but captain of detectives Charles Dullea intended to find out.

Dullea checked out the victim's home. Officers had already gone over the residence and garage without turning up anything that would lead to the identity of the heartless hit-and-run driver. After spending ten minutes on the property, Dullea declared that he thought Jessie had been murdered. His men figured the boss had lost his marbles, but Dullea was serious. He had observed tire tracks in Jessie's garage, which seemed odd to him. You see, Jessie didn't own a car. The idea of someone attempting to simulate a hit-and-run to cover over a cold-blooded planned murder had been planted in Dullea's mind. That's why he was captain of detectives.

Dullea, who was obviously part bloodhound, got down on his hands and knees on the garage floor. He believed that the concrete floor had recently been washed. Did the killer hose down the vehicle and the floor in order to dispose of any blood that might have splattered on the car? Or had someone killed Jessie in the garage?

The drainpipe of the garage was taken apart and examined. Inside, police found eight strands of grey hair. It now appeared to be a distinct possibility that someone had struck down Jessie in the garage, tossed her in the car and dumped her body where it had been found. Theories are one thing, but hard evidence is needed to solve a crime. Detectives were assigned the task of finding out who would benefit from Jessie's death.

Their investigative efforts came up with a rather unlikely suspect—none other than San Francisco public defender Frank

Egan. Egan was a reputable lawyer associated with humane charities. He turned out to be the executor and principal beneficiary of Jessie's will. On the surface, it seemed preposterous that he could seriously be considered as a suspect in a murder case. However, a check of Egan's financial status indicated that he was in debt for well over $10,000, not a small sum in those earlier times. He also had control of Jessie's money, and it was rumoured that she had recently become suspicious and wanted an accounting from him.

Detectives asked Egan where he'd been on the night of the murder. He claimed that he had attended a boxing match. When Jessie's neighbours placed him near her home on the night in question, Frank Egan became a prime suspect in the murder of Jessie Hughes.

Egan was known to help criminals after their release from prison. One such former con was Verne Doran, who worked as Egan's chauffeur. Detectives questioned Doran. He assured his interrogators that he had gone straight ever since his release from prison. He told them that although Egan owned a car, he had instructed Doran to borrow one on the day of the murder. A friend of Egan's named Postel had loaned him a Lincoln, which he had since returned. Postel verified Doran's story. He had no objection to allowing detectives to inspect his vehicle.

Police examined the Lincoln and came up with two grey hairs that matched the hairs found in Jessie's garage. A cast was made of the Lincoln's tires. The impressions were identical to those taken from Jessie's garage floor and her sweater.

When faced with this array of incriminating evidence, Doran figured it was either his neck or Frank Egan's. He chose Egan. Doran informed police that Egan had told him and his buddy Albert Tinnan that he had helped them both get out of prison and acquire jobs on the outside. If they didn't cooperate with him, he threatened, he could see that they were returned to jail.

Doran elaborated, "Egan said he was hard-pressed for money and that he could get money if Mrs. Hughes died. He phoned Mrs. Hughes and told her he was coming out with friends in a short time and that she was to have the garage door open, as she did in the past. He told me that Tinnan was to knock her unconscious by striking her in the stomach and my job was to run over her body. It was agreed that we make it look like a hit-and-run accident."

The two men drove to Jessie's residence and engaged the unsuspecting woman in conversation. They enticed her into the garage, where Tinnan punched Jessie in the stomach. He then struck her flush in the eye. Doran went on to say that Tinnan had placed Jessie under the right front wheel of the car. He gave instructions to drive backward and forward over the body. Tinnan then put the body in the back seat and the two men sped away.

They drove with the dead woman for some time, looking for a lonesome spot to dispose of the body, but every time they wanted to stop, a car drove by. Finally, they found a dark stretch of road to their liking and unceremoniously dumped the body there.

The entire unholy plot had been hatched by a man who should have known better—the public defender. The three men were tried and found guilty of murder. Frank Egan, Verne Doran and Albert Tinnan were sentenced to life imprisonment. All three were eventually paroled.

Dr. Yves Evenou & Simone Deschamps

(KNIFE)

SIMONE DESCHAMPS was a 43-year-old seamstress when she met Dr. Yves Evenou. It was an innocent enough meeting. Simone called on the doctor for a medical. Five years later, the seamstress and the doctor would provide all of France with one of the juiciest trials that country has ever enjoyed.

Simone wasn't beautiful, nor did she have a voluptuous figure. But beneath the seamstress's plain appearance beat the heart of a passionate, love-starved woman who had never fulfilled those urges we all possess in various degrees. Dr. Yves Evenou would change all that.

On the surface, Evenou was a kind and gentle doctor with a fine reputation. Tucked away at home there dwelt his ever-loving wife, Marie-Claire, and 12-year-old daughter Françoise. They had no idea that the good doctor was leading a double life. When not in his office or at home, Evenou was seldom without a glass of port in his hand. He loved the ladies and indulged in every perversion known to man with various ladies of the night. Sometimes, the doctor invented unique perversions of his own. Let's face it: he was one wild and crazy guy.

In Simone he met a lady who was easily led. After a few dates, she was not only in love with the medic, but totally under his influence. No perversion was too weird for Simone. Always half-sloshed on port, Evenou didn't treat Simone with a great deal of respect. Probably her most demeaning moments came when Evenou brought strangers to her home, to have intercourse with her while he watched. On other occasions, he would urge her to take off portions of her clothing in public places to satisfy some unfathomable personal sexual desire. Despite the humiliations, Simone was madly in love with him and did exactly as she was told.

The relationship between the odd couple grew stronger. Simone moved into the apartment building where Evenou lived with his wife and daughter. She occupied an apartment on the first floor. What could be more convenient? The doctor slipped down the stairs at every opportunity to indulge his peculiar sexual urges. Simone never disappointed. For five years the strange relationship flourished.

Something had to give. It all happened within a period of twenty-four hours one day in 1955. Dr. Evenou was slugging back his port with Simone at one of their regular watering holes, Madame Porree's Restaurant on Avenue des Allies. He brought up the subject of murdering his wife. The dear woman was ill, which would make the task that much easier. Evenou is reported to have said to Simone, "We can't go on unless she is removed. You must remove her. You have taken her place. You have a duty to me."

Simone, who after years of obedience was like one of Pavlov's dogs, listened wide-eyed. She agreed. Killing her lover's wife seemed the logical thing to do. The doctor went on, "Marie-Claire must die today. You must kill her. I will make preparations, of course. I shall see that everything is made ready. I think it would be as well if you stabbed her. Yes, that would be best."

Simone excused herself. Evenou ordered some more port. Twenty minutes later, Simone returned to the restaurant. She smiled as she showed her lover the menacing hunting knife with the horn handle that she had just purchased. Evenou approvingly took the weapon in his hand. It was perfect.

Together, the tipsy doctor and the dressmaker left the restaurant. Evenou briefed her on his plan and told her to wait in her apartment. The waiting was the hard part. Simone admitted later that although she was nervous, she never once thought of not going through with the plot to kill Marie-Claire Evenou.

A few floors up, in his own apartment, Evenou enjoyed the last dinner his wife would ever prepare. Although she was ill, Marie-Claire insisted on cooking her husband's meals. After eating, the doctor went for a short walk around the neighbourhood. No doubt he felt that he had created the perfect sex partner to share in his perversions. This would be the ultimate perversion. He had trained Simone to such a degree that she would kill for him on command.

It was a beautiful June night—in Evanou's mind, a night made for murder. Evenou returned to his apartment and called Simone. He said only one word, "Now." Simone had prepared herself as her lover had instructed. She wore only high-heeled red shoes and black gloves. She slipped her overcoat over her nude body and carefully placed the horn-handled knife into a pocket. One last touch. Simone applied bright red lipstick as Evenou had instructed. She was ready. She walked up the stairs leading to her lover's apartment, making certain that she wasn't seen by anyone.

Evenou was waiting. He removed the knife from Simone's pocket and placed her coat over a chair. He assured her that everything had been arranged. He had taken the precaution of giving his wife a sleeping pill earlier. The doctor led Simone to his wife's room. Gently, he pulled down the bedclothes. Then he pointed to his wife's body and told Simone, "Look. There is the heart. Now strike there."

As always, Simone obeyed. Nude except for her black gloves and red shoes, she struck. Maybe her mind was willing, but she hesitated. The knife came down, but it was a slow, sluggish blow that hardly broke the skin.

Marie-Claire awoke with a start. "Yves, Yves!" she cried as she looked up at her husband's smiling face.

The consoling husband responded, "I'm here, you were having a nightmare." Marie-Claire rose to get out of bed. Her husband clutched her in his arms and shouted to Simone to strike. Simone slashed out with the hunting knife. All hesitation had left her. She swung wildly time and time again. In all, she inflicted eleven stab wounds. Finally, Marie-Claire lay still in death.

In a daze, Simone returned to her apartment. She washed her blood-smeared body before turning to the incriminating knife and gloves. They too were dripping blood. Simone washed them carefully and then took needle and thread and sewed them into her mattress.

Dr. Evenou called police, but his story of an intruder didn't stand up under scrutiny. His love affair with the lady in the ground-floor apartment was discovered by police. It didn't take long for Evenou and Simone to confess to the murder, each accusing the other of being the mastermind behind the vicious crime.

Arrested and lodged in prison, awaiting trial, Dr. Evenou took seriously ill. His years of drowning himself in port, coupled with his dissipated lifestyle, had taken its toll. The good doctor died, leaving Simone alone to face the music. And face the music she did, to the fascination of the entire country.

Eighteen months after the crime was committed, Simone, now 48, stood trial for murder. The woman who sewed dresses for a living, who up to five years earlier had led a humdrum existence, stood in real danger of losing her head to the guillotine. On the advice of her counsel, Simone revealed her every thought and action from the time she had first met the evil doctor.

The details were so explicit and perverse that the judge often cleared the courtroom before allowing Simone to continue. Her defence rested on the influence the doctor wielded over her. She was depicted as nothing more than a tool in the hands of an evil man who had used her to kill an unwanted wife. But the prosecution demanded Simone's head. They claimed that cunning alone had enabled her to sew the gloves and knife into her mattress.

Simone was found guilty but displayed great remorse for what she had done. It was this remorse that provided the court with the necessary "extenuating circumstances" required to reduce the sentence from the guillotine to life imprisonment.

And that's how it all ended for the seamstress who, six years earlier, had called on a doctor for a routine medical.

Arthur Ford

(Spanish Fly)

You are forgiven if you have never heard of the drug cantharidin. Under the name Spanish fly, it has gained worldwide notoriety. What young virile male hasn't heard of Spanish fly, a substance that is supposed to enhance sexual desire in a female to such an extent that she actually craves sexual intercourse? Very few are aware that cantharidin is a deadly poison.

Arthur Kendrick Ford had served in the Far East with the British army. Aboard ship, on his way home to London, there was much lighthearted conversation among the men. Many had been away from home for years. They talked of the copious amounts of liquor they would consume and the long-legged ladies they would entice between the sheets. One of the men explained that if all else failed, he would use Spanish fly back in England. That little trick would bring the women flocking into his arms. Art Ford listened but didn't give the army jargon another thought until much later.

Art returned to his position as office manager of a wholesale drug firm, where he oversaw a staff of twenty-two women and four men. Art was typical of many men whose stint in the service was over. He adapted to civilian life. In due course, he met a pleasant young woman and fell in love. He and Marjorie married. In 1954, when our bizarre story begins, the Fords were the proud parents of two young children.

In April 1954, Art had a customer inquiry concerning cantharidin. Art's mind raced back to the shipboard conversation. He remembered well the rumoured qualities of the drug. What better way to have one of the office girls throw herself at his feet than to give her Spanish fly?

Pretty Betty Grant, 27, had been the object of Art's attention for some time. Unfortunately, his little office ploys to get her to like him had failed miserably. The girl simply rejected his every advance. So, Art had a chat with the company's senior chemist, Richard Lushington. On the morning of April 26, he asked Lushington if the firm stocked cantharidin. Art said a neighbour was breeding rabbits and had heard that the drug might help. Lushington confirmed that a bottle of the drug was in stock, adding that it was a powerful poison. Art replied, "Oh, well, if that's the case I don't want it."

Later that day, Art, by his own admission, took some cantharidin out of the bottle. With the aid of a pair of scissors, he inserted a quantity of the deadly poison into a chocolate commonly called coconut ice. The candy has a white-and-pink centre and is covered with chocolate. Art had no trouble inserting the poison in the candy, which he had purchased from a local sweetshop.

At around two-thirty in the afternoon, Art walked through the office carrying a bag of candy. He stuck his fingers into the bag and extracted a coconut ice. He gave it to Betty Grant. Other pieces were offered to other girls. Some declined. June Malins hadn't been offered a piece of candy, but was seen eating a coconut ice, which had probably been given to her by one of the other girls.

An hour later, June felt ill. Betty Grant assisted her colleague to the company's sickroom. Twenty minutes later, Betty also complained of feeling ill. At 4 P.M., Art developed a severe headache. As the afternoon wore on, the condition of the three sick employees worsened. They were taken to London's University College Hospital. Next day, the two girls died. Art's condition improved.

Autopsies performed on the two dead girls revealed that both had died as a result of poisoning by cantharidin. Detectives informed Art of the girls' deaths and received an unusual response. "Oh, dear God, what an awful thing I've done! Why didn't someone tell me? I've been a fool. Let me tell you the whole story."

From his sickbed, Art related the story of how he had heard of Spanish fly years earlier and how his memory was jarred by the customer's inquiry. He decided to try some Spanish fly on Betty Grant, and admitted that he had inserted the drug into a chocolate meant for her. He claimed that the drug must have adhered to June Malins's chocolate accidentally.

Art stated, "I gave one of the pieces to Miss Grant. We were very fond of each other. She kept putting me off and I made up my mind to give her cantharidin in the coconut ice to stimulate her desire for me. I cannot say how Miss Malins got the other piece, except that it was an accident. I am deeply sorry I gave Betty Grant the drug. I now realize that I caused the death of these girls by doing this crazy thing at the expense of losing my dear wife and children." But it was too late for self-recrimination. Two girls had died in agony because of Ford's foolish and reckless action.

In due course, Art stood trial for manslaughter in London's famed Old Bailey. Defence attorneys stated that there was no doubt in anyone's mind that Art Ford had not intended to kill the two women. Yet he had been warned by his company's senior chemist that the drug was a "Number One poison." Crown attorneys emphasized that at that point a reasonable man should have abandoned any harebrained scheme to gain a woman's affection through drug stimulation.

Marjorie Ford stood by her husband throughout his well-publicized trial and forgave his infatuation with Betty Grant. Arthur Ford was found guilty of manslaughter and was sentenced to five years' imprisonment.

Sidney Fox

(Hands)

SIDNEY HARRY FOX was a momma's boy. He was the last of four children born to Rosaline Fox. No question about it: Sid was always Mum's favourite.

During the ten years between 1918 and 1928, Sid served several short prison sentences, most of which did not exceed twelve months. In pursuit of the better things in life, he had acquired the habit of writing out cheques without having as much as a bank account. He hardly ever paid any of his bills, choosing to move rather than cough up.

Sid was not the most intelligent petty criminal in England. The fact is, he invariably got caught and was hustled off to jail. Upon his release, Momma was always at the prison gates to welcome the apple of her eye to her more than ample bosom.

In 1927, Rosaline Fox was living with a Mrs. Morris in a flat in Southsea. The arrangement was convenient for both women. Mrs. Morris's husband was a captain in the merchant navy and was always sailing around the friendly environs of China and other faraway places. Sid, as usual, was serving one of his numerous jail sentences.

When our boy Sid had completed his most recent sentence, he was greeted, as usual, at the prison gates by Momma, who brought him to her flat. Sid took one look at Mrs. Morris, stifled a yawn and proceeded to convince the older woman that he was madly in love with her. She soon thought Sid was the greatest thing since Valentino. To solidify their relationship, Mrs. Morris made out a new will cutting out her sailing hubby and making Sid sole beneficiary of her estate. To add insult to injury, Sid talked the dear lady into taking out a life insurance policy in his favour.

Soon after the necessary documentation was taken care of, Mrs. Morris woke up in the middle of the night to find her room full of gas. When police looked into the matter at the request of the gas company, they found the gas could only be turned on by a tap that was concealed by a heavy set of drawers. The near tragedy was no accident—someone had attempted to murder Mrs. Morris in her sleep. She thought she knew who. Things were never the same in the Southsea flat after that.

In fact, Mrs. Morris became downright nippy. Sid and Momma pulled up stakes and moved to more hospitable digs. However, before her departure, Sid helped himself to Mrs. Morris's jewellery. He received his longest prison sentence for this indiscretion, fifteen months.

In 1929, Sid was released into Momma's waiting arms yet again. Without Sid's petty thievery and worthless cheques to support her, she was living in a workhouse. Considerate son that he was, Sid moved his mother into a modest but comfortable hotel.

It should be pointed out that the 31-year-old Sid and his 63-year-old mother, Rosaline, believed that living in hotels was the sign of a good life. This they did constantly throughout southeast England. They never paid their hotel bill, always leaving at the first indication that management was growing suspicious. Still, it wasn't a bad setup; a few days of luxury here, a week in a resort there. It beat prison or the workhouse.

Somewhere along the line between packing and unpacking, Sid managed to take out two insurance policies on his mother's life. The policies totalled £2,000 should Momma shuffle off this mortal coil via an accidental route.

On October 16, 1929, the slippery Foxes arrived at the Hotel Metropole at Margate, Kent. Vera Hopper, the receptionist, gave them rooms 68 and 70. The rooms were side by side but had no connecting door.

After enjoying the hospitality of the Metropole for two days, Sid sneaked off to nearby Ramsgate and purchased another £1,000 of insurance on his mother's life.

Next day, a concerned Sid spoke to the Metropole's manager, Joseph Harding. It seems Momma was a bit chilled. Could they not get rooms with a gas fire? Sure they could, the manager replied. Rosaline was moved to room 66 and Sid was given adjoining room 67.

On Wednesday evening, October 23, 1929, Sid and his mother ate a hearty meal in the restaurant at the Metropole. Later that night, Sid, ever the considerate son, dashed out and purchased a bottle of port for his mother. He delivered the bottle to Momma's room.

Never one to squander a shilling, Sid had paid up Rosaline's insurance policies to midnight of October 23. It was now 11 P.M. At precisely 11:40 P.M., just twenty minutes before the policies were to expire, Sid raced down to the lobby dressed only in a shirt. He bumped into salesman Samuel Hopkins, another guest at the hotel. Sid informed Hopkins of an emergency. "I believe there is a fire," he told Hopkins.

Hopkins ran up the stairs with Sid to room 66. He opened the door and was greeted by a wall of dense smoke. Hopkins dropped to his knees and entered the room. Crawling on his stomach, he made contact with Rosaline Fox's legs. Hopkins managed to drag the heavy woman from the room before collapsing.

By this time, other guests were attracted to the smoke-filled room. One man, Reginald Reed, pulled a still-burning armchair into the hall. He reentered the room and succeeded in dragging out a portion of burning carpet that had been directly under the armchair.

Guests managed to extinguish the flames licking at the chair and carpet. Rosaline was taken to the lobby, but alas, the poor woman was dead. A doctor was called. He took one look at the body and the scene before announcing that death was attributed to suffocation. He issued a death certificate to the grieving Sid. A hasty inquest held the next day confirmed the doctor's diagnosis. Sid stayed at the Metropole one more night, just long enough to contact his solicitor regarding those convenient insurance policies. He then skipped without paying the bill.

On October 29, Rosaline was laid to rest. The undertaker's bill has not been paid to this day.

On November 3, Sid was picked up at a hotel in Norwich and returned to Margate. Suspicious insurance investigators thought Rosaline's death only moments before the policy expired smelled to high heaven. It was they who contacted Scotland Yard.

The Yard boys agreed with the insurance investigators. They had Rosaline's body exhumed. Sure enough, it was ascertained that Rosaline had gone to that great hotel in the sky as a result of strangulation rather than suffocation.

On January 9, 1930, Sid stood trial for his mother's murder. Unfortunately for Sid, his mother was a nonsmoker. It was also pointed out that the carpet covering the area between the gas fire and the burned carpet under the chair was not even scorched. There was little doubt that someone had set Rosaline Fox on fire. There was even less doubt that the culprit was her ever-loving son Sid.

The English jury took only one hour and a half to find Sid guilty of murder. On April 8, 1930, he was hanged in Maidenstone Gaol.

For years after the death of Mrs. Fox and the execution of Sid, many guests occupying room 66 at the Metropole claimed they heard mother and son arguing in the wee hours of the morning. The ghosts of Rosaline and Sid had to vacate the Metropole in 1947, when the hotel was demolished in order to widen the street.

Richard Fredericks

(MALLET)

IT'S RATHER DISTRESSING to all concerned when a supposed murder victim walks into a police station. It doesn't happen every day.

A Mexican rancher discovered the body one day in 1953 as he walked through his field. It wasn't a pleasant sight. The woman had been beaten about the head so severely that her features were beyond recognition. Most horrific of all was the absence of the victim's hands.

Mexican police were soon at the crime scene. A cursory examination of the clothing worn by the dead woman indicated that she was American. Because the body was found near Ensenada, about fifty miles south of the California–Mexican border, the Los Angeles police were notified. An American detective was dispatched to assist in the investigation.

There was precious little to help the officers in identifying the dead woman. She had been dead for weeks and the body had been ravaged by the elements. Obviously her killer had cut off her hands and had picked the isolated area to dump the body in order to make identification difficult, if not impossible.

The description of the murder victim was widely distributed in California and Mexico. She was five feet six inches tall and weighed 115 pounds. She had a mole on the right side of her neck. When found, she was wearing a red blouse and jeans. The publicity soon brought practical results. A distraught woman drove down from San Diego, deeply concerned that the murdered woman could be her daughter. She viewed the body and burst into tears. "It is Olga," was all she could say between sobs.

After giving the woman time to compose herself, detectives asked her how she could be sure, considering the condition of the victim's face. They were assured that Olga had worn an identical red blouse and jeans. The mole on the corpse's neck was further proof. During this discussion, a police doctor informed the woman that the victim had three gold teeth and indicated their position in her mouth. Sadly, the woman nodded. Now she was absolutely positive. Her Olga had three gold teeth in the same positions.

Next day, the same newspapers that had solicited information to help identify the handless body in the field revealed that her name was Mrs. Olga Carrino, a San Diego mother of two young sons, aged 5 years and 9 months.

Four days passed before a young, attractive woman walked into a San Diego police station. She told the officer in charge, "I am Olga Carrino and I am not dead. What's more, I have my two hands." With that declaration the woman pushed her hands forward to make sure the startled officer saw what she was talking about.

Olga had quite a story to tell. Her husband, Fernando, was employed on a tuna clipper fishing in the Pacific. Because he would be away for some time, she and her two young sons had moved in with her in-laws. The arrangement hadn't worked out. They had fought and she had stormed out of the house and had gone to live with a girlfriend.

Olga had only heard of her supposed death about an hour before walking into the police station. Her girlfriend had shown her details of her demise in a four-day-old newspaper. Olga had immediately informed her family that she was alive and well and then had gone directly to the police station. Yes, she wore an identical red blouse and jeans as the dead woman. Yes, she had a mole in exactly the same location on her neck as the murder victim. Most amazing of all, Olga had three gold teeth in the same places as the handless body. She opened her mouth and showed the detectives her teeth. There was no question about it—whoever had been murdered and dropped into that Mexican field was not Olga Carrino.

Detective Charles F. Stewart of the Los Angeles Police Department was studying missing persons reports in a routine manner when information on one of the documents rang a bell. He had recently read the facts and figures about a woman's body found in Mexico that were startlingly similar to the report he was scanning.

The missing woman was Ruth Fredericks. She had been reported missing by two friends who hadn't seen her in over a month. The women had made a date with Ruth to go to the movies. All had made arrangements to obtain a babysitter for their children. Ruth simply hadn't shown up.

The two friends had asked her husband, Richard, about her whereabouts. He didn't volunteer any information and seemed extremely cavalier about the whole thing, which is why they took it upon themselves to report her missing. Ruth was five feet six inches tall, weighed 115 pounds, had a mole on her neck and often wore a red blouse and jeans. She also had three gold teeth.

Stewart believed that the handless body found in Mexico was Ruth Fredericks. He interviewed the two women who had reported Ruth missing and got an earful. They had known Ruth for two years. During that time, her husband had been a holy terror. He continually screamed at his wife. Often Ruth would show up with a black eye or a bruised arm. When Ruth disappeared, they figured she must be dead, because there was no way she would leave her 5-year-old son and the two younger children.

The women informed Stewart that the 5-year-old had stopped attending school. Upon learning this, one of the women had gone to the Fredericks's home and found it vacant. She checked with the Fredericks's immediate neighbour and was told that Richard had sold his car, packed his belongings and flown to New Jersey with the three children.

Richard had worked in New Jersey before moving to California. Detective Stewart called on the insurance company where Richard had been employed. He learned that his man had been transferred from New Jersey and for a while had been a friendly, valued employee. In the past year, he had undergone a remarkable change in personality. He consistently harped about his wife being unfaithful, although, as far as anyone at the insurance company knew, Ruth Fredericks was a faithful wife and loving mother.

When an employee found a gun in Richard's locker, he had informed Ruth of his discovery. Ruth had told her husband's colleague that Richard's behaviour was so bad she was considering having him confined.

Evidently, Ruth was able to talk Richard into entering a psychiatric hospital for observation. He stayed only a week before signing himself out. After his short spell in hospital he became moodier than ever and hardly communicated with fellow employees at the insurance company. Finally, Richard confided to a co-worker that his wife was a tramp and had run away with a sailor. He wasn't sorry and took the attitude that he was better off without her.

After tracing Richard to Maplewood, New Jersey, Detective Stewart flew there for a face-to-face confrontation with his suspect. Stewart knocked on the front door of the man he believed had brutally killed his wife and then chopped off her hands. He introduced himself and was graciously invited into the house by Richard. Stewart gingerly inquired, "Your wife's name is Ruth, isn't it?"

Homicide investigators claim to have heard it all, but it is doubtful if Detective Stewart was prepared for Richard's reply: "Her name's Ruth and I killed her."

Richard went on to explain that on the previous January 6, he and Ruth were in the backyard of their Van Nuys residence. He had accused her of being unfaithful. She became furious, screaming that he was wrong and that he must be crazy. When he retreated to the garage, she followed. He saw red, picked up a mallet and struck her on the head. He couldn't stop swinging until his wife's face was nothing more than a mass of flesh.

He carried her body to a workbench, where he chopped off her hands with a hatchet. He then buried the hands in the backyard and placed Ruth's body in the trunk of his car. In an effort to dispose of the body, he drove to Mexico, crossing the international border at Tijuana. No one had searched the interior of his vehicle or asked him to open the trunk. Relieved, he drove on to Ensenada and dumped his wife's mutilated body in the isolated field.

Richard told Stewart that he thought he was home free when he read that the dead woman had been identified as Olga Carrino. When he learned that the error had been discovered, he had panicked and had fled to New Jersey.

Stewart had Los Angeles detectives dig in Richard's backyard. Sure enough, right where Richard said he had buried them, they discovered the hands of Ruth Fredericks.

Richard Fredericks waived extradition and was returned to California to stand trial. He was found guilty of murder in the second degree and received the strangely lenient sentence of one to ten years' imprisonment.

Herbert French

(SYRINGE)

ALTHOUGH IT WAS A DANGEROUS GAME, it was like an elixir. Herbert William French was having an affair. Just imagine Herbie at 45, a rather dull bloke in a rather dull job having a bona fide clandestine affair. Sure he was married, like any God-fearing office manager should be, but what the heck, his new love put spring in Herbie's gait and sparkle in his otherwise unimpressive eyes.

It had started out innocently enough in good old London town—a bit of flirting with his secretary, attractive 28-year-old Eileen Taylor, a quiet lunch and a few drinks. Sometimes, after work, they would visit a pub. There was no question in Herbie's mind. Eileen was as attracted to him as he was to her.

True, Eileen was married, but it was obvious to Herbie that she didn't get along with her husband. That made Herbie feel good. After all, he didn't want to be the cause of breaking up Eileen's marriage. When she separated from her husband and took a small flat near Hampstead Heath, Herbie didn't feel guilty at all. The natural progression of Herbie and Eileen's relationship steered a straight course to the bedroom. Folks, those two were at it all the time.

In August 1955, Eileen checked and rechecked her calendar. Convinced that no lunar miscalculation had taken place, she was certain that she was pregnant. Her unplanned condition posed a serious problem. Eileen had already left her husband. Unwed mothers were frowned upon in those days. She would have to leave her job and lose the income that provided her with the independence she treasured.

Back in 1955 in England, abortions were illegal. Eileen decided to share her little secret with Herbie. There was an outside chance that he would leave his wife and obtain a divorce. Once Eileen's divorce was final, the two lovers could marry and live happily ever after.

Fat chance. Herbie didn't take the news well. He dreaded the thought of Eileen's stomach expanding right there in the office for all the world to see. Working in the same office as Eileen would be out of the question. Moreover, he could kiss his marriage goodbye. Then there was child support to consider.

Herbie and Eileen put their heads together and came up with a solution. Herbie would pay for, and Eileen would undergo, an illegal abortion. To this end, Herbie made a few discreet inquiries. A friend of a friend gave him a phone number. That's how he met Doris Colbert. He and Mrs. Colbert came to an understanding that £40 would be a mutually satisfactory sum to do the job.

Doris agreed to perform the operation after being assured by Herbie that Eileen was no more than three months pregnant. Somewhat relieved that things might turn out all right in the end, Herbie scampered off to tell Eileen the good news. She went along with all the arrangements.

A few nights later, Eileen and Herbie showed up on schedule at a house on Bryanston Square. They were met by Doris Colbert and her assistants, Elizabeth Williams and Kathleen O'Regan. Eileen was ushered into a bedroom, while Herbie cooled his heels in the den.

The operation was to be simple enough. By means of a Higginson syringe, a soapy mixture would be inserted into the patient's womb. The sac containing the fetus would then separate from the wall of the womb. The procedure went well, but nothing happened. Eileen was made to jump up and down and to take a walk around the block. Nothing brought about the desired result.

Two days later, Eileen again subjected herself to the ordeal. This time, something went terribly wrong. Air was sucked up into the syringe with the soapy fluid and injected into the uterus. The resulting embolism caused Eileen's death in a matter of minutes.

Naturally enough, Herbie was terror stricken. He felt terrible about Eileen, but now he was faced with the problem of extricating himself from any blame in her death. The three abortionists were faced with the same problem. All four discussed their mutual predicament. Several ideas were tossed about before they decided to bury Eileen in Epping Forest.

With Herbie's help, the three women managed to carry the body down to the back seat of Elizabeth Williams's car. Eileen was propped up between Doris Colbert and Kathleen O'Regan. Anyone who has driven through the streets of London with a dead body knows it is not a pleasant experience. At last, they reached their destination. Herbie directed the women and their gruesome cargo about a half mile into the forest off Epping Road.

There are not that many people with experience in grave digging, if you discount those stout-hearted men who perform this necessary task for a living. Certainly, our ill-equipped foursome found the task tedious. It was almost dawn when what passed for a grave was completed. Eileen was lowered into her crude resting place and covered with earth.

Then something happened that was unfortunate for Herbie. He bent over and out of his pocket tumbled a yellow pencil bearing his name and the name and address of his company. Unaware of this incriminating bit of evidence left only a few metres from the grave, the foursome made their way back to Bryanston Square. They shook hands all around and called it a day.

On October 29, some three months after Eileen was unceremoniously buried, two youngsters walking in the woods saw a human hand sticking out of the earth. Police were quickly dispatched to the scene. It didn't take long to establish that the dead woman was Eileen Taylor, who had been reported missing during the early part of August.

Eileen's husband was tracked down. He proved that he had been separated from his wife for months before her estimated date of death, which had been established as being about three months before she was discovered. A post-mortem indicated that death had been caused by an attempted abortion.

And then detectives found what all detectives dream about finding at the scene of a murder. Close by the body they came across a yellow pencil with the name Herbert William French printed above the address where our Herbie was employed.

Initially, Herbie attempted to bluff his way out of his predicament by disclaiming any connection with his missing secretary. When shown that incriminating pencil, he crumbled and immediately named his three co-conspirators. When questioned, they too admitted their part in Eileen's death.

All four stood trial in London's Old Bailey. Because of absence of malice aforethought, the murder charges were reduced to manslaughter. Herbert French pleaded guilty and was sentenced to three years' imprisonment. Colbert, O'Regan and Williams pleaded guilty to using an instrument with intent to procure an abortion. Each received a one-year suspended sentence.

David Frooms

(Nightgown)

Strange as it may sound, many murderers have an uncontrollable urge to stay close to the investigation into their crimes. Some have been known to phone and even write to the police.

Before the turn of the century, Jack the Ripper wrote taunting letters to the authorities, advising them that he would strike again. In more recent times, Richard Loeb became fascinated with detectives who were searching for clues into the murder of Bobby Franks in Chicago's infamous "compulsion" case. Loeb turned out to be one of the youngster's killers.

Now we will look at the tragic death of a young English girl, Sarah Gibson, and her murderer's urge to correspond with the police.

Sarah was born into the horse-racing set. Her father, Colonel John Gibson, was a famous trainer and breeder of racehorses. One of her brothers was an accomplished rider. The family lived in the village of Lambourn in Berkshire, England. They led the good life, but Sarah wanted something different. Horses and the pleasant social life of the village didn't satisfy her.

At 19, Sarah told her mother and father that she wanted a career in the hotel business and planned on achieving success without their influence. Sarah left the genteel life of Lambourn to strike out on her own in London. Her first job was that of a domestic at the Norfolk Hotel in the West End.

A few months later, Sarah was successful in obtaining employment with the Royal Automobile Club as assistant housekeeper. This was a giant step forward in Sarah's dogged determination to carve out a career for herself. The Royal Automobile Club had a staff of 250 employees, of whom fifteen lived on the premises. Sarah was one of the huge club's live-in employees. The prestigious club had a 200-seat restaurant, 15,000 paid members and maintained eighty bedrooms for male guests only.

In 1971, the Gibson family moved from Lambourn to a beautiful restored farmhouse near Cheltenham. Sarah spent many weekends with her family. She was happy in her work and enjoyed living in London.

On Sunday, July 2, 1972, Sarah had the day off. It was one of those weekends she chose to stay in the city. That evening, Sarah had dinner in the staff dining room. A little after 7:30 P.M., she was seen strolling over to the Fun City Bingo Hall, located about 300 yards from the club. Two hours later, she was seen leaving the bingo hall, but no one saw her return to her room.

Next morning, a housemaid looked in on room 519 on the fifth floor and found Sarah's nude body on her bed. Her hands and feet were tied. A pink nightgown was knotted around her neck and a handkerchief had been stuffed in her mouth. She had been raped.

Detectives didn't take long to ascertain that Sarah didn't have a steady boyfriend. She had been a hard-working, happy young woman who enjoyed the sights of London. Her movements were traced up until she left the bingo hall, but there the trail abruptly stopped. Because nothing seemed to be disturbed in her room, it was felt that Sarah might have known her killer and had been attacked without warning.

When a list of Sarah's possessions was compiled, it was found that several pieces of jewellery were missing. Gold earrings, a travelling clock, a silver locket, a gold charm bracelet and mother-of-pearl cigarette lighter had been taken from the room. On July 7, the bracelet and lighter were sold to a SoHo jeweller.

Chief Superintendent James Neville of Scotland Yard believed that robbery might have been the motive with rape and murder an afterthought. On the other hand, he knew it was quite possible that a cunning killer could have taken the jewellery from the room to throw the police off the trail.

Of the eighty bedrooms available to males at the club, only seventeen had been occupied on the night of the murder. Police decided to check the fingerprints of not only the occupants of these seventeen, but also those of everyone who had stayed at the Royal Automobile Club since Sarah joined the staff. Their prints would be checked against those found in Sarah's room.

On July 9, Superintendent Neville received a surprise in the mail. It was an unsigned letter from the killer. It read:

I thought you might like some help in the case as it seems you are approaching it from the wrong angle. I did not like the idea of Sarah's departure but it couldn't be helped, but what can be done is to stop it happening again. I found a strange sense of power in depriving a body of life, though Sarah was a mistake.

On the night Sarah died I felt no sense of remorse or guilt so hurry up and catch me. I won't give myself up for incarceration because that would destroy me as I have a great longing for life.

Had this letter not been written, it is doubtful if the killer of Sarah Gibson would ever have been identified. Fingerprints on the letter were checked with prints on file with Scotland Yard. The prints matched those of 25-year-old David Charles Richard Frooms, a ne'er-do-well who had served several terms in prison for theft, robbery and indecently assaulting a 13-year-old girl.

Frooms was located and taken into custody. He was asked to write a few words on paper. Handwriting experts compared these words with the handwriting on the letter sent to Superintendent Neville. There was no doubt about it—both had been written by Frooms.

When confronted by this overwhelming evidence, Frooms blurted out, "I am glad you have got me. I killed her, strangled her with something she was wearing."

When asked if he had had sexual intercourse with his victim, he replied, "She was dead then."

In December 1972, Frooms was tried for murder in London's famed Old Bailey. He pleaded not guilty, claiming he had no recollection of the killing itself, although he remembered climbing through an open window and making his way up to the fifth floor looking for something to steal. He saw a bedroom door ajar and walked quietly into the room. Sarah was asleep on the bed. He took whatever appeared to be valuable.

When Sarah stirred, he stuffed something in her mouth and tied her hands and feet with her underclothing. He claimed to remember having his hands around her throat, but nothing more. He further claimed that he had no recollection of intending or wanting to kill the girl. In addition, he had no memory of having written the incriminating letter to police.

Despite his lawyer's claim of diminished responsibility, it took the English jury only half an hour to bring in a guilty verdict. David Frooms was sentenced to life imprisonment.

George Hladiy

(Hands)

IT WAS JUST ANOTHER WORKDAY for Eino De Witt and Wally Sempke on the McIntyre River. The two men were perspiring under the hot August sun that day in 1952, when Eino spotted a strange-looking object in the water near the south side of the river. The men lowered a skiff off their big derrick scow and rowed across the river.

It was the body of a man floating face downward. A half-inch rope was looped tightly around his neck with one strand wrapped across his mouth like a gag. In addition, there was a two-inch gash on the right side of the victim's head. Two heavy steel plates were tied to the dead man's neck and feet with wire. These plates were risers used under railroad tracks at switching points. They could be found stacked anywhere along the rail line, and, in fact, these two were stamped as being the property of the Canadian Pacific Railway.

Back in 1952, the twin cities of Fort William and Port Arthur were separate entities that were eventually united to form what we now know as Thunder Bay, Ontario. At the time of the murder, railway officials had become concerned about the high incidence of grain thefts from CNR and CPR railway cars. Thieves were breaking boxcar seals and carting away bushels of grain. Others were even more brazen, drilling through the boxcars and letting the grain run directly into bags outside the cars. Because of the proximity of the parked railroad cars to the point where the body was taken out of the water, officials believed that the murder could, in some way, be connected to the theft of grain.

An autopsy indicated that the unidentified man had already been dead when he was submerged in the McIntyre. In addition to being hit on the head, he had been manually strangled. His clothing proved to be untraceable and there was no documentation found on the body to assist in identification. Calluses on the victim's hands indicated that he worked at physical labour, but decomposition made fingerprinting impossible. He wore a ring engraved with the initials W.H.

Dr. A.E. Allin, chief pathologist for the attorney general's department, informed police that the dead man had a long scar along the back of his body. The scar was the result of a lung operation in which a rib had been removed. Once seen, it is doubtful anyone would forget that livid scar.

Police received a hot lead when Ignace Hyriciuk reported that a tenant of his, Josef Panok, had been missing for some weeks. Ignace explained that his tenant had recently immigrated from Europe with his wife and young daughter. They had rented a tiny house on dilapidated Simpson Street in Fort William. Ignace went on to tell investigators that the Panoks' friend George Hladiy lived with them. Ignace was taken to the morgue to view the body but couldn't say with any degree of certainty that the dead man was his tenant.

Detectives drove to the tiny house on Simpson Street. Once there, they learned that the Panoks didn't rent the entire house but occupied two cramped rooms on the second floor. Mrs. Panok, an attractive brunette, couldn't speak English. The officers' questions were translated by well-built blond George Hladiy. George explained that he and Panok were friends from the Ukraine.

With George translating, Mrs. Panok told the officers that she wasn't worried about her husband. He was in Winnipeg visiting a family named Kummel, who lived on Bannerman Street. Police suggested that she and George view the body in the morgue to assist them in their identification attempts. Mrs. Panok readily agreed.

When she looked down at the horrible sight of the decomposed corpse, Mrs. Panok cried out, but after settling down she stated that the dead man was definitely not her husband. George Hladiy agreed. Both swore they had never seen the initialled ring before.

Investigators, under the direction of Port Arthur police chief Tom Conner, learned of a missing man, a lumberjack, whose initials were W.H. Several individuals identified the ring as belonging to the missing man. After viewing the body, they all agreed that the dead man was not the elusive W.H.

This minor mystery was solved when W.H. showed up. A giant of a man, he had been on a drunken spree to end all sprees, and had found himself in Copper Cliff with a monumental hangover and no money. He had not heard of the murder until he returned to Port Arthur. W.H. stated that the ring had belonged to him and that he had given it to a man named Panok as a reward for helping him out once when he was in a fight in a beer parlour.

W.H. accompanied police to the morgue and positively identified the dead man as Josef Panok. He recognized the long scar, explaining that he had worked with Panok many times under the hot sun when both men had been stripped to the waist. But how could this be? Panok's wife and best friend had already viewed the body and had sworn they didn't know the identity of the dead man. Police, now wary of Mrs. Panok, checked out the Kummel family, who supposedly lived on Bannerman Street in Winnipeg. There was no such family.

When Chief Connor called on Mrs. Panok this time, he brought along his own translator. He asked his suspect, "Why didn't you identify your dead husband at the morgue?" Mrs. Panok replied, "Hladiy told me not to. He threatened to kill me if I did. He and Josef went out to steal wheat and only George came back."

Mrs. Panok went on to tell the officers that her husband and George had known each other in Germany, where they dabbled in the black market. When their illicit business dried up, George made his way to Canada, promising to arrange for the Panok family to follow him. True to his word, he arranged for the Panoks to emigrate and was successful in getting Josef employment on a CPR work gang.

Living conditions were primitive. She, her husband and George all slept in the same bed. Daughter Karen slept alone in the only other room, the kitchen. According to Mrs. Panok, George had asked her to leave her husband and go to Toronto with him. She had refused his offer and the tension had become unbearable in the enclosed living space.

George was picked up at his place of employment on the railroad. When presented with Mrs. Panok's statement, he agreed to it all, but he swore he had not killed Josef Panok. Lodged in jail, George made another statement to police. He said that he and Josef had gone out on the night of the tragedy to steal wheat from the boxcars. Just as George was about to break the seal and open the boxcar, Josef sneaked up behind him and put a rope around his neck. George said he grabbed at the rope with one hand and swung around with the other, striking Josef a blow to the head, which sent him reeling against the side of the boxcar. He then related that he had tied the rope and the steel risers to the body and tossed it into the McIntyre River.

Mrs. Panok filled in the rest of the evening by telling investigators that George had returned to the house around midnight, pale and shaken. Later, she would testify in court, "I couldn't sleep and I asked him again where Josef was. He told me he had killed my husband and thrown him in the river."

George stood trial for the murder of Josef Panok. He pleaded self-defence, but couldn't account for the tiny broken bones in the victim's neck, which indicated manual strangulation. The jury could not dismiss the obvious motive, that of a love triangle. They chose to believe that George had killed Josef in an attempt to possess his wife.

George Hladiy was found guilty of the murder of Josef Panok. On April 28, 1953, after all appeals were exhausted, he was hanged at the Port Arthur Jail.

Mrs. Panok, accompanied by her 5-year-old daughter, returned to Germany shortly after the conclusion of George's trial, her dreams of a fresh start in the New World shattered forever.

Mark Hofmann

(EXPLOSIVES)

MARK HOFMANN WAS BORN into a religious Mormon family in Salt Lake City, Utah. In 1973, he graduated from Olympus High School and, as is the custom in his faith, left home for two years' missionary work. Mark served his mission in Portsmouth, England, and it was here that he became interested in old books and documents pertaining to the Church of Jesus Christ of Latter-Day Saints.

His interest in such material is not altogether unusual. The Mormon church has always cherished authentic documents dating back to the founding of the faith, in 1830, by Joseph Smith. Church officials often pay well for additions to their archives. In fact, a flourishing market exists for such material.

In 1976, Mark, having completed his mission, returned to the United States and entered Utah State University. While at university, he delved deeply into the history of his religion.

Mark wed pretty Dori Olds on September 14, 1979. Dori dropped out of school to help support her husband, who was pursuing a medical career. Mark contributed a few dollars from the occasional sale of old Mormon coins and documents.

About a year after his marriage to Dori, Mark purported to find an ancient document in an old 17th-century Cambridge Bible. It was signed by Joseph Smith and contained hieroglyphics that Smith said he had copied from the Golden Plates of the Book of

Mormon. Mark took it to the church archives department, where the discovery caused quite a stir. After testing by experts, the document was deemed to be authentic.

Mark became the darling of the collection world. He gave lectures, granted interviews and received wide acclaim as the man who'd found what became known as the Anthon Transcript. Mark gave up his studies to devote all his time to tracing, trading and selling valuable documents pertaining to the Mormon faith, as well as other original material.

By 1981, Mark had a wide reputation as a tracer of extremely rare documents. Some individual sales to the church brought as much as $52,000. To finance his purchases, he often borrowed heavily. When the sales went through, everything came up roses. When there were delays or if the deals went sour, he often had difficulty meeting his financial obligations. Over and above his business debts, Mark and his wife lived well. On the surface, money didn't seem to be a problem.

In 1983, Mark Hofmann consummated the biggest deal of his career. He had in his possession a letter written by Martin Harris. The letter contained the startling information that, in 1823, when Joseph Smith found the Golden Plates on which the Book of Mormon is said to be transcribed, he came upon a salamander that turned itself into a spirit. The discovery of the Salamander Letter, as it came to be known, caused great controversy among church leaders, as it differed from official Mormon theology, which held that Smith had received the tablets from the Angel of God. Harris's signature on the letter was believed to be the only one in existence.

Steven Christensen and his associate, Gary Sheets, owned a large real estate firm. Devout Mormons, they both became deeply involved in authenticating the letter which went to the very heart of the Mormon religion. In time, Christensen purchased the

Salamander Letter from Mark for $45,000. On April 12, 1985, he donated it to the church.

Meanwhile, Mark wheeled and dealed, often in partnership with investors. He purchased letters written by Daniel Boone, describing his trek into Kentucky. On several occasions, Mark paid off his investors with large profits.

Mark slowly got in deeper and deeper. Deals had gone sour. The partnership of Christensen and Sheets also suffered from poor investments. Mark picked this time to leak the story that he had located a group of documents called the McLellin Collection. These ancient documents were hot. They cast doubt on basic church doctrine. Steve Christensen, acting for the church, would purchase the documents from Mark on behalf of investors who would donate the controversial documents to the church.

Mark desperately needed cash. He had a large amount of money invested in documents and had just purchased a $650,000 home. At wits' end, he contacted Hugh Pinnock, a devout Mormon, high church official and a member of the board of directors of the Bank of Utah. Mark managed to borrow $185,000, giving the promise that the McLellin letters would be given over to the bank for collateral. All this came to the attention of Christensen, who was owed $100,000 by Mark and who had been promised the valuable collection. Try as he might, Christensen couldn't contact Mark. He even parked outside his home for a few nights, without results. Payments on Mark's home came due, as well as payments on the bank loan from Pinnock.

Around 8 A.M. on Tuesday, October 15, 1985, Mark walked up to Steve's office. He was carrying a parcel and walked by Bruce Passey, an employee in the same building. Bruce noticed that Mark's parcel was addressed to Steve Christensen. Mark proceeded to Steve's office, which wasn't open. He left the parcel outside the door.

A few minutes later, Steve Christensen arrived at his office. He picked up the parcel. The building shook with the explosion. It blew away half his chest and killed him instantly. Detectives found thousands of nails in the vicinity of the Salt Lake City businessman's body.

Gary Sheets's wife, Kathleen, 50, had already completed her banking and was driving up her driveway at about 9:30 A.M. when she observed a cardboard box beside her garage. After parking her car in the garage, she picked up the box addressed to Mr. Gary Sheets. The motion-sensitive bomb exploded, killing Kathleen instantly. Neighbours heard the noise and peered out their windows. When they observed leaves flying in all directions, they assumed a tree had been felled. Kathleen's body was found by a friend an hour later.

No one could remember anyone ever being killed by a bomb in Salt Lake City. Now, two victims in under two hours—unbelievable.

Initially, police interviewed everyone who may have seen the man who took the box to Steve's office. They came up with Bruce Passey. Bruce was able to describe the man—medium height and build, moustache, wearing a green Olympus High School track-team jacket with a letter missing. That night, several friends jokingly thought that Mark Hofmann fit the description to a T. He often wore his old high-school jacket with the ripped-off athletic letter. All dismissed the idea as being ridiculous.

The next day, Wednesday, the main topic of discussion in Utah was the Salt Lake City bombings. It was arranged that Mark Hofmann would turn over the McLellin Collection to church officials that afternoon. They were assured that the two bombings, tragic though they were, were in no way connected with the controversial documents. Mark never showed up.

At precisely 2:41 P.M., a bomb went off as Mark got into his Toyota. Tossed into the street, he was severely injured in the chest, head and legs. Near death, he was questioned in the hospital. He told detectives that when he opened his car door, a box had fallen onto the floor. He could tell them little more.

The focus of the entire bombing investigation now pointed to a connection with the buying and selling of historically valuable documents. Soon, Mark's precarious financial position was known to police. Bank and church officials informed police of the impending delivery of the valuable McLellin Collection to the church by Mark Hofmann.

Bruce Passey identified Mark as the man who had placed the package outside Steve Christensen's office. Police located a friend of Mark's who had purchased blasting caps for him. Mark, who was recovering in hospital, became the prime suspect in the murders of Steve Christensen and Kathleen Sheets. Still, authorities didn't feel they had enough to prosecute.

On October 31, Mark was released from hospital. By the end of the year, experts revealed that the Salamander Letter, his springboard to a new career, was now thought to be a fake. Mark was taken into custody and charged with double murder as well as twenty-seven charges of fraud and forgery concerning phony documents.

On January 7, 1987, prosecution and defence lawyers met. A deal was struck. Mark pleaded guilty to two counts of second-degree murder and to a theft-by-deception count concerning the sale of the Salamander Letter. In return, all other fraud charges against Mark were dropped. In addition, the charge concerning the Sheets murder would be reduced to manslaughter if Mark revealed all details requested by authorities. Mark agreed.

He told police how he'd made the bombs. Mark confessed that he'd killed Steve Christensen so that the McLellin deal would not be finalized. He had meant the second bomb for Gary Sheets so that authorities would believe the killings were connected to real estate business transactions rather than his phony documents. He had attempted to kill himself when he became depressed over what he had done and was sure he would be apprehended. He wanted to spare his family.

Mark Hofmann was sentenced to life imprisonment in Utah State Prison with the recommendation by the presiding judge that he spend the rest of his natural life in custody.

Karl Hold

(HATCHET)

COME CLOSER. This one is really weird.

First, you should know that not all postmen in Austria are your everyday, average mail deliverers as in Canada. There are two distinct types. One performs exactly the same functions as his Canadian counterpart; the other is referred to as a money postman. He delivers all monies sent through the mails in cash. Naturally enough, one of his main tasks is delivering funds to pensioners.

On Friday, January 4, 1974, a money postman in the city of Graz disappeared. Roman Rauch was a veteran money postman who had never had any difficulty on the job. He was married and the father of two adult children. Due to the nature of his employment, his superiors immediately notified authorities that Roman was missing when he failed to report after he should have concluded his route.

Police checked out Roman's schedule of cash deliveries, all of which happened to be to pensioners. They found that he had paid out $106 to Simon Landauer, an 84-year-old pensioner, but had failed to deliver $106.34 to Leon Preis, 76. The cash had been turned over to Landauer at 12:10 P.M., but Roman had not shown up at Preis's door at the expected time of 12:20 P.M. He had $1,500 on him when he vanished.

It was reasonable for police to assume that somewhere between the two deliveries, something had happened to Roman

Rauch. A check of Roman's home life indicated that there was no other woman lurking in the wings. Roman loved his wife, family and job. How then, did he disappear in broad daylight on busy Schoenau Street? It was only a ten-minute walk between the two residences in question. Surely someone would have seen something. But no one did. All the shops along Schoenau Street were canvassed. Obviously, uniformed postmen were unseen servants of the state. They performed their tasks unnoticed by the public.

The day after Roman disappeared, the post office assigned a new employee, 20-year-old Gerhart Rosenberger, to Roman's route. The investigation continued.

Because no one had witnessed anything unusual, police had to consider that Roman could have disappeared of his own volition. But it was hard to believe that such a man would leave the wife and family that he loved for $1,500. Besides, he had left behind $5,000 in his bank account. No, it had to be murder. Roman must have vanished along his route between the Landauer and Preis residences. Both these gentlemen were frail, elderly men who were above suspicion.

Four months passed. Police were no nearer a solution to the disappearance than they were on the day Roman vanished. On April Fool's Day, Gerhart Rosenberger failed to report in at the conclusion of his route. The similarity of the two disappearing acts was uncanny. Gerhart had paid cash to Mr. Landauer but had never made it to the next pensioner on his route, Mr. Preis. He had $7,600 left in his possession.

Now, more than ever, police realized that someone had worked out a method of plucking postmen off Schoenau Street without being seen. Police checked out whether the two men had an enemy in common. They found that both men had no enemies at all. The only link between the two victims was that they were both money postmen on the same route.

There were nine shops along the ten-minute walk between the Landauer and Preis residences. All but one were owned by individual entrepreneurs. The one exception was the Sunshine Cafe, which was part of a chain. Detectives found out that three of the shops were in financial difficulty—Huber's Dry Goods, Ziegler's Second Hand Book Store, and Hold's Butcher Shop. Of the three shop owners, 26-year-old Karl Hold appeared to be the likeliest suspect because he was living beyond his means. He had a 20-year-old blond with expensive tastes stashed away in a luxurious apartment.

However, Hold had not paid off any debts since the two disappearances. His butcher shop was a modest affair. It had no back entrance or basement but did have a large refrigeration unit and a living room off the store. The refrigerator held a large number of sausage sandwiches, which Hold sold to the hordes of schoolchildren who patronized the shop each day.

Police questioned everyone along the street. They were assured that Hold had not left his premises on the two days in question. His butcher shop was a one-man operation. If he left, he had to close up. Neighbours would notice.

There matters stood until April 4, when both bodies, partially dismembered, turned up in a public dump. The bodies were individually boxed and tied with twine.

Autopsies indicated both Roman and Gerhart had been killed by a hatchet blow to the back of their heads. They had died instantly and had been dismembered with a degree of skill. It was thought that the killer could have been a doctor or butcher. When informed that each victim had consumed a sausage sandwich shortly before death, police knew they had their man.

The police officers who had searched Hold's butcher shop on two previous occasions were interrogated. They admitted they hadn't searched the large refrigeration unit because Hold had been serving food to customers directly from the refrigerator. Assorted meat may have hidden the bodies in the refrigerator from their view.

When police found one woman who swore she had seen Rosenberger go into Hold's shop and not come out, Hold was taken into custody. Once apprehended, Hold confessed. The two money postmen habitually dropped into his shop for a sausage sandwich, he told the authorities. On the day of Roman's murder, Hold had asked him if he wanted some coffee with the sandwich and had invited him into the small living room off the shop. He hit the unsuspecting postman with a hatchet, killing him instantly. The body was placed in the refrigerator and covered with meat.

When Hold discovered that Roman had only $1,500 on him, he decided to do the same thing to his replacement, Gerhard Rosenberger. The killings had been money motivated and the money had gone to keep his girlfriend in her luxurious apartment.

Karl Hold was found guilty on two counts of premeditated murder. On August 23, 1974, he was sentenced to life imprisonment.

Jack Holmes & Harold Thurmond

(WATER & ROPE)

WE LIKE TO BELIEVE that lynching became unfashionable with the demise of cowboys and cattle rustlers. It is distressing to learn that this unsavoury, if not downright nasty, practice was very much in vogue well into the 20th century in many areas of the United States.

In 1933, Alex Hart owned one of the largest department stores in San Jose, California His 22-year-old son, Brooke, had just graduated from Santa Clara University and had been made a junior partner in the prosperous business.

At six o'clock on the evening of November 9, 1933, Brooke, his father and sister were the last to leave the store. They locked up and waited while Brooke walked the three blocks to a parking lot to pick up the family's Studebaker. Alex Hart and his daughter waited for some time before deciding that Brooke must have misunderstood that he was to pick them up. They made their way home, but still there was no sign of Brooke. After calling his friends, they decided to inform police. By ten o'clock that evening, the terrible thought that Brooke could have been kidnapped coursed through the minds of the missing man's family. At ten-thirty, their worst fears were realized. Alex received a phone call—"We have your son. We want $40,000 for him. Keep the police out of this if you want to see him alive."

Alex informed police of the call, but nothing further was heard from the kidnappers for a few days. Quite unexpectedly, a young girl knocked on the Harts' front door with a note she claimed had been given to her by a stranger who had asked her to deliver it to the Harts. On the scrap of paper were the words "We have Brooke and are treating him right."

Another day passed before the Harts' Studebaker was found outside San Jose. The vehicle provided no clues leading to the location of the missing man. The kidnappers kept in touch. They again contacted Alex by phone on November 15, giving detailed instructions as to where to drop off the ransom money. This time Alex was able to keep the caller on the line long enough to have the call traced. Police sped to a San Jose garage and picked up Harold Thurmond.

Now, Harold wasn't your average run-of-the-mill lowlife. He came from a respectable family and had never been in any trouble before he tried his luck at the kidnapping game. When questioned, he told police that he had an accomplice, Jack Holmes, who was also taken into custody.

The two men confessed and told authorities the same story. Both were unemployed and had had time on their hands to hatch their amateurish plot. They had plucked Brooke off the streets of San Jose as he was getting into his Studebaker. Together with their captive, they drove in his car to the San Mateo–Hayward Bridge. Once there, one of them knocked Brooke out with a brick brought along especially for that purpose. Both men had a hand in tying Brooke up with wire and weighing him down with a slab of concrete.

Just as they were about to toss him off the bridge, Brooke regained consciousness and started screaming. It was dark and no cars passed by during the interval it took to complete the job. Brooke, screaming hysterically, was tossed off the bridge. For good measure, Harold took a few potshots at the hapless young man, but didn't think he hit his target. Brooke quickly disappeared from sight.

It was a heartless, cold-blooded recital of murder and there was great concern for the safety of the two confessed killers. They were placed in the San Francisco Prison for safekeeping. Inexplicably, six days later, they were removed to the less secure Santa Clara County Jail and lodged in separate cells on different floors.

Meanwhile, on Sunday, November 26, seventeen days after the abduction, Brooke's body was found. Two duck hunters came across the partially decomposed body about a mile south of the bridge. The concrete used to weigh down the body had come loose, allowing it to surface.

In San Jose, word of the cold-blooded cruelty of the two men in custody spread throughout the community. The Harts were a respected family; Brooke had been well liked. It was as if the city were waiting for an excuse to spring into action. The recovery of Brooke's body confirming the terrible rumours was that excuse.

A crowd, estimated at 15,000, congregated in front of the jail. Many were young men in their twenties, the same age as Brooke and the two men in custody. Some were former school chums of the murdered man. Children were held high in the air so they could get a better view of what was about to take place.

Sheriff Bill Emig was aware of the community's ugly mood. Having anticipated such an eventuality, he had enlisted the assistance of twenty county officers and state highway patrolmen. Equipped with shotguns and tear gas, they covered every window and door. Alex Hart, devastated at the news that his son's body had been recovered that day, still summoned enough strength to make an impassioned plea in front of the jail, imploring the crowd to go home. He was hardly heard over the din of the mob.

Sheriff Emig had set up barricades at the front of three alleys beside the jail. Sixty men charged the barriers and were repulsed by tear gas. On the fourth try, they crashed through. Using planks and pipes from a nearby construction site, they broke down the doors of the jail. Inside there were only three officers between them and the killers. These officers were quickly disarmed.

Deputy John Moore was forced to lead the mob to Jack Holmes's cell. Holmes, frightened out of his wits, begged, "For God's sake, give me a chance!" The mob laughed and proceeded to inflict a severe beating on their quarry. On they went, up to Harold Thurmond's cell. It was empty. Terror-stricken, Harold had managed to find a hiding place among pipes in the ceiling. He was spotted, pulled down, tied with rope and dragged down the stairs headfirst.

The two men, now almost unconscious, were taken to St. James Park. Harold was strung up on a large tree. His execution didn't go well. He choked to death at the end of the rope. Jack was made to look at his friend's body before he too was hanged. Someone in the mob knew how to make a proper hangman's knot, so Jack didn't suffer as much as his companion.

It was over. The mob pressed forward, ripping and tearing at the clothing of the dead men for souvenirs. Citizens boasted that they had taken part in the lynching. For years after, souvenirs of the event could be purchased in and around San Jose.

An inquest was held into the two deaths, but no indictments were issued and no one was ever prosecuted for the lynching. The governor of California expressed the mood of the city when he stated, "I would pardon those fellows if they were charged. I would like to parole all kidnappers in San Quentin and Folsom to the fine patriotic citizens of San Jose."

Richard Ivens

(WIRE)

IT TAKES MORE than your average riot, murder, or stuffed ballot box to gain the attention of the Chicago police. Despite past indiscretions perpetrated by the good citizens of Chicago, the year 1906 started off nastier than most. Three women—Mrs. E.F. Mize, Mrs. Maude Reese, and Mrs. A.W. Gentry—had been murdered in the last three months of 1905. The city's finest had no idea who had committed these crimes.

Understandably, the police force was under increasing pressure to solve the murders. They were totally demoralized when Fred Quimba walked into a police station and told the desk sergeant in a stage whisper, "There's a dead woman in my front yard."

Fred lived on the corner of Fullerton and Orchard Streets. Within minutes, police officers were speeding to the area to secure the crime scene. The boys back at the station house, now certain that they were dealing with murdered woman number four, were somewhat miffed when they received word that there was no body in Fred's front yard.

Fred couldn't explain the absence of his very own personal corpse. Police looked at him skeptically, thanked him for being such a public-minded citizen, and told him to be sure to give them a call if he found any more bodies.

An hour later, the very same desk sergeant who had been both aggravated and amused by Fred Quimba received a phone call from one J.H. Rush, who exclaimed, "There's a dead body in my yard." Mr. Rush went on to explain that he lived on the corner of Fullerton and Orchard. Once again, police officers were dispatched to the now-familiar area. They located Rush, but surprise of surprises, for the second time on the same day they failed to find a body.

Mr. Rush and his wife were escorted to the police station. They described the dead woman in detail. There was no doubt in their minds that they had seen the woman and she had definitely been dead. Someone must have removed the body when they left to telephone police. So insistent were the Rushes that the police agreed to return to the scene. The Rushes' credibility escalated when detectives discovered bloodstains on the ground where the couple had allegedly seen the body. Chicago flatfeet were now convinced that they were investigating the case of a body which in some mysterious way had become mobile.

Then, one day, Frank Hollister walked into a Chicago police station. Unlike Fred Quimba and J.H. Rush, Frank's approach was quite different. He said, "I'm Frank Hollister and I want to report the disappearance of my wife."

Frank turned out to be somewhat of a heavyweight. He was the owner of the Hollister Printing Co., one of the largest printing firms in Chicago. According to Frank, his wife had left their home early the previous morning. She had visited a grocery store and had left instructions for her groceries to be delivered. They had arrived at the Hollister residence at 10 A.M. She had then ordered flowers to be delivered to the Methodist Episcopal Church, where she had a 3 P.M. appointment to take part in choir practice. She hadn't shown up.

On January 13, 1906, Edward Ivens walked into a Chicago police station. He explained that he owned a carpentry shop on Belvin Avenue and a livery stable next door. He kept horses and wagons at the stable. His son Richard fed the horses and cleaned out the stable every morning at 5 A.M. Edward went on to report that Richard had found the body of a woman in the vicinity of the stable.

This time, there really was a body, that of Mrs. Bessie Hollister. She had been beaten about the head and had been strangled to death. A 48-inch length of wire had been wound around her neck. Near her body, police recovered a 12-inch length of green string.

Detectives soon learned that the wire was used by florists and the green string was of a type often used by upscale grocery stores. The Hollisters' maid was questioned. She volunteered that when Mrs. Hollister left the house that morning, she had taken along a beautiful gold clock for repair. The maid had wrapped the clock in white tissue paper and had secured it with green string she had saved from the grocer's.

A thorough search of the crime scene and adjoining areas failed to turn up the clock, but police did find a muff and purse belonging to Mrs. Hollister. The killer had obviously covered these items with leaves that had blown away.

When blood was found on the floor of one of Edward Ivens's wagons, police were convinced that someone had killed Bessie Hollister and had moved her body, for some unknown reason, from place to place, possibly using the horse and wagon in Ivens's stable. Everyone who had reported seeing the body was questioned again.

Police decided to interrogate the individual who had actually come up with Bessie Hollister's body, namely Richard Ivens. They had ascertained that Richard's brother owned a florist shop and that Richard had access to the type of wire used to strangle Mrs. Hollister. Armed with this information, they had Richard relate his every move on the day of the murder. Business had been slow, he told authorities, and he had spent much of the day and night alone. When a search of his premises uncovered a jackknife with a small length of green string adhering to the blade, Richard was taken into custody.

Richard broke down. He told police, "I've got the clock. I found it beside Mrs. Hollister. I was going to pawn it. But I didn't kill her. I had nothing to do with that." He turned the clock over to police.

Then, after only one day in custody, Richard confessed to Mrs. Hollister's murder. In his own words, he said, "I killed her. I chased her and slugged her. I took her money. She pleaded with me to take her home, said I could keep the money and she wouldn't tell anybody. I hit her again and again and then we came to Fullerton and Orchard. I saw a piece of wire in the gutter and twisted it around her neck and pulled it tight. As I walked away, I saw a man hovering over the body. When he went away, I went back. I thought she was dead and threw her over the fence and into the yard. I went away a couple of blocks and then got to worrying that she wasn't dead. I saw another man running away from the yard and figured he'd found her. I went back. I thought her leg moved and figured I'd better move her. I went back behind the fence and threw the body over my shoulder and carried it to the stable. I hitched up a team to a wagon and drove out, but didn't go far. I returned and dumped the body close to the stable."

Richard stood trial for the murder of Bessie Hollister. He recanted his confession, claiming that he had been beaten by police. He professed throughout his trial that his only crime was finding the body and stealing the clock. No one believed him.

Richard Ivens was found guilty of first-degree murder and sentenced to death. He was hanged on June 22, 1906. No evidence was ever brought forward implicating him in the murders of the three Chicago women killed in late 1905.

Bob James

(Rattlesnake)

From the very day Bob James's uncle died and left him $1,000, Bob was a big fan of insurance. The Alabama cotton picker used the unexpected windfall to finance a barbering course in Birmingham.

As they say down in Birmingham, Bob was a caution. In 1921, he wooed and wed one Maud Duncan. Now, Maud, a southern belle through and through, didn't mind it much when her new husband desired to be horsewhipped. However, when he insisted on burning her with hair curlers, that was a different matter entirely. Maud obtained a divorce.

Our Bob moved on to Emporia, Kansas, where he opened a small barbershop and took bride number two. Vera Vermillion didn't take kindly to Bob's unique sexual practices. She, too, obtained a divorce.

This time Bob landed in Fargo, North Dakota, opened a barbershop and led Winona Wallace to the altar. Winnie was still getting accustomed to whipping Bob when the accident took place. The spanking-new Mrs. James evidently suffered a fainting spell in the bathtub. Death was attributed to drowning. Thoughtful Bob had taken out a $14,000 insurance policy on Winnie's life the day before the marriage.

Bob headed back to Alabama to show the hicks just how well a local boy had done since leaving the land of cotton. While passing through the state, he married Helen Smith. Bob and wife number four moved to Los Angeles. Helen lasted longer than the previous three Mrs. Jameses, mainly because she kind of liked whipping Bob. When Bob suggested he take out insurance on her life, Helen protested. Bob said, "No insurance, no marriage," and abruptly divorced her.

Times were tough in the barbering game during the Depression and there didn't seem to be an insurable soul in sight, when a simple-minded nephew of Bob's, Cornelius Wright, showed up. He was a sailor, stationed in San Diego.

Connie was a latter-day Mr. Magoo. Disaster was his constant companion. Let's see now—he was struck by Model-T's so often that short spells in hospital became routine. Once, Connie was painting a house when the scaffolding collapsed. On another occasion, he was hit by a foul ball at a baseball game. You would think that a man with Connie's propensity for courting disaster would stay away from anything physical. Not so. He got into a fight in Honolulu and came out of the melee with a fractured skull.

Bob James welcomed his nephew like a piranha welcomes a sardine. He loaned Connie his car. Three days later, nephew Connie was deader than a mackerel. Seems the steering wheel failed, plunging Connie over a cliff near Santa Rosa. Bob had taken out a $10,000 insurance policy on Connie's life and collected without question.

Flush with cash, Bob opened a luxurious barbershop in downtown Los Angeles. Naturally, he took a wife; number five if you are keeping score. Mary Bush, a manicurist by profession, was only 25 when she became Mrs. James.

It was in the hot summer of 1935 that Bob James hatched the scheme that would forever cast him as one of the most bizarre murderers of all time.

Charles Hope was sitting in Bob's barbershop when Bob casually inquired if Charlie knew anything about rattlesnakes. If he did, Bob assured him he could earn an easy hundred bucks. Charlie didn't know a rattler from a Lippizaner stallion, but he was down to his last quarter and decided to bluff his way toward that hundred bucks. "There isn't a man alive who knows more about rattlers," Charlie replied.

Bob went on to explain that he had a friend with a nasty wife. The friend wanted a rattler to bite the wife and teach her a lesson. Of course, you and I know there was no friend. That Bob was up to his old tricks.

Charlie was successful in locating two rattlers at a circus sideshow. He rented the snakes and presented them to Bob. Bob decided to test out the rattlers by placing them in a cage with a chicken. He was furious when he returned and saw those mean rattlers curled up in a corner while the chicken made threatening noises.

Undaunted, Bob went forth in search of snakes. Finally, he located Snake Joe Houtenbrink, who guaranteed that his little pets, Lethal and Lightning, would kill at the least provocation.

The die was cast. Charlie was invited over to the James residence for dinner. Bob told Mary that Charlie was a physician. Mary, who was pregnant, felt that Bob was thoughtful to invite a doctor. No doubt he was concerned about her condition. In a way she was right. Bob wanted her condition to change from living to dead.

During dinner, Charlie remarked that he didn't like the way Mary was carrying. Charlie thought that the delivery of the baby would kill Mary. He suggested an abortion. Simple-minded Mary questioned just how they should proceed. Charlie suggested they do the abortion right there and then. Mary could alleviate any discomfort with several slugs of whisky. As soon as Mary, who was a bit of a lush in training, heard the reference to whisky, she agreed.

It wasn't long before Mary was higher than a kite. Then she passed out. In a flash, the two slippery stars of the show, Lethal and Lightning, were fetched from the garage.

Bob positioned his wife's leg in a box with the snakes. Then he and Charlie retired to the garage for a few slugs from the same bottle that Mary had almost finished. Bob revealed to his confederate that Mary's life was insured for $10,000. He promised Charlie a payoff of $2,000 as soon as Lethal and Lightning completed their job.

Over the next few hours, Bob and Charlie checked on Mary. The snakes had done their work. Mary had been bitten several times and her leg was grossly swollen but, darn it all, she wasn't dead.

Bob gave up on the snakes. "I'm going to drown her," he declared. Mary regained consciousness and figured she had just had an abortion, but even the not-too-swift Mary couldn't fathom the lack of pain in one area and the excruciating pain in her swollen leg.

In the wee hours of the morning, Bob suggested a nice warm bath to alleviate the pain. When Mary was nicely relaxed in the tub, Bob paid a visit. He lifted his wife's legs high in the air, resulting in her head disappearing under the water.

Bob later dried off Mary's body, dressed her, and lugged her out to the small lily pond beside the house. He arranged her head so that it was submerged in the water. At eight o'clock that morning, Bob was dispensing shaves and haircuts in his barbershop as if nothing had happened. That evening, after work, Bob James "found" his dear wife dead. Obviously, she had taken a dizzy spell and had fallen into the lily pond.

A doctor and police were soon at the scene. It appeared that Mary had died as a result of drowning. The doctor figured that something must have bitten Mary to account for the swollen leg. Bob was not suspected of having anything to do with the tragedy.

Isn't there always one nosy cop who takes that second look at deaths that appear to be accidental? In this case, Detective Jack Southard decided to look into Bob James's past. When he learned of the multitude of past wives and insurance payoffs, he knew he was on the right track.

Southard canvassed the Jameses' neighbours and learned that a green Buick had often been parked outside the James home during the few days before Mary's death. He was able to trace the Buick to Charlie Hope.

Inside Charlie's apartment, detectives found a receipt for two rattlesnakes. That receipt led them to Snake Joe Houtenbrink, who told them he had sold Lethal and Lightning to Charlie. When Charlie was questioned, he couldn't wait to spill the beans.

Bob was apprehended at a motel, in the company of a 19-year-old beauty who was using the whip Bob loved when detectives broke into the room.

Bob James was tried and found guilty of his wife's murder. He was sentenced to hang. Charlie Hope turned state's evidence and was sentenced to life imprisonment. Rattlesnake Bob, as he came to be known in prison, fought for his life on San Quentin's death row for seven years.

While Bob was awaiting death, the State of California changed the method of execution from hanging to the gas chamber. Because he was convicted under the old law, Rattlesnake Bob became the last man to be hanged in the state. He was executed on May 1, 1942.

Doreen Jeffs

(Hands)

Up until November 22, 1960, not that much had happened to Doreen and Gordon Jeffs. The young couple and their 3-week-old baby, Linda, occupied an airy, comfortable home in Eastbourne, England. Doreen was a stay-at-home mum, and Gordon made a fine living as a butcher.

The day started like most days since the baby's arrival. Doreen prepared breakfast. Gordon left for work, after which Doreen attended to her housework and the baby's needs. The couple's close-knit circle of friends knew Doreen to be a meticulous housekeeper. That afternoon, she decided to take Linda out for a walk in her carriage. At the same time, she would attend to a few errands. Since the baby's birth, Doreen had often felt depressed and liked to get out in the cool, fresh air.

At ten minutes after four, Doreen walked into Dale and Kerley's Furniture Store in the centre of town. She inquired about the price of a vacuum cleaner. Outside, sleeping peacefully in her gleaming new carriage was 3-week-old Linda. Three minutes later, Doreen left the store and was shocked to discover that the carriage and Linda were nowhere in sight.

The distraught woman ran up and down the street screaming, "My baby, my baby, where is she?" Passersby could do little to comfort her. Hysterically, Doreen ran back to the store entrance. She stood there shouting, "Please, have you seen my baby, a little girl in white woollens with a pink bow?" Busy shoppers paused, shook their heads. No one had seen her baby.

Seven minutes later, police and civilians were actively searching for the missing child. Hours passed. Kidnapping for ransom was eliminated; the Jeffs were not a wealthy family. The dreaded thought that the child had been kidnapped by professionals who sold children to illegal adoption agencies was considered, as well as the possibility that some deranged woman who wanted a baby of her own might be the abductor.

All theories were discarded at 8 P.M., about four hours after the kidnapping, when a police officer peered into some bushes in a park in Hartfield Gardens, about a half mile from the furniture store where the child went missing. There lay little Linda Jeffs in her carriage. She had been strangled to death.

Upon being told of her daughter's death, Doreen Jeffs collapsed. Her husband, Gordon, was devastated. Police immediately launched an intensive investigation into the murder. A house-to-house survey was conducted in an attempt to find anyone who may have noticed someone wheeling a carriage away from the front of Dale and Kerley's store. No one volunteered any useful information. About the only clue the police had to work with was a very faint footprint found in grass near where the baby's body was recovered. The print was believed to have been made by a shoe with a stiletto heel, but there was no guarantee that it was connected with the murder.

So distraught was Doreen Jeffs over the murder of her daughter that it was four days before she could be fingerprinted in order to eliminate her prints found on the baby carriage. Unfortunately, no other prints were found on the carriage, leading detectives to believe that the killer had worn gloves.

Gordon Jeffs accepted the cruel hand he had been dealt. Doreen didn't seem to be recovering from the trauma of losing her only child. Her eyes were bloodshot from weeping. Seldom was she seen without a handkerchief.

As the investigation wore on, Scotland Yard detectives became troubled by one undeniable fact. It didn't seem reasonable that not one person could be located who had seen the baby carriage outside the furniture store at a few minutes after four. After all, the streets had been crowded. Several people were located who swore they were there at that time, yet no one had seen a thing. Detectives measured off the distance from the furniture store to where the body was found. It was a fifteen-minute walk. Several shoppers were in the area at the time. Not one had noticed a woman wheeling a baby carriage.

Realizing they were treading on sensitive ground, detectives became convinced that the baby carriage had never been placed outside the furniture store by Doreen Jeffs. Could this woman, who was genuinely heartbroken, have murdered her own child?

Discreetly, Gordon Jeffs was questioned. Without revealing their suspicions, detectives learned that Doreen had been terribly depressed since the baby's birth. They also discovered Doreen's obsession to keep her house in an almost sanitary condition. Was it possible that her depression, coupled with the ordinary disruptions associated with caring for a newborn, had caused Doreen Jeffs to become mentally deranged? Had Doreen Jeffs killed her own child?

Detectives approached Gordon once more, this time revealing the possibility that Doreen might be the killer. They also explained that she would receive a great deal of sympathy from any court, as she was obviously suffering from a mental illness. Gordon agreed that it would be in the best interests of his wife for him to co-operate with police.

A meeting was held in which Gordon urged Doreen to tell her story one more time in an effort to assist the authorities. Once again, Doreen repeated the story she had related on the day of the baby's disappearance. Gently, police explained that they had had cases where mothers, mentally ill after giving birth, had killed their own children. They told Doreen that none of these women had been convicted of murder.

For the first time, Doreen wavered. She indicated that she was afraid of being condemned by her husband. Gordon assured her that he understood. Doreen broke down. She told police she had been burping the baby that day when the child turned blue and stopped breathing. She placed Linda in the carriage and went out. Doreen couldn't remember going into the park, nor could she account for the baby's fractured skull, which had been discovered in a post-mortem. She had no memory of concocting the phony kidnapping, but remembered going through with the made-up story.

Doreen Jeffs was charged with the murder of her daughter. On November 28, she was released under custody to attend Linda's funeral. Weeping uncontrollably, Doreen collapsed at graveside.

The murder charge was soon dismissed and Doreen was charged with infanticide. She was allowed bail, conditional on her being confined to the Hellingly Mental Hospital until March 17, 1961, the scheduled date of her trial.

The trial was brief and to the point. Doreen pleaded guilty to infanticide. She was sentenced to one year's probation, again conditional upon her remaining in Hellingly Mental Hospital for the full year.

Gordon and Doreen Jeffs resumed their life after Doreen's release from hospital, but Doreen never fully recovered from the horror of taking her own child's life. On January 6, 1965, Doreen disappeared. Two days later, police found her coat folded on the edge of a cliff near Eastbourne. Days later, her body washed ashore at Folkestone, Kent.

Genene Jones

(Heparin)

GENENE JONES was a good ol' Texas gal who had once pursued the hairdressing profession to earn a living. But all that was behind her. In June 1976, Genene took a one-year course to become a licensed vocational nurse. In some states, LVNs are known as practical nurses.

After one bad marriage, several boyfriends, and two children stashed away with her mother, Genene gained employment with the Methodist Hospital in San Antonio. Five months later, she was dismissed. It seems our Genene liked to overstep her bounds as a practical nurse, whose main function was to assist doctors and registered nurses. Genene liked to tell them what to do. Undaunted, 28-year-old Genene caught on at Community Hospital. She was forced to resign after five months to undergo elective surgery.

At her third hospital, the Bexar County Hospital, Genene was assigned to the pediatric intensive care unit. She soon gained a reputation as a dedicated, intelligent nurse, if a bit too enthusiastic. All in all, Genene was considered a fine addition to the ICU.

Despite her admirable work habits, there were some flaws in Genene's behaviour. Actually, there were eight official complaints against the nurse, ranging from being intoxicated while on duty to setting an IV solution at an improperly high rate. For these indiscretions, Genene received nothing more than mild reprimands.

The rash of deaths began in May 1981. All the babies were extremely sick cardiac patients. Chris Hogeda was one of Genene's favourites. Many mornings she would stay long past her shift to care for the little boy, who was attached to tubes and arm restraints. Genene cried unashamedly at Chris's funeral.

For the next 120 days, the series of unexplained deaths continued. Terry Lynn Garcia was only 3 weeks old when she was admitted to hospital for vomiting and diarrhea. A month later she was transferred to the ICU and placed under Genene's care. Two days later, the child died.

Patricia Sambrano, a 3-month-old, was rushed to hospital following a seizure. Placed in a respirator under Genene's care, Patricia went into cardiac arrest. Doctors revived the child and, for the next two nursing shifts, the little girl was reported to be stable. Genene arrived back on duty. Patricia died a few hours later.

And so it went. Four-month-old Paul Villarreal died during Genene's shift when blood poured out of a tube placed down his throat. Two-year-old Rosemary Vega died after it was discovered that a breathing machine was feeding her too little oxygen. The machine had inexplicably been altered. Placida Ybarra, 4 months old, entered hospital after suffering a heart seizure. Her respirator was found to be supplying 100 percent oxygen, an extremely rich mixture. A few days after being admitted, Placida died.

Of course, the rash of deaths and unusual occurrences was noticed. The average rate of resuscitations had been three or four a month. In those few months in 1981, the statistics went haywire. There were nine cardiopulmonary resuscitations in August, and thirteen in September. Something was drastically wrong. Stranger still, most of the deaths had taken place on the 3-to-11 shift when the children were under the care of Genene Jones. Around the hospital, Genene's colleagues referred to her as the death nurse.

Rumours concerning the series of deaths drifted up to the hospital's hierarchy. They received reports about the excessive amount of bleeding occurring in their young patients, such as blood streaming out of old needle punctures, mouths, and rectums, causing blood pressure to drop and straining tiny hearts until they stopped.

Some doctors thought that the drug company that manufactured the anticoagulant Heparin had made a mistake in its strength. Others believed that digitalis, which can bring on a change in the heart rate, may have caused the deaths. Still others felt they need look no further than Genene Jones. Nothing was done about the problem through that fall and winter. The great number of resuscitations and deaths continued.

Bexar County Hospital, which had just changed its name to Medical Center Hospital, admitted 1-month-old Rolando Santos. Rolando had pneumonia and was placed on a respirator. The baby improved over the next two days, but during the 3-to-11 shift the child suffered a seizure and his heart stopped. Doctors managed to revive the child and ran tests on his heart and brain. The results were normal.

Two days later, Rolando was in such good shape, doctors planned to take him off the respirator. Without warning, the child passed an unusual amount of urine, so that he became dehydrated and sluggish. Fluids were immediately administered, but the doctors couldn't help but wonder if someone was giving unauthorized drugs to their little patient.

Genene Jones took three days off. Rolando improved remarkably. Upon her return, the baby began to bleed and went into cardiac arrest. Electric shock started his heart up again. Blood samples were tested, indicating excessive amounts of Heparin. Rolando's arterial line was removed, eliminating the possibility of an overdose of any drug by error. The child was moved out of

Genene's care and other nurses were instructed to guard the patient. Within a week, Rolando was released from hospital.

In March, the administration of Medical Centre Hospital changed its policy. The LVN positions in the pediatric ICU were eliminated and replaced by registered nurses. When offered a position on another ward, Genene Jones resigned. She was given a glowing recommendation by the hospital.

Genene was hired at a new one-doctor pediatric clinic in the town of Kerrville, Texas. Dr. Kathy Holland had just recently opened the clinic and thought herself fortunate to obtain someone with Genene's qualifications.

Crises became the order of the day at the new clinic almost immediately. Children who were taken there would have sudden seizures. One-month-old Brandy Lee Benites was brought to Dr. Holland's clinic with bowel trouble. The doctor left the baby with Genene. In a few moments, the baby had stopped breathing. Dr. Holland resuscitated the baby and rushed her to a local hospital. Later, while being transferred to a hospital in San Antonio, the child was almost lost again. Accompanying her was nurse Genene Jones.

Six days later, completely well, Brandy Lee was discharged from hospital. The mysterious attacks went undiagnosed. Everyone was pleased at the baby's recovery.

On September 17, Chelsea McLellan, 15 months old, arrived at the doctor's office for a checkup and inoculations. Genene sat the child on her mother's lap. She injected a needle into the child's arm. Chelsea convulsed and turned blue. Rushed to hospital, Chelsea recovered somewhat. Dr. Holland felt the little girl should be transferred to a better-equipped facility.

Genene was in the ambulance while the doctor followed in her car. Little Chelsea's heart stopped. The ambulance pulled over. Dr. Holland frantically commenced massaging the child's heart.

By the time they reached the hospital, the baby was dead. This was certainly a strange occurrence for a child who was taken to the doctor's office for a checkup and her shots.

The rash of emergencies and unusual deaths continued at Dr. Holland's private clinic. It was probably Dr. Duane Packard, chief of medical staff at Sid Peterson Hospital where many of Dr. Holland's emergencies ended up, who first took steps to uncover why so many children were arresting at Dr. Holland's clinic. He had another doctor check out Dr. Holland and her nurse, Genene Jones. For the first time, the medical community in Kerrville heard of Genene's trouble at the Medical Center Hospital.

Dr. Holland was questioned. She gave straightforward responses but, despite her professional and logical answers, her privileges to work at Sid Peterson Hospital were lifted. The investigation focused on Genene Jones. Dr. Holland also began to suspect her nurse. When she checked the clinic's records and found that Genene had ordered more succinylcholine than she had used in her practice, she knew her worst suspicions were well founded.

Faced with accusations that she was a baby killer, Genene took an overdose of pills in an attempt to commit suicide. She was unsuccessful. Upon recovering, she submitted to a polygraph test, which indicated guilty knowledge of the baby deaths. She was dismissed from Dr. Holland's clinic.

On October 12, 1982, a grand jury was called to investigate the death of Chelsea McLellan. It was proven without a doubt that succinylcholine had been given to Chelsea, causing death. Genene was also charged with injuring seven other children, who survived. At her trial, it was proven that she surreptitiously purchased succinylcholine and administered it without Dr. Holland's knowledge or permission. The Texas jury found Genene Jones guilty of murder.

In San Antonio, authorities virtually had their pick of which case to prosecute. They chose to prosecute Genene on the case of Rolando Santos, who had been injected with the blood-thinning agent Heparin and had survived after being taken out of Genene's care. Genene was found guilty of this offence and sentenced to sixty years' imprisonment.

It is estimated that Genene Jones murdered sixteen children. Today, she is incarcerated in the Mountain View Unit for Women at Gatesville, Texas. Her accumulated sentences total 159 years.

Bahar Kandlbinder & Wolfgang Grunwald

(HATCHET)

INGE HERMANN was only 19 years old when she fell in love with Wolfgang Grunwald. Her mother was fit to be tied. Mrs. Hermann simply didn't understand how an attractive girl like her daughter could fall for a no-goodnik like Wolf. The boy had no job and no prospects. Besides, he had an atrocious complexion. Surely, with all the eligible boys in Munich, Germany, her Inge could do better.

Mrs. Hermann's opinion became academic when Inge, due to an unfortunate miscalculation, found herself definitely pregnant. Quick as a bunny, she and no-goodnik Wolf became husband and wife.

The marriage, born out of necessity, was not a happy one. The responsibilities of married life didn't change Wolf one iota. Two years after he and Inge tied the knot he still had no job and no prospects. When he chose a mistress, Inge felt it prudent to pack up her baby and go home to Momma.

Wolf's mistress, Bahar Kandlbinder, a 32-year-old Turkish woman, was gainfully employed as a masseuse in a sex shop that featured massages of a specialized nature. Folks, you know what I mean. Living with Bahar had one positive effect on Wolf. He got a job in a manufacturing plant. When Inge filed for divorce, Wolf didn't oppose the action. In fact, considering that he was the recipient of all those massages on a regular basis, we must assume that he was rather pleased with the way things were working out.

On June 19, 1974, Inge failed to arrive home from her job at a gas station at her regular time of 4 P.M. Her mother immediately reported her missing to police. Inge had always arrived home promptly since she and her baby had moved in with her mother.

Wolf was located at home watching television with Bahar. He told detectives he had no idea where his estranged wife could be located. There were no new developments for two days.

The possibility that Inge might have run away was eliminated when a lock tender on the River Isar in Munich found a woman's purse containing some money and identification papers belonging to Inge Grunwald. The river was dragged but nothing further was uncovered.

The next day, a man, walking in the woods about nine miles from the city, came across Inge's body lying below a steep incline. He ran to the nearest telephone, which was some distance away, and called the police. Inge had been hacked to death with a hatchet. Her scalp was virtually split open. The blows had been struck from behind. She was fully clothed and had not been sexually interferred with in any way. An investigation of the crime scene indicated that Inge had been killed beside a logging trail at the top of a steep incline. Her body had been rolled down the incline to where it was found.

The logging trail was closely examined. Casts were made of tire tracks and footprints leading to the edge of the incline. One set of footprints belonged to the victim. The other two had been made by a man and a woman.

Detectives were able to reconstruct the circumstances of Inge's murder. Accompanied by a male and female, she had walked twenty-five yards from the car that had made the tire tracks. Here she was struck several times from behind with a hatchet. Inge had fallen, bleeding profusely. She was then dragged the rest of the way to the steep slope and pushed over the edge. The body rolled some distance, finally coming to a stop.

A list of clothing worn by the murdered woman when she went missing was given to authorities by her mother. The body was dressed in all the clothing listed with the exception of a red velvet jacket.

The logical suspects were hubby Wolf and his mistress, Bahar. The tires on Wolf's Opel Kadet were checked against the cast made of the tire tracks at the scene of the murder. Much to investigators' surprise, they didn't match. Although the suspects' shoes were the correct sizes, they did not match the prints taken near the logging trail. The suspects' clothing was examined for blood but none was found.

Munich police had no idea why Inge had been murdered, but they were sure her husband and his mistress were the culprits. They set up additional investigative procedures, which lack the glamour of the fictional murder investigation, but which more often than not snare the killer in real life. Dry-cleaning establishments were canvassed in an attempt to find out if Wolf or Bahar had deposited any bloodstained clothing. Hardware stores were checked for the purchase of a hatchet before the date of the killing. It was also felt that Wolf may have been cunning enough to have purchased new tires immediately after the murder.

Sometimes one connecting clue is uncovered in a massive investigation. On this occasion, everything attempted by the police came up aces. The hardware store where Wolf had purchased a hatchet on June 13 was found only four blocks from his apartment. The clerk who had sold him the hatchet knew him by sight. Police also located the tire shop where Wolf had purchased new tires. Inge's missing red velvet jacket was not located in a dry cleaning establishment, but the bloodstained garment was found in a playground near the River Isar.

Wolf was informed of the evidence pointing to his guilt and immediately confessed to his involvement. He vehemently denied that he had killed Inge, claiming that Bahar had struck the fatal blows. According to Wolf, his wife had threatened to commence proceedings to have Bahar confined to a mental institution. Although Inge had no legal right to take such action, Bahar believed it was possible and decided to kill her antagonist.

The pair picked Inge up and drove out to the woods, ostensibly to discuss the impending divorce. Wolf had purchased the hatchet at Bahar's instructions. He had waited in the car while Bahar struck the fatal blows. His mistress had then summoned him to help her drag the body to the edge of the slope and push it over. Wolf admitted that he should have informed police of the murder, but by the next morning he believed that it was too late. That's when he went out, changed the tires of his Opel Kadet and threw away both his and Bahar's shoes.

Now it was Bahar's turn. She too confessed involvement, but named Wolf as the killer. According to Bahar, the reason for the killing was Inge's threats to inform Wolf's employer that he had stolen goods and money from the plant. To complicate matters, Bahar had attempted to break off her relationship with Wolf. For her trouble, he had beaten her black and blue. After that little episode, Bahar never again mentioned leaving him. She claimed that it was she who had stayed in the car at the time of the murder and that it was Wolf who had inflicted the blows with the hatchet.

Police believed Bahar's story. She was a short, tiny woman. Tests indicated that it would have been impossible for her to have inflicted the fatal blows without standing on something like a box or stepstool.

Bahar Kandlbinder was found guilty of being an accessory after the fact of murder. She was sentenced to two and a half years' imprisonment. Wolfgang Grunwald was found guilty of murdering his wife and was sentenced to life imprisonment.

Kreisberg, Murphy, Pasqua, Marino, Green & Bastone

(GAS)

TONY MARINO RAN A GIN MILL in the Bronx back in 1932, when 15 cents would buy you a slug of rotgut. For two bits, you could knock back two slugs. Those who were hungry bellied up to the free lunch, which consisted of stale bread and salted herring.

Tony moaned to his regulars that it was tough to make a living, what with the Depression and all. His good friend, undertaker Frank Pasqua, couldn't agree more. He voiced the opinion that folks were becoming too cheap to die. It was enough to make him think of turning in his embalming equipment and taking up another, more lively occupation.

Bartender Red Murphy expressed similar sentiments. Tips had become scarcer than hens' teeth. The bums he rolled every Saturday night didn't carry enough cash to make that age-old profession a paying proposition.

The three men grumbled, but there was little they could do about their predicament. Or was there? It so happened that an old codger named Michael Malloy had become a fixture around Marino's. Malloy told Irish jokes all night and was able to beg enough drinks to maintain a buzz most evenings. When the last drunk staggered out of the gin mill, Malloy curled up in a corner to sleep off whatever horrors the wee hours provided. For this privilege, he swept out Marino's every morning.

By the merest of coincidences, an insurance salesman dropped into Marino's one day and proceeded to give the proprietor his number-one pitch. Marino paid attention, not that he had any intention of insuring his own life, but because he thought it would be a great idea to insure the life of Michael Malloy, whose only aim on earth was to avoid work and stay drunk. Wouldn't it be fortunate for beneficiaries if Malloy's life were insured and he were to meet with an untimely death? Of course, it wouldn't be so fortunate for Malloy, but you can't make everyone happy all the time.

Undertaker Frank Pasqua, with visions of a funeral dancing like sugar plums in his scheming head, thought that any untimely death had a silver lining for him. Marino talked things over with Pasqua and Red Murphy, the bartender. Malloy had no relatives and wouldn't be missed.

It wasn't difficult for Marino to insure Malloy's life for $1,200, with himself as beneficiary. For a hundred bucks Red agreed to feed Malloy radiator antifreeze until the old codger was deader than last week's herring. Undertaker Pasqua anted up the first quarter's premium in return for the imminent undertaking job.

The Christmas season was approaching. Even the stiffs at Marino's treated their fellow derelicts to a 15-cent slug of booze now and then. Red was overgenerous with Malloy. He poured him enough legitimate booze to put a gorilla away before he doctored a drink with 90 percent antifreeze. Six slugs of antifreeze later, Malloy, with a smile on his lips, slid off his bar stool to the sawdust-covered floor.

When sunlight made its way into Marino's humble watering hole, Malloy should have been dead. Instead, he woke up, shook his head, and proceeded to sweep out the place as usual. The conspirators were downcast, but not discouraged. All that week, Red fed Malloy enough antifreeze to pulverize an ox. Each morning, Malloy woke up, whistled an Irish tune and went about his sweeping.

Red Murphy is credited with coming up with the idea that was sure to terminate Michael Malloy's stay on Earth. He would see that Malloy died of ptomaine poisoning. Red opened a can of sardines and let it sit for several days until it smelled to high heaven. Marino added a nice little touch. He laced the little fishes with metal filings from a machine shop.

It being the Christmas season and all, Red, who normally kept Malloy away from the free lunch, offered the old bird a sandwich. Malloy's eyes filled with gratitude as he wolfed down the freebie and topped it off with a slug of antifreeze. The three larcenous gentlemen watched in horror as the ptomaine metal–laced sandwich and antifreeze had absolutely no effect on their intended victim. If anything, Malloy proceeded to whistle and sing those annoying Irish ditties louder and more off-key than ever.

It was time for drastic action. The three schemers enlisted a fourth member into their deadly endeavour. Cab driver Hershey Green would sell his mother's false teeth if the price was right. His main accomplishment in life was his ability to drive a car.

Christmas had come and gone. It was now January 1933. The boys waited until a bitter-cold night to give it another try. They lingered until Malloy had passed out under his bar stool. Marino and Pasqua carried him to Green's cab and off they drove to Claremont Park. Malloy was dumped into some bushes. His coat was removed. His shirt was opened. For good measure, Pasqua poured a few gallons of water over his head.

Next day, Pasqua had a terrible cold when he went down to Marino's to celebrate. He was scanning the newspapers with Red and Marino for a report of a body found in the park, when Malloy waltzed into the joint. He had a wild story to tell. He had awakened in Claremont Park shivering like the dickens but none the worse for wear. He had no idea how he had gotten there, he said, but he had often awakened in worse places. Malloy went on to declare that a slug of rotgut would fix him up just fine.

A regular customer at Marino's, one Anthony Bastone, became the fifth member of the inept murder squad. Bartender Red, in a moment of frustration, had confided to Bastone that it was getting under everyone's skin that they couldn't put Malloy away. Bastone suggested trying a fake hit-and-run accident. When Marino and Pasqua were told of the scheme, they wondered why they hadn't thought of it themselves. Bastone wanted a hundred dollars to hold Malloy upright while he was hit by Hershey Green's cab.

A few days later, at 3 A.M., the unconscious Malloy was driven to a deserted street. Bastone displayed a degree of dexterity when he jumped clear of Green's cab as it plowed into Malloy.

Next day, the plotters scanned the newspapers. There was no mention of a body being found on the street. The boys checked the morgue and hospitals but failed to come up with Malloy, dead or alive.

It was Anthony Bastone who put forward the super idea of finding another drunk as a substitute for Malloy. This proved to be no easy task, but a Malloy clone was found in the person of an Irish gentleman named McCarthy. With a dry run under their belts, the gang had no difficulty dispensing of McCarthy. Bastone did the holding, Green did the driving. To make doubly sure, Hershey drove over McCarthy's limp form as it lay on the deserted Bronx street.

Routinely, the plotters looked through the following day's newspapers, but once again they could find no mention of a body. This time, a check of hospitals brought results. McCarthy was not dead, but almost. He was not expected to live. While the gang was digesting this latest bit of disconcerting news, who should stroll into Marino's but Michael Malloy. He informed his startled companions that he had been in an accident but was now feeling just fine. It was enough to make a grown man weep. More bad news—McCarthy's condition had improved dramatically and he was now given a good chance to pull through. It was getting so that you couldn't kill a man in the old-fashioned way anymore.

The conspirators were on the horns of a dilemma. Should they wait months until McCarthy recovered and then knock him off or should they try again to kill Malloy? It was decided that Malloy would suffice.

A fruit dealer, Daniel Kreisberg, was recruited to get Malloy drunk in his own room. Red Murphy was called in to lower the boom. He arrived at Kreisberg's with a length of rubber hose. He attached one end of the hose to a gas jet and held the other end to Malloy's mouth. At last, Michael Malloy was truly dead. An alcoholic medic attributed the cause of death to pneumonia. Next day, undertaker Pasqua planted Malloy. The insurance company paid off the $1,200.

From conception to execution, it had taken five months of tedious plotting and hard work to kill Michael Malloy. With so many people in on the scheme, the payoff money didn't go far. The conspirators argued among themselves about the distribution of the insurance money. One of the plotters was eliminated when Anthony Bastone was killed in an unrelated incident.

Cabbie Hershey Green complained bitterly to anyone who would listen that his cab had been damaged when he had hit Malloy, and he hadn't been paid extra. The loose talk came to the attention of the police. When questioned, Hershey spilled his guts. Malloy's body was exhumed. Surprise! An autopsy proved he hadn't died of pneumonia at all, but had been gassed.

The entire gang was rounded up. Green got off with a prison sentence, but the others weren't as fortunate. Kreisberg, Murphy, Pasqua and Marino were all put to death in Sing Sing's electric chair.

Anders Larson

(SAUNA)

FOR THE WEAK AT HEART, I hasten to point out that some portions of this narrative would be best read after mealtime. Forewarned is forearmed. Shall we get to it?

Anders Larson drove a cab for a living in the Swedish village of Overlida, which, to be geographically accurate, lies some thirty miles east of the city of Gothenburg. As a young man with normal glandular drives, Anders fell hard for a young girl who hailed his cab. Karine, obviously, felt similar vibes. Despite inclement weather, the young couple made their way to an open field, where they commenced to do what young couples have been doing since Adam took a bite out of that apple. Both had been married before and divorced, but this was different. This was true love.

Precautions were thrown to the wind. In due course, Karine was informed that the pregnancy test was positive. Both were delighted to marry before their son, Eric, was born.

For years Anders and Karine led a quiet existence in the village. Then it happened again. Gerda Anderson jumped into Anders's cab. Impulsive Anders liked what he saw. History repeated itself that July 1976, but Anders, being a wiser man, made sure no births resulted from his extramarital activities.

Gerda and the cab driver carried on a prolonged affair. I mean years. Everyone in the village came to know and accept the fact that Anders Larson had a wife, son and mistress. But Gerda really loved Anders. She was forever bugging him to get a divorce and marry her. Anders ignored her pushy demands. Karine, obviously, knew of her husband's affair. While the tenuous situation fostered arguments between husband and wife, Karine managed to live with the status quo.

That's where matters stood in July 1984, when 17-year-old Eric Larson returned home at 3 A.M. He was shocked to find his father slumped over the kitchen table with his head in his arms. Initially, Eric feared his father had suffered a heart attack, but as he drew closer he realized his dad was drunk as a lord, close to unconscious. Eric shouted, "Where's Ma?" Anders mumbled, "Quarrel, gone to sit in the sauna." It all made sense to the teenager. His parents had had a squabble. His father, who was not a heavy drinker, had drowned his sorrows in liquor. His mother had stormed off to the sauna in the basement.

Eric made his way to the sauna and opened the door. There lay his mother on the sauna floor. Her nude body had turned dark brown. Eric was not shocked by Karine's nudity. He was quite accustomed to seeing his parents nude in the sauna. Now Karine's shapely body lay among lava rocks and an overturned wooden bench. Her hands were encrusted with dried blood.

Trembling with fear and shock, Eric attempted to remove his mother from the sauna by pulling at her arms. They came off in his hands. Overcome with horror, Eric dropped the arms and raced outside. Neighbours found the hysterical teenager gesticulating wildly. He was rushed to hospital, where he remained for some days, recovering from his traumatic experience.

Meanwhile, neighbours entered the house. They found Anders at the kitchen table. They continued through the house, eventually reaching the sauna, where they came upon the body of Karine Larson, whose arms were now separated from her body.

They frantically called an ambulance. It was the ambulance attendants who called police.

Officers did their best to sober up Anders. He managed to tell them what he had already told his son. There had been a quarrel and Karine had stormed off to the sauna. He appeared to be genuinely distraught when informed of his wife's death.

A doctor joined police. He expressed the opinion that Karine had literally been cooked to death. Because Eric could not be questioned, the detached arms were a complete puzzle to the investigators. Police, however, were able to figure out other aspects of the case.

The sauna had been at room temperature when the body was discovered. Because of the charring of wood near the heating unit, experts figured that the temperature had been set extremely high for a lengthy period of time. Although the door to the sauna was working perfectly, Karine had not been able to get out. By law, sauna doors in Sweden must swing open from the inside.

Someone had raised the temperature, then fastened the door in some manner from the outside and succeeded in cooking Karine Larson to death. Police surmised that as the heat became unbearable, Karine had attempted to ram the door with the sauna bench. She had picked up lava blocks and pounded the door, but no one heard her and the sturdy door didn't budge. Who had turned the temperature up, and later, after Karine was dead, turned it back down? How had that same person kept the door from opening?

Naturally enough, Anders was suspected, but there was no proof that he had murdered his wife. Laboratory testing proved most difficult, as there was no record of a similar crime ever having taken place in Sweden. However, using the bodies of animals and the Larson sauna, doctors were able to ascertain that Karine had been in the sauna for three hours before losing consciousness. Other evidence indicated she had entered the sauna at 7 P.M. and was most certainly dead by 1 A.M. Two hours later, her body was discovered by Eric. The killer must have turned down the temperature around 1 A.M. in order for the sauna to cool to room temperature by 3 A.M.

When detectives learned of Anders's prolonged affair with Gerda Anderson, they realized he had a strong motive for murder. Gerda was taken into custody and questioned. She admitted to her affair with Anders but denied any involvement in the murder. In fact, she and Anders had pretty well broken off, but there was one juicy tidbit the police had not uncovered. According to Gerda, Karine wanted to divorce Anders because she, too, had a lover. Gerda stated that Anders knew of his wife's affair. Gerda, who was just full of information, provided police with the name of Karine's lover, Dr. Arnold Joestrom.

Investigating officers called at Dr. Joestrom's office just outside of Overlida. While waiting for the doctor, they questioned his secretary. She told police that Anders Larson had recently marched into the doctor's office while Karine was there. He walked past her into the doctor's examining room and caught his wife and the good doctor in the act of intercourse.

Karine, who was obviously a realist, told her husband that it was just as well he had proof of her infidelity. She was planning to divorce him, anyway. Then, before the startled secretary and Anders, the doctor and Karine resumed right where they had left off when they were so rudely interrupted.

Police were certain they had their man but couldn't figure out how Anders had kept that sauna door closed from the outside. A team of laboratory technicians was dispatched to the Larson residence to examine the place from top to bottom. A seemingly unimportant pile of lumber was found at the other end of the Larson basement. The planks were closely examined for nails or screws. None were found, but one alert officer noted that the ends of two of the planks had been cut at an angle. By placing these two planks in an X across the sauna door frame, police discovered they could be wedged tight. Two sturdy police officers were placed inside the sauna. They couldn't budge the wedged planks.

Anders was arrested and charged with his wife's murder. When told of the strong evidence against him, he broke down and confessed. In essence, he didn't want to lose his wife to the doctor, he told police. If he couldn't have his Karine, nobody could. He drank himself unconscious as his wife cooked to death in the basement sauna.

On May 10, 1985, Anders Larson was found guilty of murder and sentenced to death.

Georgi Markov

(UMBRELLA)

IN LONDON'S NEW SCOTLAND YARD, there is a tiny pellet measuring about one and a half millimetres in diameter that has baffled the most sophisticated forensic minds in the world. This innocent-looking pellet was an instrument of murder.

Georgi Markov, 49, was a successful novelist and playwright in his native Bulgaria. He was also an avowed enemy of the Communist Party, then in power. In 1971, it was necessary for Markov to leave Bulgaria and seek refuge in England. He soon gained employment with the BBC. His radio program, broadcast over Radio Free Europe, was one of the most popular on the air. He continued to expose the corrupt Communist regime, as he had done back in Bulgaria.

The first sign that the Communists were not taking kindly to Markov's broadcasts came in 1977, when he received an anonymous phone call threatening him with what he told a friend was an extraordinary death. The strange call upset Markov to a degree, but didn't deter him from continuing his broadcasts.

On September 7, 1978, Markov parked his Simca near Waterloo Bridge, as he customarily did, to catch a bus across the bridge to his office. While he idly stood at the bus stop, he felt a sharp sting on the back of his right thigh. He glanced over his shoulder and saw a man bend down and pick up an umbrella. The man, unknown to Markov, mumbled an apology in a foreign accent, hailed a taxi, and disappeared into traffic.

Markov continued to his office. He told a colleague what had happened at the bus stop and complained that the sting was causing him some distress. His colleague was interested enough to take a look. He saw blood on Markov's jeans and observed a red pimple-like mark on the back of his thigh. By the time Markov reached his home in Clapham that evening, he was generally feeling weak. He told his wife, Annabel, about the incident.

The next day, Markov was rushed to hospital. He was vomiting, had a high temperature and could hardly speak. His thigh was X-rayed, but nothing unusual was detected. Twenty-four hours later, Markov's condition rapidly deteriorated. He was transferred to intensive care. He vomited blood; his white-cell count rose dramatically. At 10:40 A.M., he was declared dead.

An autopsy indicated that death was due to blood poisoning. The attending pathologist, who had been made aware of the incident at the bus stop, cut away a block of flesh surrounding the angry red dot on the victim's thigh. It was sent to the Metro Police Forensic Science Lab, who in turn sent it to the government laboratory in Wiltshire.

An examination of the piece of flesh revealed a metallic bead located just under the skin. The pellet had two tiny holes, drilled at right angles to each another. Daylight could be seen through one hole. The other was clogged. The entire pellet measured one and a half millimetres in diameter and could contain about half a milligram of material.

No poison was found in the body. Doctors went about eliminating bacterial and viral infections as the cause of death, as well as diphtheria and tetanus toxins. Endotoxin was also eliminated. Dioxin was considered, but the death had not been characteristic. Natural toxins, such as snake venom, were also considered, but death due to these types of poison usually occurs more quickly.

Finally, one doctor had come across a death similar to Markov's. It had been brought about by ricin, which is found in castor-oil plant beans, more specifically, the seeds in the beans.

The pellet was sent back to the Metro Police Forensic Science Lab. It was tested and found to be made of an alloy consisting of 90 percent platinum and 10 percent iridium. It was ascertained that the tiny hole in the pellet could have been made by a well-equipped jeweller.

When X-rays were again taken of the piece of flesh from Markov's thigh, doctors realized how they had missed the pellet on the first X-rays; it was visible, but looked like a speck of dirt. The amount of poison in the pellet was estimated to be 0.2 milligrams. Most experts believe that ricin was the agent used to kill Markov. In 1978, experiments using the poison had been conducted on pigs. None survived.

Markov's friend and fellow Bulgarian defector, 26-year-old Vladimir Kostov, had received a letter from Markov warning him to be on guard. Twelve days before the attack on Markov, Kostov, along with his wife, Natalia, had been on an escalator in Paris when he felt a sharp pain in his back just above the belt line. When he turned around, he saw a man carrying a bag who quickly disappeared into the crowd. The next day, Kostov had a fever so high he went to the hospital but was told he was in no great danger. Three days later, his discomfort subsided.

Naturally enough, Kostov was alarmed to learn that only days later, his friend Markov had died. The similarity of the attacks was obvious. He informed Parisian police, who immediately provided police protection. He was X-rayed, and sure enough, a tiny pellet was found just under the skin of his back. An operation using local anaesthetic was performed and the pellet removed. It was identical to the one taken from Markov, with one slight exception. The holes were .01 millimetres in diameter, somewhat smaller than those in the pellet found in Markov's thigh.

It has been theorized that Kostov survived because the amount of ricin in the pellet was smaller. It is possible that when Kostov failed to succumb, the holes in the Markov pellet were made larger, enabling the amount of poison to be increased.

One must turn back the clock to the 1970s to understand a motive for the murder of one broadcaster and the attempted murder of another. At the time, Russia was having difficulties within its own country as well as in Poland and Czechoslovakia. Both victims had been personalities on Radio Free Europe. Both were actively agitating the population with anti-Communist broadcasts. It is quite possible that word came down from the Kremlin to silence them both forever.

It has been twenty-six years since Markov was shot on the streets of London. The file on the unsolved murder is still open at New Scotland Yard.

Don Mason

(BELT)

DONALD MASON was a proper young man raised in a proper religious family. Smoking, drinking and cursing were what other boys did, not Don. The Bible was the word of God and the Good Book was the most influential factor in his life. Sex before marriage was unthinkable.

Don met Ruth Ragatz, a stunning blond, at a church convention. Don was smitten, but there was a complication. Ruth was seeing another boy. However, she and Don continued to see each other at church functions until finally Ruth terminated her relationship with Don's rival. The pair married in July 1983.

The honeymoon preyed on Don's mind. Although he had been a virgin, he discovered that Ruth was not. The thought of his wife in bed with another man festered in his mind. He couldn't get it out of his head. As the months wore on, he began to worry that since Ruth had not been chaste before their marriage, how could he be sure she had been faithful since their wedding day?

Three years of doubts and suspicions passed. Don thought of divorce, but with his religious background that was out of the question. There was another way—he would murder his wife. Lesser men than he had committed murder and avoided detection. Murder was definitely the answer to his dilemma. He would plan the details and he would kill his wife. It would be the perfect murder.

In October 1986, Don took out an insurance policy on his life for $100,000 and one on Ruth's for the same amount. The scheme not only would be perfect, it would pay handsomely as well.

Don was 27 years old. He and Ruth lived in a trailer park in Plattekill, New York. Both worked at the AT&T complex in Ramapo. They were well liked, conscientious employees. No one knew what dark thoughts Don Mason harboured in his warped mind.

In March 1987, Don underwent a hernia operation and was off work for a couple of weeks. What an opportune time to put his well-thought-out plan into action. He would use a belt to strangle Ruth. No gun, no knife, no discernible murder weapon. How clever, Don thought. It would look like a robbery with sexual assault as an afterthought. He would receive sympathy from friends and co-workers, even from some police officers whom he knew personally.

On Tuesday, March 24, after Ruth came home from work, Don playfully told her, "Turn around and close your eyes." Ruth may have thought she was about to be given an unexpected present. When she turned her back on her husband, he quickly looped a belt around her neck and pulled tight. Ruth, eyes bulging, managed to turn around. She scratched at Don's face, but it was no use. He pulled tighter until Ruth stopped breathing.

Don bent over his wife and ripped jewellery from her body. Then he dragged her out to her car. It was tough sledding. After all, Don had recently had a hernia operation and he didn't want to dislodge his stitches. Soon, he was speeding along the thruway. As far as any onlooker was concerned, it seemed as if Ruth were catching a few winks in the passenger seat. At the toll booths, no one gave them a second glance.

Don pulled into the Caldor Shopping Center in Ramapo and drove up beside a trash-disposal unit behind the Shop-Rite

Supermarket back door. He dragged his wife's body out of the car. Don realized one thing had gone wrong, but there was nothing he could do about that now: Ruth had managed to scratch his face. Systematically, Don went about breaking Ruth's fingernails, knowing that it was his flesh under those nails. It was a tedious task and dangerous, too. Someone could walk out of the Shop-Rite at any moment. Don quit breaking the nails. He ripped at Ruth's blouse and tore away her brassiere. Then he pulled down her pantyhose. Working frantically now, he removed her coat and purse before driving away.

It had all gone smoothly, with the exception of the scratches on his face. Don drove Ruth's car to the parking lot of a King Kullen Supermarket in Suffern, where he transferred to a rental car he had previously placed there. As he approached his home at the trailer park, he threw away Ruth's coat and purse along with the belt he had used to kill her.

Don washed his hands and face. It was time to prepare a hot meal for Ruth. After all, since he was recuperating from his hernia operation, he had been in the habit of preparing the evening meal. It was the least he could do.

That evening, Don called a friend, Bob Parks. He was concerned. Ruth hadn't come home from work. He and Bob drove around looking for Ruth's Chevy Sprint, but couldn't locate it. The folks at AT&T told him she had left the facility at 5:30 P.M. Don called the police, but they said they couldn't do anything for twenty-four hours.

Next morning, Don Mason was beside himself with worry. Tearfully, he reported his wife missing to the Ramapo police. Within an hour a truck driver making a delivery to the Shop-Rite Supermarket came across the body of Ruth Mason. As soon as she was identified by an AT&T employee, a detective informed Don that his wife had been murdered. He burst into tears.

That night, Ruth's vehicle was found. Nothing of importance was discovered in the car, but its location puzzled investigators. Who would dump a body where it could be found at any moment and then abandon the victim's car some miles away? It appeared to investigators that the killer would have to have had a second car in order to get away from the shopping centre where Ruth's car was found. It just didn't add up. Was rape the motive or was it robbery, or as sometimes happens, a combination of both? Why take the dead woman's purse? Where had she been attacked?

Don, understandably distraught, was requested to visit the Ramapo police station to assist the authorities. Detectives couldn't help but notice the scratch on his face, but didn't comment about it at the time. An autopsy performed that same day indicated that Ruth had not been raped. Death was attributed to asphyxiation due to ligature strangulation. It was believed that the murder weapon was something smooth, like a belt.

One of the detectives mentioned that Don would be wise to have the doctor who had just performed the autopsy take a look at that nasty scratch on his face. Don agreed. The doctor treated the scratch and informed detectives that it had been made by a fingernail and was surrounded by makeup. Don told police he didn't remember how he had received the scratch, but admitted that he had applied makeup so that the scratch wouldn't be so noticeable.

Detectives believed that Don Mason had killed his wife. They asked him to agree to a polygraph test and were surprised when he quickly acquiesced. While waiting for arrangements for the test to be finalized, a detective informed Don that his version of his wife's disappearance didn't make sense. Don surprised those present by blurting out, "I killed her. I did it in our trailer as soon as she came home from work." He went on to describe his obsession with his wife's infidelity. The thought had eaten away at his mind until he had turned to murder to solve his problem. He told detectives that he had hidden his wife's jewellery and a $100,000 life insurance policy under his bed.

Don wondered out loud whether he would have gotten away with murder had Ruth not scratched him. No one told him that his credit card had already been traced to the agency where he had rented the getaway car.

Don Mason pleaded guilty to his wife's murder. He was sentenced to a term of twenty-two years to life.

Jerry McFadden

(PANTIES)

JERRY MCFADDEN WAS A BAD MAN. Let's just look at his record.

At age 18, McFadden, of Haskell, Texas, who liked to call himself Animal, tried his hand at burglary. Two years later, in 1968, he was arrested for destroying private property. By the time he was 24 he had reached a height of well over six feet and weighed a bulky 250 pounds.

In 1972, big bad Jerry graduated to rape. While the rape charge was pending, he viciously assaulted another young woman and was sent to prison for fifteen years. Five years later, he was paroled and managed to stay clean for a year, one of the longest trouble-free periods of his life.

In 1979, Jerry kidnapped an 18-year-old secretary from her office and kept her prisoner for a full day. He raped the girl several times, finally choking her and leaving her for dead. The girl eventually regained consciousness. A passing motorist found her running hysterically down the highway near the town of Lueders. For this offence, McFadden was sentenced to fifteen years' imprisonment.

Once again, this vicious habitual criminal was released under the mandatory-supervision program after serving one-third of his sentence. He settled in Wood County, where he had relatives. When McFadden's release became known, the locals petitioned to have him removed to his home area of Haskell. Their efforts brought no results. McFadden was so feared that his female parole officer refused to visit him unless accompanied by armed escorts.

No wonder Jerry McFadden was suspected when three outstanding young people from the small town of Hawkins went missing. Suzanne Harrison, 18, Gena Turner, 20, and Bryan Boone, 19, went for a drive around Lake Hawkins in Bryan's blue pickup. The three popular honours high-school students told their parents they wouldn't be home late. They planned to have supper, drive a bit and return home.

By midnight, their parents were concerned. At 1:20 A.M., a relative of Bryan Boone's spotted his abandoned pickup by the lake. That same day, police and concerned citizens combed the area but failed to turn up any sign of the missing youths.

Authorities were apprehensive for two reasons. The girls had left their purses containing small sums of money in the pickup. Whatever had happened to them had not been triggered by robbery. Second, that same night, a young couple from Tyler had been parked along the lake when they were held up by a huge man brandishing a handgun. The shirtless intruder was a wild-looking specimen with a bushy, unkempt beard and several weird tattoos. He wanted drugs. When he was told they had none, he searched the couple's car.

Obviously satisfied that they were telling the truth, the gunman lingered for some time, hinting at sexual escapades with the terrified woman. As suddenly as he had appeared, the giant of a man left in what the couple thought was a blue Ford Bronco. The young couple had been frightened out of their wits but were otherwise unharmed. This incident had taken place only a half mile from where Bryan Boone's truck was found abandoned.

Police attempted to trace the last movements of the three missing youths. They learned that they had eaten at a restaurant in town before driving to the lake. At 9:30 P.M., they were observed parked at the lake. Then nothing until the pickup was found.

Tragically, it wasn't long before the fate of one of the girls became known. Suzanne Harrison's body was found by a state cleaning crew in a recreational park near the town of Gilmer. Suzanne had been raped and strangled with her own panties. Her body had been found about thirty miles from where she had been parked with her two friends the previous evening.

The search for the other two missing young people was continuing when police learned that a wild, bushy man had been sighted in a blue Bronco and had been taken into custody. The couple who had been terrorized the night before identified the man as their antagonist. He turned out to be the area's bad boy and parolee, Jerry McFadden. He denied any knowledge of Suzanne Harrison or her friends. He was held in custody, charged with attempted robbery and parole violation.

The search for Gena Turner and Bryan Boone intensified. Hundreds of volunteers combed the area where Suzanne's body had been found. They interrupted their efforts only to attend Suzanne Harrison's funeral. The small town was devastated by the tragedy. Almost all the stores in town closed on the day of the funeral.

A week after their disappearance, Gena's and Bryan's bodies were found in a ravine a mile outside the small town of Ore City. Bryan was fully clothed, but Gena was nude from the waist down. She had been raped. Both had been shot to death. Once again, the tiny community had funerals to attend.

Texas authorities went about building a case against Jerry McFadden. On May 22, 1986, the sheriff's office issued a statement that McFadden had been charged with the murder of Suzanne Harrison. Law enforcement officials, as well as the general public, were enraged that a three-time convicted rapist had been released after serving only one-third of his sentence. Texas had the death penalty and McFadden, if convicted, was in real danger of paying the supreme price. But Jerry McFadden had not played out his vile string just yet.

On Wednesday, July 9, 1986, at 6:30 P.M., McFadden was cooling his heels in the Gilmer County Jail, as he had every evening since his incarceration in May. On duty that evening was jailer Ken Mayfield, 53, along with radio dispatchers and jailers Rosalie Williams, 24, and Stacy Mullinix, 27.

In Texas, regulations at all county jails allow prisoners to be removed from their cells to make phone calls. McFadden had made several during his weeks in jail. On this particular evening, he requested a call. Jailer Mayfield, following correct procedure, removed his holster and placed it outside the jail area. He unlocked McFadden's cell and escorted him to the phone. Suddenly, McFadden swung at Mayfield's head with a piece of sharp metal. Unknown to all, he had managed to dislodge a piece of his cell window frame and had used it as a club. Mayfield fell to the jail floor, bleeding profusely.

The two women were in an adjacent control room. The door was not locked. In a split second they were facing wild Jerry McFadden. Barking commands, McFadden ordered the two women to drag Mayfield into a cell. After this was accomplished, he had Rosalie Williams lock up Mayfield and Mullinix. McFadden, acting as wild as he looked, propelled Rosalie to a strongbox where prisoners' money was kept. This strange man counted out $162, the exact amount he had credited to his name. Other cash was left untouched.

Quickly, McFadden armed himself with a .38-calibre service revolver and changed his white jail garb for a sweatshirt and blue jeans. Down an elevator he and his hostage travelled five floors and out into the hot Texas night. Rosalie was forced into her own Datsun. With McFadden behind the wheel, the pair drove away.

When officers radioed the sheriff's office and received no response, they sped to the jail. There, locked in a cell were Stacy Mullinix and Ken Mayfield, who was slowly regaining consciousness. Mayfield was taken to hospital, where sixty-six stitches were required to close the wound in his head.

Convicted rapist and suspected triple killer Jerry McFadden had a female police officer as a hostage. Rosalie was married to state trooper Eddie Williams, who took an active part in the search for his wife. The Williamses had a 3-year-old child. One can only imagine Trooper Williams's thoughts as he hunted for his wife and a man with McFadden's record.

Roadblocks were thrown up. Helicopters scanned the area from the sky. Prison bloodhounds were pressed into service. As the search intensified, 700 law enforcement officers were actively engaged in the hunt.

McFadden had made one mistake. He had escaped from jail in his stocking feet. He and Rosalie left the Datsun at 6 A.M. the following morning near the town of Big Sandy. As they slogged through the woods, they could hear helicopters overhead, but the choppers didn't sight McFadden and his hostage.

As the morning wore on, the heat became oppressive. The terrain was rough. Sometimes they walked through poison ivy. McFadden's feet were taking a beating. Rosalie felt that sooner or later her captor would turn on her. She was terrified, but kept her wits about her. She had recently completed a course on hostage taking, never dreaming that she would have first-hand experience so shortly after finishing the course.

On an isolated railway siding, McFadden spotted an empty boxcar. Near exhaustion, with his feet a horrible mess, the wanted man took refuge there. As the day wore on, he and Rosalie could hear searchers, particularly helicopters. Both captor and captive were hungry, but more important, they were becoming dehydrated.

Nightfall relieved the heat somewhat, but did nothing for their thirst. Rosalie was having difficulty breathing. McFadden appeared to be affected by the deteriorating condition of his hostage. He decided to leave the boxcar to look for water. Before he left, he warned Rosalie to stay put.

Rosalie weighed her chances. When she felt McFadden was far enough away from the boxcar, she decided to make a run for it. At that exact moment, a dog accosted McFadden. As the dog snapped at him, he attempted to ward it off with a stick. Rosalie made a dash out of the boxcar and ran down the railroad track to a house some distance away. She rushed through the unlocked door of the farmhouse and was met by its occupant, who recognized her immediately from photos he had seen on TV.

Police were phoned with the startling and welcome news that Rosalie Williams was alive and unharmed. The wanted man's location was now known, but he still managed to stay at large for two days, when he was finally sighted in an abandoned house by two deputies. He gave up without a struggle.

In July 1987, Jerry McFadden was convicted and sentenced to death for the murder of Suzanne Harrison. On October 14, 1999, he was executed by lethal injection in Huntsville, Texas. The man who called himself Animal declined to make a last statement.

Joe Medley

(WATER)

THERE WASN'T MUCH of anything good to say about Joseph Medley. He passed a few rubber cheques and rolled the odd drunk. Nothing big. Our Joe was an inept practitioner of the illegal professions and, as a result, served several short sentences in a variety of Michigan jails.

Joe graduated, in a manner of speaking, when he teamed up with Jane Edwards, a young lady who enjoyed the finer things in life but had a distinct aversion to anything remotely resembling work.

One fine night in 1944, when Jane was knocking back a few in a nightclub near Battle Creek, Michigan, she struck up a conversation with Louis Brooks. Maybe Louis had had one or three too many, but boys will be boys. He divulged that he was the owner of a prosperous manufacturing facility. Talkative Louis even told Jane that he had been mayor of nearby Marshall. To Jane's way of thinking, she had a big fish in a little pond just aching to be reeled in.

Jane told Joe of the big one who frequented the local watering hole. Joe was all ears. The pair of connivers evolved a scheme to relieve Brooks of at least some of his cash. Next night, as Brooks was enjoying a few, Jane sidled up to his table. The evening wore on. In Brooks's eyes, Jane became more attractive with each slug of Glenlivet. Around midnight, when she was positively gorgeous, she suggested a pleasant drive in the country. Brooks figured he had come up lucky. The pair drove away into the night.

They had only gone a short distance when who should force Brooks onto the shoulder of the road? None other than Joe Medley. Joe tied up Brooks and Jane and ordered Brooks to direct him to his plant. Under threat of death, Brooks was forced to open a safe and hand over $12,000 in cash and $33,000 in bonds. Joe hightailed it out of there with the loot, figuring that he and Jane had pulled off the perfect robbery.

He was wrong. Brooks managed to free himself and went straight to the police. Things just didn't stack up for the boys in blue. How did the robber know Brooks and Jane would be driving down a lonely road late at night? How did he know Brooks had a manufacturing plant located nearby? They decided to rake Jane over the coals. What was a girl to do under such pressure? Jane confessed to her part in the abduction and robbery. She told detectives her accomplice was Joe Medley. Unsuspecting Joe was immediately picked up, tried and found guilty of kidnapping. He was sentenced to thirty to fifty years' imprisonment.

At the time of Joe's incarceration, the Second World War was at its ugliest. While the boys behind bars had to sit out the action, they did whatever they could for the war effort. Joe was a leader at Michigan State Prison in raising money for war bonds. He was also a model prisoner and, as such, was allowed to go into the town of Jackson, accompanied by a guard, to purchase war bonds for his fellow inmates.

Convinced that Joe had no intention of escaping, a gullible guard let him out of the prison vehicle to purchase the bonds. While the guard parked the car, Joe, with $750 stuffed in his pockets, walked to the bank and right on by.

Who knows what thought processes converted Joe Medley from an inept thief to a far more serious criminal? He was at large for a month when an incident occurred that was to catapult Joe onto a direct line to doom.

Mr. and Mrs. D.J. Stafford were staying at the De Soto Hotel in New Orleans. On Christmas Eve, 1944, Mr. Stafford called the hotel's housekeeper, advising her that he and his wife would be away for several days and that it would not be necessary to make up their room. What a considerate guest, thought the housekeeper. She passed along the information to her staff. One chambermaid was not told of the special instructions and it was she who entered the Staffords' room two days later. Peering into the bathroom, she saw a sight she would never forget. There was Mrs. Stafford, sitting nude in the bathtub, rigid and dead.

The chambermaid spread the alarm. Soon police and other officials were swarming over the Staffords's room. A coroner confirmed that Mrs. Stafford had been murdered. Her head had been submerged under the water in the tub until she had drowned. From the hotel's registry, detectives learned that D.J. Stafford's address was 4611 Hazel Ave., Chicago.

The story of the murder in the bathtub made headlines in the New Orleans papers. Furious, the real D.J. Stafford walked into a police station. By the merest coincidence, while passing through New Orleans, he had picked up a newspaper and realized that someone was using his good name. After being told of the address on the hotel register, he had a good idea as to the identity of the culprit. Stafford told police that twenty years earlier, a young man had worked for him when he owned an automobile dealership. The young man had lived at 4611 Hazel Avenue. His name was Joseph Medley.

Routine police work uncovered the real identity of the woman in the bathtub. The red-haired victim had been an Austrian immigrant, Laura Fischer.

The hunt was on for Joe. Unknown to police, he had made his way to Chicago. Now that he had murdered one woman, he apparently decided to rob and murder women as his full-time occupation.

J.H. Hanan checked into the Atlantic Hotel in Chicago. Hanan claimed that he was a cattleman from out West. He was often seen with assorted ladies on his arm. Funny thing, most of them were redheads.

Blanche Zimmerman was a redhead. A maid ignored the Do Not Disturb sign on Mr. Hanan's doorknob, entered his room, and found Blanche's body in the bathtub. She had apparently died from an overdose of benzedrine. Hotel employees were shown photographs of Joe Medley. He was indeed J.H. Hanan, and he was long gone with whatever he could carry of Blanche's belongings.

Joe next showed up in Washington, D.C., using the name Joseph Fischer. He made the acquaintance of a woman in a restaurant. When Joe told her that it had been a long time since he had had a home-cooked meal, she invited him to her place for a meal like Mother used to make. While Joe was partaking of the culinary prowess of his new friend, an acquaintance of hers paid a visit. The ill-fated woman, by coincidence, had red hair. Her name was Nancy Boyer.

A few days after this chance meeting, Nancy was found shot to death in her apartment. Her jewellery and furs were missing. Those of you who are paying attention should note that Joe often used aliases that had some connection to him. When he checked into the De Soto Hotel, he used the name of a former employer and his own old address. In the case of Nancy Boyer's murder, he used his own first name and the surname of his first victim.

Like all murderers, Joe couldn't just go on and on killing red-haired women forever. Something had to give. Once again, coincidence reared its head, this time to the consternation of Joseph Medley.

Dr. James Elder, an observant university professor, spotted a man in a hotel restaurant having lunch with an extremely attractive woman. He remembered seeing that face somewhere. Dr. Elder raced home, dug out an old newspaper, and there was the man's photograph—Joseph Medley, wanted for murder. Elder called the authorities immediately.

Police converged on the restaurant, but Joe and his companion were gone. They learned that the man who had eaten there was registered as a guest at the hotel. Upon checking the register, police came across the name James H. Hanan. They rushed to Hanan's room. A man answered the door. The police had arrived in the nick of time. Joe's lady friend was preparing her bath. She was, of course, a redhead.

Joe Medley, the strange killer of red-haired women, was taken into custody. He was tried and found guilty of the murder of Nancy Boyer.

On December 20, 1946, Joseph Dunbar Medley paid the supreme penalty when he was put to death in the electric chair.

Penelope Mitchell

(Hatchet)

PENELOPE BAMFORD WAS ONLY 17 when she wed Alan Mitchell on April Fool's Day, 1971. Penelope had jumped at the chance of marriage for the very good reason that she came from a family where child abuse was the norm rather than the exception. Her dad was a drunken lout who regularly beat his wife and children. He was happy to learn that he would have one less mouth to feed.

Penelope and Alan settled into a small but comfortable home in Paarl, South Africa, a city famous for its exported wine in less troubled times. For ten years the Mitchells led an apparently happy life. There were two additions to the family, daughters Natalie and Jane.

Now, I'll let you in on a little secret. By the time Alan was 44 years old, his sexual interest in his wife had diminished to such an extent that it was almost nonexistent. Penelope, 27, was diametrically opposite to her husband when it came to the birds and bees. Folks, the woman was frustrated.

It was quite a shock to neighbours Natalie and Harley Brown when they heard Penelope give a blood-curdling scream shortly after Alan had driven up to his home. The Browns dashed outside and observed Penelope standing over her husband's fallen form. His head had been split open and he was near death. So near that he died shortly after being rushed to hospital.

Detectives were soon at the scene searching for the murder weapon. Whoever had killed Alan had apparently carried away the instrument of death.

When questioned, the Browns told a straightforward story of having heard Penelope scream and of running to assist her. They were immediately eliminated as suspects. Penelope, who was under sedation, told police she'd heard her husband slam the door of his car. When he failed to enter the house, she had gone outside and had found him on the path beside a hedge.

Dr. Brian Cheevers, the criminal investigation's medical officer, examined the body. He told detectives that the blow to the back of the head had probably been delivered by a hatchet. Because of the severity of the wound, he felt that the murderer had most probably been a man. Penelope, a petite woman, had never really been considered as a suspect. She was now totally dismissed.

Police had difficulty establishing a motive for the murder. Alan Mitchell was not a wealthy man. He carried only enough insurance to provide a decent burial. Nothing had been removed from his person at the time of the attack. His friends and relatives were checked out. He had no known enemies. Yet, someone had waited for him behind a hedge in front of his home and had struck him on the back of the head with a hatchet.

The Mitchells' family life was investigated. There was no hint that they were anything but a happy, loving couple. The only thing a bit unusual was Penelope's hobby. She had received some local acclaim as a hypnotist.

Penelope held meetings at least twice a week in her home. When she had good subjects, she often had them act out ridiculous scenes and find hidden objects. Everyone enjoyed the entertainment. Besides, she didn't charge for the fun. Discovering that the wife of a murder victim is an amateur hypnotist didn't help the investigation one little bit. However, when detectives received an anonymous tip that a butcher might be involved, that was a different matter.

Police checked out where the Mitchells usually purchased their meat. They found that the butcher, a man named Borken, was over 70 years of age and towered at five feet four inches in height. Borken could not have inflicted the fatal blows, but his delivery boy was strong, good-looking Noel Hatting.

For some time police couldn't figure out why no one in the Mitchells' neighbourhood had reported seeing a stranger. They surmised that the killer must have been someone who wouldn't be noticed, someone who had every right to be there, someone like Noel Hatting.

Noel was taken into custody and questioned. He had quite a story to tell. He stated that he had been having intimate relations with Penelope for some time. They were usually rushed affairs, due to the fact that her husband and two children had to be out of the house. Whenever he made a meat delivery, Noel also delivered other goods to Penelope. The first time he had delivered meat, Penelope had seduced him. She had told him that her husband wasn't interested in sex. Conversely, she just loved it. Noel was her boy.

Penelope had also told her lover that divorcing her husband was out of the question. Alan was a deeply religious man who would never consent to a divorce. When Penelope suggested that the only way to get rid of Alan would be to murder him, Noel was aghast. He would never be a party to murder.

On the day of Alan's murder, Penelope had hypnotized him. He was an excellent subject and had often allowed her to put him under in the past. This time, he came around and discovered, to his consternation, that he was standing on the path in front of the Mitchells' house holding a bloody hatchet. Alan Mitchell was lying at his feet with a horrible wound in his head.

Penelope told him that he had killed Alan, but that everything would be all right. She took the hatchet and urged him to go home, wash, and burn his blood-spattered clothing. She had promised to hide the hatchet and had assured him that there were now no obstacles to their being together forever and ever. Noel claimed that he had no recollection of the actual killing. Dazed and confused, he had thrust the hatchet into Penelope's hands and had run home.

Penelope was taken into custody. Her story was in sharp contrast to the one told by her lover. According to Penelope, it was Noel who had seduced her. She had attempted to break off their affair, but Noel had blackmailed her by threatening to tell all to her husband. On the afternoon of the murder, she had heard her husband arrive home. When she went outside to greet him, she had found Noel, bloody hatchet in hand, standing over her husband. She had not told the true story earlier because she felt Noel would implicate her. She feared separation from her children and life in prison.

There you have it—two diverse stories, but the police were not taken in by either yarn. Experts agreed that while Noel was an excellent subject for hypnosis, no one could be persuaded to do something under hypnosis to which they were morally opposed. No, Noel had known full well what he was doing.

Detectives proved that the murder weapon belonged to the Mitchells. Noel could not have obtained possession of the hatchet without Penelope's knowledge. The two conspirators had planned and executed the murder together.

On January 8, 1982, Penelope Mitchell and Noel Hatting were found guilty of murder. Each received fifteen-year prison terms.

Stella Nickell

(CYANIDE)

FRUMPY 44-YEAR-OLD STELLA NICKELL first saw the light of day in Portland, Oregon. Her family was poverty stricken and Stella was left pretty much to her own devices during her formative years. By the time she was 16, she was married and the mother of a bouncing baby girl, Cynthia.

Stella got into minor scrapes with the law. Let's see now, there was the silly scam the law called fraud, and the small-time wallpapering operation, which an inconsiderate prosecuting attorney deemed to be forgery.

Eventually, Stella shed her teenage husband and married Bruce Nickell, a heavy-equipment operator with a drinking problem. For a while, Bruce and Stella had fun bar-hopping their lives away. It was kind of a shock to Stella when Bruce took the cure. To Stella's way of thinking, the good times stopped and boredom set in.

In the early 1980s, Stella and Bruce lived in a trailer in Washington State. Money was scarce. Bruce was unemployed for long stretches of time. Daughter Cynthia, who had married and divorced, was bringing up her child in Stella's trailer. Right beside the Nickells' trailer lived Stella's elderly mother. All in all, Stella had her hands full. Life was a bowl of cherry pits.

In 1982, Stella confided to her daughter that she would like to get rid of hubby Bruce. She vaguely told Cynthia that she was thinking of insuring his life and collecting on the insurance. Then she would purchase the land the trailer was on and open a tropical-fish store. Cynthia listened to her mother but dismissed the conversation as the ramblings of a woman who had missed the boat.

But Mother wasn't kidding.

In 1985, Stella took out a $40,000 insurance policy on Bruce's life, with herself as sole beneficiary. Bruce, who often worked for the state, had an employment policy that paid his wife $136,000 in the event of accidental death. The same policy paid only $31,000 if death was due to natural causes.

One fine day in June, Stella took a bottle of Excedrin capsules down from a shelf in the kitchen. She laced several of the capsules with cyanide. Just like in an Agatha Christie novel, Bruce came home from work complaining of a headache. He reached for the Excedrin and gulped down four pills. Stella watched. Bruce turned on the TV. Nothing happened.

He then got up and went outside. Suddenly, Bruce screamed, "I feel like I'm going to pass out!" True to his word, Bruce bit the dust. Stella did the wifely thing. She called paramedics and watched as a helicopter flew her seriously ill husband to Harborview Medical Center in Seattle. A few hours later Bruce was dead.

When informed of Bruce's death, Stella had the distasteful duty of breaking the news to Cynthia. She felt obliged to tell her daughter that she'd had nothing to do with the unexpected tragedy.

A coroner failed to detect any poison in Bruce's body and attributed death to pulmonary emphysema. Stella had committed the perfect murder. But our Stella was far from pleased. In fact, she was downright depressed.

Remember those insurance policies? Stella stood to collect $40,000 and $31,000, for a total of $71,000, which everyone will agree is a tidy sum. But darn it all, if only the death had been accidental, the payoff would have been a whopping $176,000. There simply had to be a way to get at the big bucks. Stella thought and thought. Then the idea struck her. Why not murder someone else? Authorities would be convinced that her husband had been killed by some nut who ran around snuffing out strangers.

Stella opened three bottles of Extra Strength Excedrin and Anacin-3 and emptied some of the capsules. She refilled them with cyanide. The poisoned headache remedies were surreptitiously placed on the shelves of three nearby stores. (Because of this case, as well as one other, medicine containers were made more secure.)

Within a week, one of the bottles was purchased. Sue Snow, 40, was the assistant vice-president of the Puget Sound National Bank branch of Auburn, Washington. She had recently married for the third time. Husband Paul Webking, 45, was a truck driver, who dearly loved his new wife.

Somewhere along the line, Sue had heard that caffeine in Extra-Strength Excedrin would give you a boost to start the day. It was her habit to take two capsules each morning. On June 11, 1986, Sue got up around 6 A.M., took her capsules and collapsed on the bathroom floor. Six hours later, Sue was dead.

This time, Stella's handiwork was uncovered. Doctors stated that Sue had been poisoned by the administration of cyanide placed in Excedrin capsules. That same morning, Sue's husband, Paul, who suffered from arthritis, had taken Excedrin from the same bottle as Sue. He suffered no ill effects; no thanks to our Stella. By sheer luck, his capsules had not been doctored.

Now Stella went after those accidental-death insurance dollars. Exhibiting more gall than brains, she informed authorities that her husband had also taken Excedrin the day he died. An examination of skin tissue indicated that Stella's suspicions were well founded. Bruce Nickell had been poisoned.

The Bristol-Myers Co., manufacturers of Excedrin, acted swiftly in removing hundreds of thousands of bottles of their products off store shelves. Paul Webking filed a wrongful-death suit against Bristol-Myers. Bold as brass, Stella Nickell filed a similar suit.

In all, five poisoned bottles of headache remedy were uncovered. Because two of the five were found in Stella's home, she received close attention from detectives attempting to crack the case. It wasn't long before they discovered the insurance policies on Bruce Nickell's life. Stella was given a lie detector test, which indicated she was not responding truthfully.

The case was solved when Stella's daughter Cynthia, now 28 years old, came forward and agreed to testify against her mother. Stella was taken into custody.

At Stella's murder trial, Cynthia was the state's star witness. From the witness stand, she reviewed the family history. She revealed that her mother had told her that her life had become empty and boring when Bruce stopped drinking. Her mother had stated that she was contemplating killing Bruce. Why had Cynthia not revealed her mother's intentions before Stella committed double murder? For one thing, Cynthia never dreamed that her mother would actually kill anyone.

Defence lawyers suggested that Cynthia had been tempted by the $300,000 reward for the killer's identity put up by the Non-Prescription Drug Manufacturers Association. (An official of this organization has informed me that, as of this date, no one, including Cynthia, has applied for the reward.)

After deliberating for more than five days, the Washington jury found Stella guilty of causing death by product tampering. She was the first person convicted in the United States under a new law covering product tampering, instituted in 1983 after seven people were killed in the Chicago area by bottles of poisoned Tylenol. The Tylenol killer has never been apprehended.

Stella Nickell was sentenced to ninety years' imprisonment. She will be eligible for parole in 2018, when she will be 74.

Fred Nodder

(STRING)

LITTLE 10-YEAR-OLD MONA TINSLEY left the Wesleyan School in Newark, England, at four o'clock as usual. Then she disappeared off the face of the earth.

Although it was a rather nasty January day in 1937, Mona's parents were not unduly alarmed when their daughter didn't arrive home at her usual time of 4:20 P.M. The Tinsleys had several children. One of them was always late for something or other.

At 7 P.M., Mona's parents grew apprehensive. They called on relatives and neighbours. At 9:30 P.M., Mr. Tinsley reported his daughter missing to police. That night, abandoned buildings were searched. Vehicles were stopped and their drivers interrogated. Next morning, school principals asked their pupils to come forward if they had seen Mona after 4 P.M. the previous day.

Several children erroneously believed they had seen the missing girl, but one youngster's story was taken seriously. William Plackett, 11, lived close to Mona and knew her well. He claimed that he had seen her at a quarter to five near the bus station in the company of a man. The little boy gave a vague description of the man, but said that he would recognize him if he saw him again.

The investigation intensified. Scores of officers scoured the town, inquiring if anyone had seen the missing child. At the time of the disappearance, Newark's population was 10,000. Mona's disappearance seemed to affect the entire community.

One woman, Mrs. Hird, came forward with the ominous information that she had seen a man loitering about the school at four o'clock when the children were dismissed. To Mrs. Hird, the man seemed to be staring at the Wesleyan School door. She not only observed him, but believed she recognized him as a man who had at one time lodged with the Tinsley family.

Detectives questioned the Tinsleys, who recalled Fred Hudson, their well-liked lodger. He had been like a member of the family and had stayed several weeks with them about fifteen months earlier. When he couldn't pay his rent, he had left, but the parting of the ways was amicable. Mrs. Tinsley told police that her sister, Mrs. Grimes, knew Hudson well. She believed her sister still saw him on occasion.

While police were pursuing this avenue of investigation, bus driver Charles Reville informed the authorities that on the day in question, a little after 4 P.M., he had picked up a little girl near the Wesleyan School. She had been accompanied by a man. They had boarded his bus and had taken the twenty-two-mile trip to Retford. The man had purchased a return ticket for himself and a one-way ticket for the child.

The man named Hudson appeared to be untraceable until police questioned Mrs. Tinsley's sister, Mrs. Grimes, who told them she often visited Hudson in the village of Hayton. She also informed them that he sometimes used the last name Nodder.

This casual statement was the break the police required. Frederick Nodder proved to be a married man with two children. He had fathered a child by another woman. When his wife heard of Fred's dalliances, she left him. Meanwhile, the mother of the child born out of wedlock obtained a court order forcing Fred to pay for the support of their child. In order to avoid making payments, Fred moved from Sheffield to Hayton.

Fred was living in Hayton, in a house named Peacehaven. Before calling on Fred, police made some inquiries of neighbours. They learned from a Miss Whittaker that on January 6, the day after Mona went missing, she had observed a little girl standing at the back door of Peacehaven. That same day, she had seen Fred digging a hole in his garden.

Detectives called on Fred. They let him know they were inquiring about the missing Mona Tinsley. Fred, cool as a cucumber, replied, "I know nothing about it." He went on to give an account of his movements on January 5, but portions of his statement proved impossible to verify.

Fred, now strongly suspected of murder, was taken into custody, although there was precious little direct evidence against him. His garden was dug up, but no body was found. A search of his home turned up one concrete clue. Police found a piece of paper with a child's scribbling on it. The writing was identified as that of Mona Tinsley. Fred said he must have carried away the piece of paper when he moved out of the Tinsley home.

Everyone who claimed to have seen Mona with a man the day she disappeared was asked to view a line-up. Half identified Fred as the man they had seen with Mona and half picked another man.

Under intense pressure to confess, Fred abruptly changed his story. He now said that he had lied when he had first been questioned. He admitted meeting Mona after school. She had been extremely happy to see him, calling him Uncle Fred, as she had done when he was a lodger at her home. Mona had expressed a wish to visit with her cousin Peter, Mrs. Grimes's baby son. Fred said he had foolishly agreed to take the little girl to visit her cousin. He explained that he had expected Mrs. Grimes to visit him the next day and, at that time, Mona could accompany her to her home and visit with her cousin. When he arrived home, he received a phone call from Mrs. Grimes telling him that she wouldn't be visiting him the next day. Strangely, there was no mention of Mona during this conversation.

Fred swore that he and Mona had slept in separate beds. Nothing of a criminal nature had taken place, although he realized the precariousness of his position. Fred claimed that he had accompanied Mona on a bus partway to Mrs. Grimes's home on the following evening. He had then put the little girl on a bus to Sheffield, with a letter to Mrs. Grimes explaining his actions. Fred swore that was the last time he had seen Mona. She was alive and well and quite excited about seeing little Peter for the very first time.

On January 10, Fred Nodder was taken into custody and charged with taking Mona Tinsley away from her home by force or fraud. In March 1937, an English jury deliberated only sixteen minutes before finding Fred guilty. He was sentenced to seven years' imprisonment.

Three months later, with Fred securely behind bars and the town's traumatic experience slowly fading, the case again hit the headlines. Walter Marshall, his wife, sons and friends set off for a sail down the River Idle. It was Mr. Marshall who noticed the strange-looking object stuck in the mud near the shore. The unusual object proved to be the body of Mona Tinsley. A post-mortem revealed that the child had been strangled with a ligature such as a string or tape. Fred Nodder was taken from prison and charged with the murder of Mona Tinsley.

On Monday, November 22, 1937, Fred pleaded not guilty. The prosecution presented many of the same witnesses who had appeared at the previous trial. Mona's parents, the bus drivers, and Fred's neighbours all repeated their previous evidence. There was a difference this time around. This time there was a body.

The defence offered only one witness—Fred Nodder. Fred told the same story he had related so often. He claimed his problems had all started when he met Mona, who had greeted him with a cheerful, "Hullo, Uncle Fred." Fred detailed his trip to his home with Mona and went on to tell how he had eventually sent her on her way to her aunt's house with a letter of explanation. He stuck to his story throughout his trial.

When asked why, on a rather nasty night in January, he hadn't dispatched Mona to her parents promptly, Fred could only lamely respond that it had not occurred to him. He said that he knew he was in trouble and wanted Mrs. Grimes to act as mediator. Fred had difficulty giving a logical reason why he had waited until nightfall of the second day before sending the child to her aunt.

Defence attorneys theorized that Mona may have been lured off her bus by a stranger after Fred had left her and that this stranger was responsible for the child's death. They also put forward an accidental-death theory. They suggested that Mona might have caught her dress on the branch of a tree. Hanging at the edge of the river, her dress could have caused her to strangle before her body plunged into the river. It was a far-fetched, implausible theory that was ridiculed by the presiding judge in his summing-up.

Fred Nodder was found guilty of the murder of Mona Tinsley. On December 30, 1937, he was hanged at Lincoln Prison.

Beatrice Pace

(sheep dip)

HERE'S YOUR OPPORTUNITY to be a judge at a murder trial. I'll lay out the facts much as they were put before an English jury back in 1927. Was the defendant guilty or not guilty? Ready? Here we go.

In 1909, Harry Pace, 17, of Coleford, England, married Beatrice Martin, who was also 17 and hailed from the nearby village of St. Briavels. Right from the beginning, the marriage didn't work. Well, it worked a little. The couple had ten children. Five of the Pace offspring had died of natural causes by the time 1927 rolled around.

There is some evidence that Harry beat his wife when the urge overtook him. Much-maligned Beatrice often left her sheep-farmer husband, but always returned to the beatings and pregnancies. Those who knew of the turbulent lifestyle of the Paces claimed that Harry cared more for his sheep than for his wife and children.

It was during the spring of 1927 that Harry took ill. He had severe tummy pains and complained that his legs felt funny. Harry was confined to bed, where Beatrice cared for his every need. By August his condition had deteriorated to such an extent that he was placed in the Gloucester Infirmary. The Paces' family physician, Dr. Dupre, diagnosed Harry's trouble as peripheral neuritis, a condition which is rather painful and results in loss of use of the affected limbs. The hospital doctors, as well as Dr. Dupre, were stumped as to the cause of their patient's illness.

Harry's health improved gradually until October 17, when he was released from hospital under the care of Dr. Dupre. Christmas was a red-letter day in the Pace household. Papa was able to come downstairs to take part in Christmas dinner. Harry felt so good about the whole thing he beat up his wife and kiddies. After that, his condition worsened. Actually, it did more than worsen. Harry died on Tuesday, January 10, 1928.

Dr. Dupre signed the death certificate. Harry Pace had died of natural causes. Beatrice went about attending to the funeral arrangements. But hold the phone: Harry's nosy brother, Elton, smelled a rodent. He thought Harry might have been poisoned. He told police how he felt and they in turn checked out the Paces' rather violent home life.

The funeral was held up while an autopsy was performed. Some of Harry's vital organs were forwarded to Bristol University for pathological examination. Based on the findings of the autopsy, Beatrice was arrested and charged with the murder of her husband. An inquest jury felt there was enough evidence to hold Beatrice over for trial.

In July 1928, Beatrice stood trial for the murder of her husband. Much sympathy was displayed toward the widow. No one really likes a man who beats his wife and children. A defence fund was hastily organized and succeeded in raising £1,300, which, in those long-ago days, was sufficient to hire a top lawyer. Well-known defence lawyer Norman Birkett was retained to do battle with the Crown's best.

The prosecution pointed out that Harry had kept sheep dip on the farm. This arsenic-impregnated dip is commonly used to rid sheep of vermin. Beatrice had access to the poison, as well as the opportunity to administer it to her husband. As to motive, the Crown stated that the beatings Beatrice and the children had endured had become unbearable.

From the witness stand, Beatrice's 10-year-old son, Leslie, described the family's joyous Christmas dinner. He also told of having seen his father place a packet of sheep-dip powder in his bedroom bureau drawer. Another Pace offspring, 17-year-old Dorothy, described how her father beat her mother. He sometimes beat Dorothy as well. She told the court, "I remember Father beating Mother at the bottom of the stairs about a year ago. He got a walking stick and beat Mother across the back."

Harry's mother testified that Beatrice had never left her alone with her son during his long illness. Harry's brother, Elton, told of having heard his sister-in-law say many times over the years that she wished Harry were dead. Elton went on to say that a man named Les Sayce frequently visited Beatrice during Harry's illness, clearly implying that Beatrice had been an unfaithful wife. Under cross-examination, it was learned that Mrs. Sayce often accompanied her husband to the Pace farm, as she was Beatrice's best friend.

Charles Fletcher had been a patient at Gloucester Infirmary at the same time as Harry and had known him for years before that. Fletcher stated that Harry had once told him that he believed he had become ill because of the sheep dip. He felt that somehow he had ingested the arsenic-laced solution while delousing his sheep.

Inspector Alan Dent told the court that he had taken Beatrice's official statement. She had told a straightforward story of an unhappy marriage. She claimed that her relationship with Les Sayce had been that of a dear friend, nothing more. She readily admitted to having purchased packages of sheep dip, which was rather natural for the wife of a sheep rancher. Beatrice went on to state that she had conscientiously cared for her husband during his prolonged illness.

Dr. Dupre testified as to his patient's illness. He related that Harry's mother had suggested her son get another opinion. Dr. Ram Nath Nanda had concurred with his diagnosis.

Dr. C.O. Carson, who had performed the autopsy, stated irrevocably that Harry had come to his end via the arsenic-poisoning route. Mr. Rowland Ellis, the Gloucester County criminal analyst, agreed. According to him, four times the fatal dose had been found in Harry's organs. However, Mr. Ellis, who also analyzed the packets of sheep dip in the Pace residence, found them to contain only insignificant quantities of arsenic.

No evidence of food poisoning was found in the dead man's organs. There was, however, toxic irritation of the stomach, bowels, liver, heart and kidneys. There was evidence arsenic had been imbibed over a period of six months, with the last dose being taken within six to forty-eight hours before death. To add to the drama, Beatrice, listening to the condition of her husband's insides, let out a wail and collapsed.

The defence established that arsenic can be absorbed through the skin. Norman Birkett further pointed out that, as the experts had stated, extreme care should be used in the process of sheep dipping in order to prevent self-poisoning. Moreover, the defence explained, after dipping sheep, one must scrub up carefully to avoid transferring the poison from the hands to food. In this way, the famed lawyer introduced at least the possibility that Harry had been poisoned by accident.

Dramatically, Birkett addressed the judge, suggesting that the evidence was as consistent with being self-administered as it was with being given by someone else. He went on to state that the fact that his client had the opportunity to give poison to her husband was meaningless. After all, he said, sheep dip could be found on most sheep farms. Admitting that Harry had taken arsenic forty-eight hours before his death did not necessarily point to Beatrice as the killer.

The judge listened to the defence motion and invited the prosecution to respond. The prosecution attorney stated that he had presented the case and had nothing further to add. The judge then charged the jury. His statement weighed heavily on the jury's verdict. What do you think it was?

The judge pronounced, "In my opinion, there is no case to go to the jury, and I shall advise the jury to return a verdict of not guilty." The jury did as the judge advised.

Beatrice Pace, accompanied by her children, left the courtroom a free woman. A crowd of hundreds of cheering spectators greeted her outside.

All of this leaves us with the perplexing problem of who actually done in Harry. There are four possible options:

1. Did Harry take his own life? I don't think so. Why would he allow himself to suffer over such a long period of time when he could have killed himself outright and avoided the prolonged agony?
2. Was he accidentally poisoned? This was the most popular theory at the time, but I have a hard time agreeing. The small amount of arsenic in the sheep-dip solution that might have accidentally entered his body would hardly have killed him.
3. Did someone other than Beatrice do the job? Very unlikely. Although the children could hardly love such a man, there was no evidence that any of them had anything to do with their father's death. The attending physicians were also above suspicion.
4. Did Beatrice get away with murder? I believe she did. While no one saw her do it, she did have the opportunity and those beatings surely were motive enough. Quite possibly, an arsenic-based poison other than sheep dip could have been the murder weapon. In my opinion, an astute lawyer saved Beatrice's neck.

Alferd G. Packer

(HATCHET)

TO NORMAL FOLK, the practice of cannibalism is downright disgusting. After all, the consumption of a fellow human is not compatible with pleasant dining, nor does it do anything for one's digestive system. Despite the repulsive nature of cannibalism, the subject does hold a certain fascination. Usually it is associated with another crime, such as murder. Rarely do we humans kill each other for the sole purpose of a good nourishing meal. All of which brings us to the subject of today's story, Alferd G. Packer.

In the fall of 1873, Alferd, together with nineteen inexperienced prospectors, trudged from Salt Lake City deep into Colorado's San Juan Mountains, searching for gold. Alferd had some knowledge of the area, but his fellow travellers were strangers to one another and to the region. Unfortunately, the party had no success in its quest for the elusive yellow metal. For weeks the prospectors searched until, with little left in the way of supplies, they stumbled, half starved, into the Indian camp of Chief Ouray. The chief not only fed the ragtag group, but he also provided them with enough food to continue their prospecting venture.

A problem arose. Ten of the men wanted to give up the hunt for gold and return to Salt Lake City. Their close brush with death had given them their fill of the prospecting game. After many arguments, these ten men decided to return to Salt Lake City. Alferd, who had headed the faction wanting to continue prospecting, became the unofficial leader of the party. He led the remaining men to Los Pinos and beyond, figuring that the rumours of gold strikes up the Gunnison River would at last bring riches to himself and his group. After the party had trudged along the river for weeks, supplies ran dangerously low. Four men elected to return to Los Pinos and on to Denver. Alferd and the remaining five men left the riverbank for the treacherous mountains. Their names are worthy of mention, mainly because no one ever saw Swan, Bell, Miller, Noon and Humphreys alive again.

In February, Alferd made his way out of the frigid cold back to Los Pinos. He looked terrible and was practically in rags. Someone thrust a bottle of whisky into his gnarled fingers. Alferd greedily consumed huge gulps from the flask. When he was offered food, Alferd said that he wasn't that hungry; the booze would do just fine, thank you.

Alferd had a story to tell. He said that he had become ill and that his five companions had left him in the mountains to die. Instead of dying, however, he had recovered and, miraculously, had made his way to Los Pinos. He figured that the lure of gold had affected the good judgment of his companions. No doubt they had starved to death in the unforgiving mountains.

Alferd stayed at Los Pinos recuperating for ten days. He had an abundance of money, which allowed him to stay well oiled most of the time. In due course, fit as a fiddle, he left and made his way to Saguache. Word of his remarkable feat had preceded him, along with the nasty rumour that he had a lot of money for a man who had started out broke. Then there was the insinuation that he was extremely well nourished for a man who had spent so many weeks in the wilderness.

On April 2, 1874, two of Chief Ouray's men arrived in camp with the distressing news that they had found strips of frozen meat from white human beings in the snow just outside the camp. When faced with the gruesome evidence, Alferd broke down and confessed. He claimed that supplies had run out. The men were desperate. One day, when he returned to the group after collecting firewood, he found that Swan had been killed by a blow to the head. The four remaining men were in the process of cooking portions of his body and dividing up the $2,000 removed from the dead man's pockets.

Assorted parts of Swan lasted only a few days. The men eyed each other suspiciously. Little intrigues and cliques developed. Who would be the next to go? Answer: Miller. When he wasn't looking, one of the men split his head open with a hatchet. In time, Humphrey and Noon were killed, roasted, and eaten as well. Alferd claimed that he and Bell agreed that they wouldn't attack each other, but would remain together even if it meant starving to death. Despite the agreement, Bell went out of his mind and attempted to club Alferd with the butt of his rifle. Alferd overpowered his adversary and killed him with his trusty hatchet.

Our boy wasn't telling the absolute truth. We know that for a fact, because early in June artist John A. Randolph, while traipsing through the mountains doing sketches for *Harper's* magazine, came across the bodies of the five men. Noon, Humphreys, Swan and Bell had been shot in the back of the head. Miller's body, sans head, was found some distance from the others. The head was found nearby and showed evidence of having been hacked with a hatchet. Now for the bad part. Strips of flesh had been removed from the chest areas of each body.

Shortly after the bodies were discovered, Alferd escaped from custody. For nine years he led an exemplary life in Salt Lake City under the name of John Schwartze. It's quite possible he would have remained at large forever had he not had the misfortune to run into one of the original members of his ill-fated prospecting trip on the streets of Salt Lake City. Alferd was immediately arrested and brought to trial on April 3, 1883. He claimed that he had killed only Bell and in self-defence. Part of his statement is startling: "When I came to Los Pinos, I threw away the strips of flesh I had left and I confess I did so reluctantly, as I had grown fond of human flesh."

No one believed Alferd's story and he was found guilty on five counts of murder. His lawyers managed to obtain a new trial on a technicality. This time he was more fortunate, being convicted of five counts of manslaughter. In 1885, twelve years after the murders, Alferd was sentenced to a total of forty years' imprisonment. He served sixteen years in prison before being paroled in 1901. Alferd died of natural causes in Denver on April 24, 1907.

You may be interested to know that Alferd's name will live on. Students at the University of Colorado in Boulder have named their cafeteria the Alferd G. Packer Grill. They commemorate his dubious deeds each spring with an Alferd G. Packer Day. One of the major events on that special day is the students' raw meat–eating contest.

Mary Perkins

(ARSENIC)

SOMETHING STRANGE was happening on Plant Street in Selma, Alabama, back in 1957. At first, folks only whispered about it. Then they became fearful that a sinister curse had befallen them. You see, people on Plant Street were dying without any logical reason. Doctors said the cause was pneumonia, but the folks on Plant Street knew better than the doctors. A devil was loose among them.

No one thought much about it when 42-year-old Sam Davis died, although Sam went to his great reward without giving much of a warning. Healthy as a horse one day, dead as a mackerel the next. There were those who said that pneumonia could take a man that way. Only a few weeks after Sam gave up the ghost, Beulah Moutre was struck with a bad case of pneumonia. Nothing the doctors did could save her. Within days Beulah joined Sam down at the local graveyard.

When Charlie Perkins died, some folks called the illness that was killing their neighbours "The Plant Street Plague"; others claimed it was the work of evil spirits who would eventually carry them all off to their maker. Children were told to play close to their homes. The elderly sat in their rocking chairs on their verandas shaking their heads. Truly the devil was afoot.

The deaths continued. Gloria Jean Montgomery was only 10 months old when she died suddenly. She was followed by

Della Davis and Ed Johnson. The unusual rash of deaths was brought to the attention of the police. Could it be coincidence that six healthy individuals living on the same street had all died of natural causes, and all of pneumonia?

It was coroner Bailey Green who first brought up the subject of arsenic. He informed police that the doctors could have been mistaken about cause of death if they had not examined the internal organs of the deceased. Large quantities of arsenic would cause the dilation of blood vessels, which could cause a seepage into the lungs, very much like pneumonia. A large dose of arsenic would cause death before telltale symptoms of the poison became evident.

Based on the coroner's suspicions, detectives were dispatched to investigate and question members of the dead individuals' families. Gloria Jean Montgomery's parents were still distressed at the unexpected death of their infant daughter. The baby had been perfectly normal, but had taken ill so suddenly that she'd died before the doctor reached their home. Gloria's mother swore she had been with her baby all the time. On the day of the child's death, she had fed her the usual things—some broth, milk, and a bit of water. When asked if she had insured her baby's life, Mrs. Montgomery was straightforward in informing the officers that she had a $250 policy on her child's life.

Sam Davis's widow cried profusely as she related how her husband had eaten a hearty meal the night before his death. Sam had even boasted that he had never felt better in his life. Like Gloria's mother, Mrs. Davis couldn't see how anyone could have put any foreign substance in her husband's food. She readily admitted that Sam had carried a small insurance policy on his life. Mrs. Davis firmly believed that someone had put a curse on her husband.

The investigation continued, but the questioning of the families of the other victims brought no concrete results. There matters stood. The six deaths stretched coincidence to the limit. Any thinking person had to know that these six neighbours had not died from natural causes. Police felt so strongly about their suspicions of foul play that they pressed for the exhumation of at least some of the bodies.

While rumours spread along Plant Street that the dead were not to be allowed to rest in peace, another death took place. Seven-year-old Charlie Perkins Jr. was the son of one of the men who had died of pneumonia. Mary Perkins, the dead boy's mother, had been questioned the previous day. Only hours later, her young son had died. A doctor had rushed the boy to hospital, where he had died within hours of being admitted.

Detectives arrived at the Perkins home to find Mary in hysterics. Between violent outbreaks of sobbing, she related how her son had had a sudden attack and she had called the doctor. He took the boy to hospital and that was the last time she had seen her son alive. "It's a curse. I'm sure it's a curse. First my husband, then my little boy, and I'll be next," Mary said.

Mary described all the food young Charlie Jr. had eaten the day before. She swore she had eaten the same food. When asked who else had been in the house around mealtime, she told detectives that a total of seven people had been in and out of her home. She mentioned the name of one woman who had fixed some herbal tea for her son that evening. This woman was questioned extensively and proved without a doubt that she had had nothing whatever to do with Charlie's death.

While this tangent of the investigation was being conducted, police received a visit from Dr. R.L. Reynolds, who was aware of the investigation involving the deaths on Plant Street. He had a patient, elderly Mary Lanier, whom he believed had been poisoned.

Miss Lanier lived just one block removed from Plant Street. Detectives were dispatched to the Lanier residence. Miss Lanier was amazed that the authorities felt she had been poisoned. She told them that she carried a small policy insuring her life for $300. She had no visitors at all, but did admit she often visited friends on Plant Street, particularly her good friend Mary Perkins.

Miss Lanier gave police the names of friends she had visited. All the victims' families were told to list the names of people who had called on them or people they had visited. Three names appeared on all the lists. Two were quickly eliminated, leaving just one—Mary Perkins. Meanwhile, the results of autopsies performed on Gloria Montgomery, Della Davis, and Charles Perkins Sr. indicated that they had died from the administration of arsenic poison. An autopsy on Charlie Perkins Jr. showed that he had not been poisoned. But how could that be? If Mary Perkins was involved in poisoning the others, how had her son died of pneumonia? He had displayed the very same symptoms as the other victims.

One of the detectives remembered that when Mary had discussed her husband's death, she had been composed and rather cool. Yet, when discussing her son's death, she had been hysterical. Had an unbelievable coincidence taken place? Had she murdered her husband, only to have her son die of pneumonia shortly thereafter? Police hurried once more to Mary Perkins's modest home. No one responded to their knocks, and with good reason. Mary had shot herself. She had been taken to hospital with a bullet wound in her chest. For a while her life hung in the balance, but she gradually recovered.

While Mary was still in serious condition, police looked for a motive for the three proven murders and the three suspected ones. Somehow, they felt, insurance had to be involved. They brought an insurance investigator into the case. He knew very well that at that time in Alabama, all you had to do to insure someone's life was to fill out a coupon in a magazine. The insured individual would never know that their life had been insured. The investigator suggested that the police search Mary Perkins's home.

The search produced over a hundred life insurance policies. Mary had insured every one of the victims and was a one-woman killing machine. Although she earned only about $25 a week as a cleaning woman, she was paying out much more than that each week in insurance premiums. Considering that all the policies she had purchased were in the amounts of $200 to $2,000, she had to keep on killing to make her scam pay off.

As soon as Mary was well enough to talk, she confessed to her crimes. She told police that her victims had either visited her or she had gone to their homes. She had become an expert at inconspicuously adding arsenic to food after it was portioned out to one individual. Mary had purchased a large quantity of arsenic a year before her killing spree. When officers had checked stores that sold rat poison, her name had not popped to the surface as a recent purchaser. When she was questioned the second time about her husband, she had thrown her remaining supply of rat poison away.

On November 13, 1957, Mary was charged with three counts of murder. Shortly after she shot herself, three more of her acquaintances succumbed to arsenic poisoning. While it was never proven that Mary was the culprit in these cases, officials firmly believe that she was responsible for these deaths.

Mary was tried and found guilty of three counts of murder. She was sentenced to three consecutive life sentences, to be served at the Julia Tutweiler Women's Prison in Wetumka, Alabama. On May 22, 1977, Mary Perkins was transferred to the Elmore County Hospital, where she died of a heart attack after having served nineteen years in prison.

Craig Peyer

(ROPE)

CARA KNOTT WAS a beautiful young San Diego State University student. On December 27, 1986, she phoned her parents from her boyfriend's home in Escondido to tell them that she was leaving for home. It was a forty-five-minute drive to El Cajon, where she lived with her parents. Cara never made it.

When she didn't arrive home, Cara's parents, Joyce and Sam Knott, immediately became alarmed. It simply wasn't like their daughter to take a side trip without phoning them. The Knotts called police but were told that they would not institute a search until twenty-four hours had elapsed. Sam Knott jumped into his own car and spent the night crisscrossing the route his daughter would have taken to travel from Escondido to El Cajon. So did Cara's sister, Cynthia, and Cynthia's husband, Bill Weick.

It was dawn when Bill and Cynthia drove off Interstate 15 down an unused off-ramp. The road led nowhere, but there, under the expressway, they spotted Cara's white Volkswagen. The vehicle was empty. They shouted Cara's name, but soon gave up and called police. Officers searched for some hours for a trace of the missing girl.

At a little after 8 A.M., an officer peered over a bridge railing. The bridge was about a mile from where Cara's car had been found. There, in a brook, about sixty feet below, was the body of

Cara Knott. An examination of the body revealed that she had been strangled and thrown from the bridge.

Homicide detectives studied Cara's Volkswagen and the area where the body was discovered. Who had enticed Cara to drive off the road to a ramp that was clearly marked "Road Ends 300 Feet"? Her family and friends insisted that she would never stop for a hitchhiker. A computerized gasoline receipt was found on the front seat of the car. Cara had stopped for gas at a Chevron station at precisely 8:27 P.M. It was estimated that she was killed no more than an hour and forty-five minutes after stopping for gas.

Cara had not been robbed or sexually molested. The passenger door was locked. Despite it being one of the chilliest nights of the year, Cara's window was partially rolled down. Detectives deduced that somewhere on that road Cara had stopped for someone she knew or for some authority. They believed from the outset that a police officer might have stopped Cara that fateful night.

Official suspicions were reinforced when several citizens came forward claiming that they had received tickets for minor infractions along Interstate 15. Traffic tickets were checked. One such ticket was written on the night of the murder at 9:20 P.M. It had been made out by California Highway Patrol officer Craig Peyer.

Craig Peyer, 38, was an unlikely suspect. His record was unblemished. He was a career police officer who had served thirteen years on the force. Craig had been patrolling the same stretch of highway for more than four years. He was married and the father of two children. He took his job seriously and was known to give out tickets for the slightest traffic violation. He often appeared on radio and television, lecturing on safety and urging drivers not to pick up hitchhikers.

The investigation into Cara Knott's murder focused on Officer Peyer. The evidence against him mounted, resulting in his arrest and dismissal from the state police force. Not everyone was sure of Craig's guilt. Family and friends were convinced that the conscientious police officer had been dragged into a web of circumstantial evidence simply because no other suspect could be found. Several mortgaged their homes in order to raise the million dollars in bail needed to gain Craig's freedom until his murder trial.

Craig's trial proved to be one of the most sensational ever held in San Diego. Here was a veteran police officer with a spotless record. What possible motive could he have for killing the beautiful student? In January 1988, the murder trial began. An array of attractive women testified that Craig had stopped them on the interstate. Their traffic violations were minor ones. It had appeared to them that the officer had engaged them in unusually long conversations, but all stated that he had made no improper advances. Most damaging of all was the testimony of the two female witnesses who had been on the job at a nearby service station on the night of the murder when Craig had driven up for gas. They testified to having seen scratches on his face. When Craig completed his shift at 10:30 P.M., a colleague noticed that he appeared dishevelled, which was very unusual. Craig told another officer that he had taken a bad fall while putting gas in his patrol car.

Experts took the witness stand. A fibre expert stated that a minuscule gold thread on Cara's sweatshirt was the same type of thread found in Craig's gold shoulder patch. A serologist testified that genetic markers in a single drop of blood taken from Cara's boot could be found in the blood of fewer than 1 percent of California's population. Craig was in that group.

One woman testified that on the night before the murder Craig had stopped her, invited her into his patrol car to give her a ticket and chatted with her for more than thirty minutes. The incident was strange, but the woman admitted that, other than chat and pass the time with her, Craig had not done or said anything of a personal nature.

The damaging evidence against Officer Craig Peyer mounted. Inside the trunk of Craig's patrol car, police recovered a nylon rope that could have been the murder weapon. Marks on Cara's throat generally matched the nylon rope. Despite the volume, however, all the evidence was circumstantial. That little oversight was corrected by Michelle Martin, who came forward a year after the murder and testified that Craig was the officer she had seen stopping what she described as a light blue Volkswagen on Interstate 15 on the night of the murder. The colour of the car was wrong, but Ms. Martin was the only witness to place the defendant at the scene of the crime.

Defence attorneys challenged the testimony of the serologists and fibre experts, claiming that the testing was faulty. Witnesses took the stand and swore they had seen a dishevelled madman waving money on the highway on the night of the murder. He had practically thrown himself in front of several cars attempting to get a lift. It was pointed out in court that Cara's vehicle was found a mile from where Craig was accustomed to stopping traffic violators.

Was Officer Craig Peyer a conscientious policeman who liked to chat up pretty girls to break the monotony of long hours on duty or was he a cold-blooded killer who'd accosted Cara Knott only to be repulsed? To avoid exposure, had he strangled her and thrown her body into the shallow brook?

The San Diego County jury took seven days to deliberate the case. Their verdict: seven guilty, five not guilty. A mistrial was ordered by the presiding judge.

In June 1988, a second trial was held. This time, the verdict was unanimous—guilty. Craig Peyer was the first California patrol officer in the history of the state to be convicted of murder while on duty. He was sentenced to twenty-five years to life imprisonment, a sentence he is presently serving.

Priscilla Phillips

(SALT)

THERE WAS NOTHING UNUSUAL about Priscilla and Steve Phillips. They met in university and married after Steve completed his stint in Vietnam. By 1974, they had two young sons, Eric and Jason. Steve had a good position with the Department of Vocational Rehabilitation in Oakland. When Priscilla had a hysterectomy, they decided to adopt a little girl.

At the time, there was a great deal of publicity concerning the children of American servicemen and deserted Vietnamese women. It appeared to the Phillipses that their chances of adopting one of these children would be far greater than adopting an American child. They applied through several agencies and were delighted when they were informed that a 6-month-old Korean infant girl was available to them.

Little dark-eyed Tia was an immediate hit with the Phillips family. She was christened Tia Michelle Phillips. Tia received a medical examination as part of the adoption procedure. Other than a severe rash, she was a healthy, normal infant. However, almost from the time Priscilla Phillips had her new daughter at home, medical complications developed. There was an irritating ear infection that cleared up but always came back. A urinary tract infection proved to be more serious, as were the child's persistent bouts of diarrhea.

Priscilla brought Tia to the clinic at San Raphael's Kaiser

Hospital. Dr. Evelyn Callas assured Priscilla that there didn't appear to be anything seriously wrong with Tia. They would keep her for a few days for testing. The doctor also informed Priscilla that it was a policy of the hospital's to have mothers participate as much as possible in their child's care while the patient was confined to the institution. Mothers often helped out by giving infants their bottles and that sort of thing. Priscilla was pleased that she was allowed to pitch in.

Tia never did improve. For four straight months she stayed in hospital. Priscilla got to know the staff well. They had difficulty recalling a more loving parent than Priscilla Phillips. Tia continued to suffer from diarrhea, so dehydration was a threat that constantly had to be combatted. When she wasn't suffering from diarrhea, Tia vomited, experienced cramps, and often developed a fever. She became lethargic and stared into space for long periods of time.

Various theories were put forward as to what was causing the child's illness. Irritation of the intestinal lining was considered. In order for the infection to heal, Tia was fed intravenously. On April 1, 1975, she was transferred to the Kaiser facility in San Francisco, where she could receive better care. Priscilla drove with her daughter in the ambulance. Once there, Tia improved to the point that Priscilla requested the child be returned to San Raphael. Her request was granted.

At San Raphael, Tia's diarrhea returned. Her weight dropped until she was an emaciated thirteen pounds. Tests were continually being conducted to find the cause of Tia's illness, but nothing seemed to get to the root of her problem.

Central venous hyperalimentation was attempted—a catheter was inserted surgically into a vein leading directly to the heart. During the night, Priscilla, who often slept beside her daughter, excitedly reported that the child had pulled the tube out. The catheter was replaced.

Tia was transferred to San Francisco for a second time. She improved dramatically. Slowly, she gained weight until she reached an all-time high of seventeen and a half pounds. Doctors now had her on solids. On July 28, Tia was released from hospital after spending five long months in institutions. The Phillipses' long ordeal appeared to be over. Their little girl, who had been through so much, was on the mend. They would have her home forever.

Priscilla took Tia back for her first post-hospital checkup. The little girl was now 15 months old and attempting to walk. While her illness had never been diagnosed, everyone was extremely pleased at her improvement. Then, without warning, it happened. Priscilla rushed Tia to hospital. She was suffering from diarrhea and vomiting. She had lost two pounds overnight, was lethargic and stared straight ahead. Tia was in shock. Every conceivable test and emergency procedure was used to save her. The most puzzling of all test results was the presence in the child's body of excessively high sodium levels.

For no apparent reason, the little girl rallied. Experts across the country were consulted. More tests were conducted, more theories explored. Little Tia underwent exploratory surgery in search of a tumour. Nothing was found. She recovered from surgery and the Phillipses were thankful for that. By now, Priscilla was well known around the hospital and was on a first-name basis with doctors and nurses. They told her that Tia might never be really well. Eventually, Tia was released from hospital.

Three weeks passed without incident. Tia's progress was so encouraging there was talk that she might grow out of her delicate condition. Unfortunately, such was not to be the case. In the middle of the night, Tia had an attack of diarrhea and vomiting. Priscilla rushed her to hospital, where doctors frantically worked over her. It was no use. The little girl's heart stopped beating.

Shortly after Tia's funeral, the Phillipses decided to adopt another child. A year later, Priscilla and Steve became the proud parents of their second adopted Korean child. Mindy Phillips was sickly right from the beginning. At 13 months, she was diagnosed as having congenital cytomegalovirus and intermittent cyanosis. Since her first birthday, she had been hospitalized several times with chronic diarrhea. Various treatments were attempted but nothing seemed to help.

Because her sister Tia's case had been so unusual and because many of the same doctors and nurses had tended Tia, all felt very close to Mindy and her mother Priscilla. It was common knowledge that Tia and Mindy were not natural sisters. This was deemed important because it ruled out the hereditary factor in diagnosing the child's illness.

Doctors took pains to explain to Priscilla exactly which procedures they were following to find the cause of Mindy's condition. Priscilla insisted on being informed of every detail. As with Tia, Priscilla was constantly at Mindy's side. She helped hold the child and stroked her straight black hair. She slept beside her baby. The hospital staff's hearts went out to the mother who so obviously loved her adopted daughter.

And still, the doctors were puzzled. What was causing the diarrhea? No matter what they put into Mindy and no matter what method they used, the state of her gastrointestinal tract did not reflect her diet. Could an evasive parasite that did not show up on tests be the culprit? So, more tests. More remedies. As before, nothing helped.

The first break in the vomiting and continual diarrhea occurred when a doctor ordered a stool sodium list. The doctor knew the child's intake had been 14 milliequivalents of sodium, which should have equalled the test results of the stool. Mindy's stool sodium level had reached an incredible 251 milliequivalents. The doctor did all the necessary checks. There were no defective products given to the child. The only non-staff member with access to her had been her mother. The shadow of little Tia's death now loomed large. Why had no one suspected the mother before? But why should anyone suspect Priscilla, worn to a frazzle because of her sick children? Doctors seek cures; they don't play detective with patients. Their aim is to make sick patients well.

The doctor's suspicions were related to the head of pediatrics, Dr. Evelyn Callas. She had recently read about Munchausen's syndrome by proxy, a hideous malady that manifests itself in individuals seeking to be the centre of attention. They arrive at hospital emergency wards complaining of excruciating pains, complete with fictional medical histories. They long to be hospitalized. Some have studied the symptoms of serious illnesses and, as a result, undergo unnecessary operations. Many hospitals in the United States keep names and photos of these people in the emergency room so that they can be spotted before they take up valuable hospital space.

Could Priscilla Phillips be suffering from Munchausen's syndrome by proxy? Could she be seeking attention for herself by introducing salt into her daughter's diet? It seemed the only answer. All tests indicated that Mindy was receiving large quantities of sodium from an external source.

Dr. Callas met with the Phillipses. They were told that Priscilla would be allowed to see Mindy under supervised conditions for only five minutes an hour. The child was watched constantly and given nourishment by staff only. The improvement in her condition was dramatic. As soon as Priscilla was cut off from Mindy, the child's condition improved rapidly. Dr. Callas called in police. Mindy recovered and was placed in a foster home until the investigation into Tia's death was concluded. After a thorough investigation, Priscilla Phillips was charged with the murder of Tia Phillips and the attempted murder of Mindy Phillips.

On March 19, 1979, Priscilla stood trial for murder and attempted murder in Marin County Superior Court. After a two-month trial, the jury deliberated for two days. They found Priscilla guilty of murder in the second degree in the death of Tia Phillips and guilty of endangering the life of Mindy Phillips. She was sentenced to five years to life for murder and two years' imprisonment for endangering life, the sentences to run concurrently.

Priscilla was released on bail, appealed her conviction and lost. She was returned to prison to serve out her sentence.

Dale Pierre & William Andrews

(GUN)

DALE PIERRE AND WILLIAM ANDREWS never adjusted to air force life. Both had been in and out of scrapes and both had applied for early discharge from the U.S. Air Force. In April 1974, they were assigned to janitorial duty at Hill Field Air Force Base near Ogden, Utah, as punishment for minor infractions.

Pierre was a short, powerful man with delusions of grandeur. The air force wasn't for him. He would get out, make a lot of money any way he could and live in luxury. Andrews was a follower rather than a leader. Much taller than Pierre, he was the type of individual who went along with the tide. He and Pierre spent a great deal of time together performing janitorial duties at the base.

The two men planned a robbery. Andrews owned a van. They would rob the Hi Fi Shop in Ogden and stash their loot in a storage warehouse. It should be easy. They would tie up the owner, drive the van up to the back door and be gone before anyone was the wiser. There was some talk about what to do should there be any eyewitnesses who could later identify them. Pierre felt they should kill any such witnesses. Andrews agreed. A third airman, Keith Roberts, was brought in to help drive the van and load the equipment.

On April 22, 1974, just before 6 P.M. closing time, the three airmen drove up to the Hi Fi Shop in Ogden. They pulled into the alley behind the store. Stan Walker, 20, was in charge of the shop that day. The owner was in San Francisco attending an electronics show. Stan and clerk Michelle Ansley were about to close when they looked up to see two African-American men armed with handguns.

As Stan and Michelle stood there transfixed, the door to the shop opened. In walked a mutual friend, 16-year-old Cortney Naisbitt. He was told to keep his hands high. Cortney obeyed without question. All three young people were pushed downstairs into a sound studio. Their hands were tied behind their backs and their feet secured with electric wire. Two hours passed while the robbers loaded turntables, amplifiers and speakers into Andrews's van. The three captives lay in mortal fear for their lives. It was now 8 P.M.

Meanwhile, at the Naisbitt residence, Cortney's mother, Carol, was concerned. At around 6:30 P.M., she mentioned to her husband, Dr. Byron Naisbitt, that it wasn't like Cortney to be late for dinner. Dr. Naisbitt, an obstetrician, thought his wife was making a mountain out of a molehill. But Carol didn't see it that way. She jumped in her car and did the rounds, looking for her son.

Stan Walker's father dropped by the Hi Fi Shop to see what was keeping his son. Tentatively, he walked through the shop only to be confronted by the intruders. He too was tied hand and foot and placed in the downstairs sound studio. Carol Naisbitt was next to arrive at the store in her search of Cortney. She opened the back door and peered directly into the barrel of a revolver. Mrs. Naisbitt was tied and placed on the floor beside her son and the other captives. In all, there were now five helpless victims lying on the floor in the small basement room.

Dale Pierre produced a cup of foul-smelling liquid. He propped Carol Naisbitt into a sitting position and put the cup to her lips. Carol was told the liquid would put her to sleep. She was forced to take a gulp and immediately commenced to spit, cough and vomit. Soon her mouth and lips started to burn. The liquid in the cup was Drano.

Each of the five captives was made to drink the drain-cleaning chemical product. The last, Mr. Walker, recognized the smell of the caustic. He allowed his captor to pour the liquid in his mouth, but only pretended to swallow. Once his head was placed back on the floor, he silently let the liquid pour out of his mouth.

Systematically, the five captives were stripped of wallets, purses, and jewellery. William Andrews left the shop. Dale Pierre then stepped over the sprawled forms on the floor. He felt for Mrs. Naisbitt's head, placed his gun to the back of it, and pulled the trigger. She was killed instantly. Her son, Cortney, was next. Then Stan Walker was shot in the same way. His father was shot in the back of the head as well. Michelle Ansley begged for her life. Pierre untied her feet and forced her into an adjoining room. There he raped the helpless girl before returning her to the floor beside the other four victims.

One individual remained conscious throughout the nightmarish incidents in the Hi Fi Shop. In spite of having been shot in the back of the head, Mr. Walker never lost consciousness. Pierre sensed he was not dead. He strung a cord around Walker's neck and tied it three times, as tight as he could. Walker tensed his neck muscles. After Pierre had finished knotting the rope, Walker found he could still breathe. Walker was playing dead. Pierre then leaned over Michelle and fired a shot into the back of her head. She died instantly.

Orren Walker believed he was the lone survivor. Lying helpless, his mouth and lips burning from the Drano, a bullet in his head, he fought to retain consciousness and yet appear not to be breathing. His tormentor wasn't through. Pierre pushed a ballpoint pen into Walker's ear. He stomped on the pen once, twice, but the pen didn't enter Walker's head. Walker felt the pen point angle down into his throat. Then his assailant was gone.

Mrs. Walker was waiting at home, beside herself with worry. Her son Stan hadn't come home from work at the Hi Fi Shop. Her husband had gone looking for Stan and had also failed to return. Together with her strapping son Lynn, she decided to visit the shop. When they got there they heard Orren screaming for help. Young Lynn kicked down the door and summoned the police. His father embraced him. Orren Walker had a ballpoint pen sticking out of his ear.

One other victim of the Hi Fi Shop massacre lived through the ordeal. Cortney Naisbitt was barely breathing when rushed to hospital. Doctors were undecided whether to put him on life support or not. The decision was made to take heroic measures. After numerous operations and years in hospital and convalescent homes, Cortney recovered.

Within twenty-four hours the perpetrators of the heinous torture and murder were themselves apprehended. An informant at the air force base revealed that he had heard three men plan the robbery. He named Dale Pierre and William Andrews. Orren Walker identified Pierre from a photograph.

At the same time, two youngsters, 12-year-old Charlie Marshall and 11-year-old Walter Grissom, were hunting for empty bottles in a trash dump at the Hill Field Air Force Base. They found wallets, credit cards and other documents, all taken from the five victims before they were shot. The Dumpster was located thirty feet from Pierre's barracks.

Pierre and Andrews were taken into custody. Pierre's room was searched. Detectives found a white envelope under the carpet. It contained a rental agreement between Dale Pierre and Wasatch Storage, located only a few blocks from the Hi Fi Shop.

Pierre had rented space on April 22, the day of the murders. Inside Pierre's storage facility, detectives found the equipment carted away from the Hi Fi Shop. They also found a large bottle of Drano.

Pierre, Andrews and Roberts were charged with three counts of first-degree murder and two counts of aggravated robbery. Pierre and Andrews were found guilty of all charges. The jury couldn't agree on the murder charges concerning Roberts. He was found guilty on the two counts of aggravated robbery.

Orren Walker, despite his ordeal, was not as badly injured as Cortney Naisbitt. He survived to testify against Pierre and Andrews. Mr. Walker still resides in the Ogden, Utah, area. Near death when taken from the Hi Fi Shop basement, Cortney Naisbitt miraculously survived months in a coma to graduate from high school. He is presently employed at the Hill Field Air Force Base, the same base where his assailants were stationed.

After spending thirteen years in Utah State Prison, Keith Roberts was paroled on May 12, 1987. Dale Pierre survived several execution dates before being put to death by means of lethal injection on August 27, 1987. William Andrews was executed in July 1992, eighteen years after the horrendous crime.

Pauline Rogers

(ARSENIC)

MORRIS AMOS WAS A BIG, healthy specimen, never sick a day in his life, until he took the miseries in the winter of 1977. Morris would bend over and complain that his bouts of cramp would be the end of him. On a good day, Morris could give Nostradamus a run for his money. He was dead on in regard to his future.

Morris's wife, Pauline, was a rock. Folks from Kentucky are like that. Whenever Morris complained, there was his Pauline with an encouraging word. When he began to lose serious weight, about thirty pounds in a few weeks, ever-loyal, ever-faithful Pauline was there at his side with piping-hot chicken soup. It shouldn't have hurt, but it did. Morris complained of a burning thirst that wouldn't go away, so Pauline brought him quarts of strawberry ice cream.

Louisville neighbours were amazed at Morris's rapid deterioration. He went from a good old boy with a substantial layer of suet cascading over his belt, to a gaunt, feeble man, all in a few months. Diarrhea on a daily basis will do that to a fellow.

Pauline insisted that Morris see a physician. The doctor took one look at him and agreed that something was drastically wrong with his 46-year-old patient. He prescribed vitamins and a high-protein diet. I would like to report that Morris's condition improved, but such was not the case. His condition worsened to such an extent that he had difficulty walking. The tips of his fingers turned blue and his face took on a grey, pasty look. On a second visit to the doctor, it was suggested that Morris reduce his workload, which was kind of redundant, since Morris was now too weak to do much more than breathe.

A week after the doctor's latest advice, Morris was admitted to Suburban Hospital, where his illness was considered something of a mystery. Physicians couldn't figure out what was causing Morris to waste away to nothing. There were various suggestions, from muscular dystrophy to a virus, but eventually, all these conditions were ruled out.

On February 17, 1977, two days after being admitted to hospital, Morris died. Doctors believed that death had been caused by a heart attack, but they weren't positive. They approached Pauline, suggesting a post-mortem, which would clear up any doubts and reveal the cause of her husband's rapid deterioration. Pauline wouldn't hear of it. She told the doctors, "My Morris would never approve of such a thing."

The death certificate was duly signed. Morris was laid to rest, accompanied by the usual formalities. It was a sad affair. Pauline wept into a dainty handkerchief while her husband was lowered into his final resting place. The grieving widow received the proceeds of a modest life insurance policy as well as social security cheques. Life went on.

Five years after Morris's death was little more than a dim memory, Luther Rogers, an assembly worker down at the Ford plant in Louisville, was admitted to hospital. He complained of severe diarrhea and a burning thirst. Doctors tried everything, but Luther went rapidly downhill. After several days in hospital, his health showed a marked improvement. In fact, Luther was so strong he was released into the loving arms of his wife.

Two months later, Luther showed up at the hospital again. He could hardly walk. Tests indicated a drastic decrease of white blood cells, but medics were stumped as to the cause. They met and discussed every possibility. Someone asked if Luther had ever been tested for poison. It was a long shot, but the doctors decided to conduct several tests. In the meantime, Luther's food intake was being carefully monitored.

Luther's wife visited as usual. She asked her husband's nurse if she could feed him some ice cream. After all, he complained constantly of extreme thirst. The nurse could see no harm in ice cream. Luther looked up gratefully as his wife spoon-fed him heaping tablespoons of the refreshing delicacy. It was strawberry, his favourite flavour. When Luther polished off the ice cream, his wife tossed the empty container into the wastebasket. After she left the hospital, Luther's lab tests were completed and given to his attending physicians. Normal urine tests contain 200 milligrams of arsenic. Our boy's sample contained 20,000 milligrams. Someone was poisoning Luther. Doctors called in the police.

Detectives inquired about Luther's food intake. They were assured that his entire diet was supervised and carefully monitored. Nevertheless, the nosy detectives wanted to question Luther's nurses. The nurses told them that no one, absolutely no one, had fed Luther anything other than his prescribed nourishment, much of which was administered intravenously. Of course, they said, his wife was an exception. She had fed him strawberry ice cream. As a matter of fact, they went to report, she had been there earlier in the day and had tossed the empty ice cream container into the wastebasket.

The container was retrieved. Large traces of arsenic were found. Luther's home was searched for arsenic but none was uncovered. Finally, his wife Pauline's background was investigated. Well, son of a gun. Quicker than you could consume a mint julep, it was learned that Pauline Rogers's previous husband,

Morris Amos, had died five years before under exactly the same circumstances that surrounded Luther's illness. Both had been healthy, robust men who had wasted away in a matter of weeks for no apparent reason. In each case, Pauline had fed them strawberry ice cream. It was all too much of a coincidence.

County coroner Richard Greathouse was made aware of the facts of Morris's death. Since arsenic remains in the hair and fingernails of deceased persons, he authorized the exhumation of Morris Amos's body. In June 1982, the body was transferred to University Hospital. A day later, the results were delivered to the coroner's office. Morris had not died of a heart attack. Arsenic had been found in the body; 460 milligrams in hair, 470 in the stomach and 18,000 milligrams in the liver. From the hair it was ascertained that Morris had been systematically poisoned for more than a year.

Pauline Rogers was taken into custody and charged with the murder of Morris Amos. Next day, she raised bail of $2,500 and was released from jail. That same evening, she was hospitalized with severe stomach cramps. Pauline had poisoned herself. She recovered, but the incident revealed that she was an avid gardener and had access to arsenic-laced pesticides.

In August 1982, Pauline Rogers was indicted on charges of murdering her first husband, Morris Amos, and the attempted murder of her second husband, Luther Rogers. She was found guilty on both charges, although she never revealed the motive for her actions. She was sentenced to twenty years' imprisonment for murder and received the maximum sentence of twenty years for attempted murder. The sentences were to run consecutively.

James Ruppert

(GUN)

THE CARNAGE TOOK PLACE on Easter Sunday, 1975, and to this day no one is sure why it happened.

James Ruppert was an inoffensive little man who weighed in at 135 pounds. He lived with his mother in an ordinary two-storey, wood-frame house on an ordinary street in the ordinary community of Hamilton, Ohio. Inside James Ruppert there was a fuse burning. It had burned for years, gradually growing in intensity until it consumed his very soul. Finally, the bomb at the end of the fuse exploded, causing havoc and death.

James was always tiny. As a little boy, he suffered from asthma, which limited his physical activities. He was often taunted by other children for not being able to keep up in sports. As a result, he became a shy, introverted youngster who didn't attend dances or social functions. He had little contact with members of the opposite sex.

James's father repeatedly told him that he would grow up to be a failure. When James was 12 years old, his father died of tuberculosis. His older brother, Leonard, offered no support to James. Quite the opposite. Leonard, who stood well over six feet, towered over his younger brother. Moreover, Leonard excelled in school and sports. Teachers often berated James for not being more like his brother. Then, when James turned 16, he attempted to hang himself. He failed in his suicide attempt and ran away from home, but returned, tired, hungry and totally defeated.

Leonard attended night school and graduated as an electrical engineer. He obtained a secure, responsible position with General Electric. James flunked out of college during his second year. Thereafter, he moved from one menial job to another. Leonard married and proceeded to have eight children. James had only one serious girlfriend, who dropped him suddenly. He moved in with his mother.

By the time James was 30, he was a frustrated man with a deep hatred for his older, successful brother. He remembered more vividly than ever the childhood taunts, the pranks and tricks played on him that were nothing more than jokes to Leonard but were barbs that cut James to the quick. He remembered being locked in a dark closet and being tied up with rope. He remembered Leonard's laughter as he cried to be set free.

Leonard wasn't the only focus of James's innermost thoughts. James was also convinced that the FBI and other law enforcement agencies were persecuting him. In particular, he felt these lawmen were following him when he was out driving his car. In his paranoid state, he became convinced that they were spreading rumours about his sexual preference, telling everyone he was a homosexual.

James decided to get back at everyone. He knew that the people at the local library were talking behind his back. He would get his revenge by making an obscene phone call to one of the female clerks. The call was quickly traced to him. When the Hamilton police questioned him, James confessed that he had made the call. He was thoroughly convinced that his brother and mother had informed on him.

The fuse kept burning. The frustration mounted. James had only one hobby. He collected guns and practised target shooting.

Probably his happiest moments were spent shooting at tin cans along the Great Miami River. On the Saturday night before Easter Sunday, 1975, James walked into the Nineteenth Hole Cocktail Lounge. He often chatted with the employees. On this particular night, he confided to Wanda Bishop that his mother had issued an ultimatum. He would have to leave home because he wasn't contributing to the rent. James was devastated. He was unemployed and now his own mother was throwing him out on the street. He told Wanda that he had to take care of the problem. At 2:30 A.M., when the bar closed, James left.

This Easter Sunday would be different. James stayed in his upstairs room until 4 P.M. as his entire family gathered at the house for their usual Easter festivities. When James came downstairs, Leonard engaged him in conversation. Nothing seemed to be amiss. Nephews and nieces scampered about gathering up Easter eggs. Leonard passed one of his sarcastic remarks about James's Volkswagen, but there was nothing unusual about that.

James excused himself and said he was going target shooting. The fuse was burning dangerously close to the bomb. Leonard would never again mock him. His mother would not throw him to the wolves. They would all be made to pay. James went upstairs and returned with a .357 Magnum and a pair of .22-calibre handguns. He also lugged an 18-shot rifle, which he propped up against the refrigerator door.

The shooting started and it didn't stop. First to fall under James's fire was brother Leonard. His sister-in-law, Alma, and his mother, Charity, were the next to be shot. Methodically, he shot at his nieces and nephews. Leonard's children fell one by one: Ann, 12; Leonard Jr., 17; Michael, 16; John, 4; Thomas, 15; Teresa, 9; David, 11; and Carol, 13. If the first shot only wounded, James went about the house shooting his victims in the head at close range. The smell of powder and death permeated the now eerily silent house. Inexplicably, James waited three hours before calling police. Over the phone, he said only, "There's been a shooting here."

When the police arrived at the scene, they couldn't believe their eyes. Eight children between the ages of 4 and 17 lay sprawled like lifeless dolls throughout the kitchen and living room. Their parents and grandmother had been gunned down in the kitchen. Only James Ruppert was alive. No one appeared to have struggled. No one had attempted to escape. The only piece of furniture out of place was an overturned wastebasket.

James was waiting for police inside the front door of his home. He was quietly taken into custody and refused to talk about the crime. Later, he pleaded not guilty by reason of insanity. The family's friends, the police and indeed the entire community of Hamilton were at a loss to explain the killing spree. Frustration is one thing, but not every frustrated individual goes about killing eleven members of their family. Detectives delved into James's past and discovered his deep feelings of rage and rejection. They also learned that James Ruppert may have been a master criminal who had plotted and carried out his monstrous crimes for monetary gain. At his trial, this was the tack the prosecution followed.

The Ruppert estate was substantial. As sole heir, James stood to inherit the entire proceeds of his brother's life insurance, as well as his mother's estate and half the property of his brother's children. James's mother's modest home was valued at $14,000. Leonard's home was worth $40,000. A General Electric company policy covered Leonard's life for $62,000. A personal life insurance policy had been taken out by Leonard for $100,000. Leonard had other property valued at $19,500. A total of $30,000 was found in various family savings accounts. Unemployed, in debt and on the verge of eviction from his mother's home, James could have used the money.

Did James plan to cop an insanity plea, be confined to a mental institution and, upon being released, collect well over $300,000, or was he a mentally deranged man who had acted without having control of his faculties, as he claimed? If found not guilty by reason of insanity, he would eventually be freed a rich man. If found guilty of murder, he would end up in prison forever.

A three-judge panel found James guilty of eleven counts of murder. He was sentenced to eleven life sentences to run consecutively. However, James was granted a new trial on a technicality. On July 23, 1987, James Ruppert, 47, was found guilty of murdering his mother and brother and was sentenced to two consecutive life sentences. He was found not guilty by reason of insanity on the nine other murder charges. The court evidently reasoned that James knew exactly what he was doing when he killed his brother and mother, but was in a crazed state when he went on to kill his entire family.

James Ruppert is currently serving his sentence in the Ohio State Penitentiary and is ineligible to inherit his family's worldly goods.

Suchnam Singh Sandhu

(Hammer)

WHAT IS IT ABOUT England that compels some inhabitants of that tight little island not only to kill their friends and relatives, but to dissect their bodies and spread the assorted parts around the countryside?

Today's sojourn into the realm of cutting and chopping came to official notice on April 5, 1968, when a lone suitcase arrived at Wolverhampton and remained unclaimed on a cart. It was taken into the left-luggage office, where an attendant, Leslie Stevens, peered inside. He was greeted with the distressing sight of a torso of a young Asian woman severed at the waist. The torso was attired in a pink cardigan, a blue Indian-style dress embroidered in white and a bra manufactured in India. On her left arm were four Indian-style bracelets. The suitcase was manufactured in England.

Scotland Yard was immediately immersed in tracing the route of the suitcase. The Yard quickly established that the train had left Euston Station in London at 10:40 P.M. and had stopped at Rugby, Coventry and Birmingham before arriving at Wolverhampton at 12:52 A.M. They questioned a gentleman with the great name Terrance Proudman, a passenger guard on the train. Proudman was able to tell investigators that there were 160 people aboard the train when it left Euston Station. When it pulled out of Coventry, there were 129 passengers, but most had disembarked in Birmingham, leaving only twelve passengers on the Birmingham-to-Wolverhampton run.

The train, which had originated in Liverpool, had been thoroughly cleaned in London. No suitcase had been left on the train when it was cleaned. It was reasonable to assume that the suitcase had been placed on the train at Euston Station or any of the stops on the way to Wolverhampton. Detectives questioned ticket taker William Faux at Euston Station. He remembered that a man had presented a ticket and had boarded the train for Wolverhampton carrying a suitcase. Faux recalled the man well, because a few minutes later he got off the train and left without the suitcase. A passenger was located who remembered seeing an unattended suitcase on the train. He had planned to report it, but after arriving at his destination, decided not to bother. He had forgotten the entire incident until questioned by Scotland Yard.

All the information I have revealed here was garnered on the same day that the torso was discovered. Later that same day, another suitcase showed up under a bridge spanning the Roding River in Ilford. Inside was the lower torso and legs of a young woman. They matched the upper body found in Wolverhampton.

A Scotland Yard pathologist pointed out that one ankle of the mystery woman bore a surgical scar. He thought the scar was compatible with the type made when a surgeon gives an intravenous transfusion if veins in the arms collapse following hemorrhaging. Coupled with the fact that the victim's pubic hair had recently been shaved, investigators were led to believe that the victim may have visited a gynecologist, possibly for an abortion, before she was murdered. In addition, it was learned that the stomach of the murder victim contained the equivalent of thirty half-grain tablets of phenobarbitone. This would have been a fatal dose, but the slow-acting phenobarbitone had not had time to be absorbed into the system before the woman met her death.

Scotland Yard distributed a description of the man who had placed the suitcase on the train as well as a description of the clothing found on the torso. These flyers were printed in English and in the Indian dialects of Urdu, Punjabi and Gujerati.

On May 8, a month after the initial discoveries, a cyclist spotted a duffel bag in a field in Ilford. When he opened the bag, a human head wrapped in white linen tumbled out onto the ground. The head had sustained two fractures which a Scotland Yard pathologist later determined had been inflicted by a hammer. All the body parts of the unfortunate woman had now been found.

Since there was some evidence that the victim had gynecological problems, hospitals were checked in an attempt to find out if any patients fit the dead woman's description. Sure enough, one Sarabjit Kaur had been examined by Dr. Joan Watts, a gynecologist at Barking Hospital. Dr. Watts remembered that her patient had been very concerned that she was pregnant. In the doctor's opinion, Sarabjit's pregnancy was under twenty weeks' duration. She had been referred to Dr. Watts by Dr. Gabriel Merriman, who had diagnosed Sarabjit's pregnancy and who now positively identified the dead woman. Sarabjit had insinuated to the doctor that she planned to terminate her pregnancy. She had visited both doctors on one occasion only and had not returned for subsequent appointments.

Detectives were given Sarabjit's address on Uphall Road in Ilford, but she had moved. Her former landlady was able to provide the address of the young woman's father, Suchnam Singh Sandhu, a 39-year-old machinist. When first questioned, he denied being Sarabjit's father. After several hours of interrogation, he admitted that he had three daughters, the eldest being the dead girl. A former teacher, Suchnam was an intelligent, articulate man with an excellent command of the English language. He wasn't co-operative with the police and refused to identify any of his daughter's clothing or jewellery.

After one night in custody, Suchnam requested to make a formal statement. His entire demeanour had changed from one of truculence to total co-operation. He stated that Sarabjit had visited with him when his wife and two other daughters were out of the house. She told her father that she was in love with a married man. Suchnam had heard of this man before and had forbidden Sarabjit to have anything to do with him. According to Suchnam, his daughter had urged this man to either kill or divorce his wife. When he refused, she had taken poison and now planned to write a suicide note blaming her death on the real culprit of the piece, her father.

Suchnam saw red. A hammer lay close by. He brought it down with all his might on Sarabjit's head. She crumpled to the floor. He then went out and purchased a hacksaw. Suchnam described in detail how he had dismembered his daughter and had then gone to great lengths to distribute her body parts to three different locations. Hardened Scotland Yard detectives listening to the confession considered it to be the most horrible and cold-blooded they had ever heard.

Although it was never proven, there is some evidence that Sarabjit's father took her to an Indian doctor who aborted her baby. Detectives learned that Suchnam was employed at a pharmaceutical laboratory and had access to phenobarbitone tablets. It is believed that he may very well have poisoned his daughter. When the poison didn't immediately end her life, he had killed her with a hammer.

Suchnam Singh Sandhu was tried in London's Old Bailey. He was found guilty of murder and sentenced to life imprisonment.

Tony Shook

(SUGAR WATER)

TONY SHOOK WAS AN INTELLIGENT, conscientious nurse at Baptist Hospital in Winston-Salem, North Carolina. There were those around the hospital who thought he was a bit arrogant. Maybe Tony felt he knew as much as the doctors, but everyone agreed he was a top-notch nurse.

A U.S. Navy veteran, Tony had once worked as a paramedic before enrolling in the nursing program at the University of North Carolina, where he graduated with a bachelor's degree in 1981. After graduation, Tony worked at several hospitals before joining the staff of Baptist Hospital. Now a mature 36, Tony found his niche in the intensive-care unit of the hospital. He impressed everyone who came in contact with him, yet there was that superior air which tended to grate on people's nerves.

On April 18, 1986, Peggy Lou Epley was admitted to the hospital's ICU. Mrs. Epley had undergone intestinal surgery in Lexington, Kentucky. When her blood pressure dropped and her kidneys failed, she became comatose and was transferred to Baptist Hospital. Gerald Epley, husband of the gravely ill woman, was totally distraught over his wife's illness. He visited the hospital every day and grew to dislike nurse Tony Shook. For one thing, Tony kept telling Mr. Epley that his wife could die at any moment. Gerald felt that Peggy Lou's condition always seemed to deteriorate immediately after Nurse Shook completed his shift.

In September, after Peggy Lou had been in hospital for five months, there was a crisis. Her blood pressure dropped dramatically, but she pulled through. After this incident, Gerald asked hospital officials to have Nurse Shook removed from caring for his wife. Evidently, this request was granted. Tony was not responsible for Peggy Lou's care until October 9—the day she died.

Gerald Epley arrived at the hospital for his regular daily visit with his wife. He chatted with one of the nurses, who advised him that his wife's condition was the same as usual. Gerald caught a nap on a couch waiting for visiting hours to begin, but was awakened by a nurse who told him that Peggy Lou had just died. When he learned that Tony Shook had cared for his wife during her last night, he was furious.

It must be pointed out that, at best, Peggy Lou Epley's condition was grave. She was comatose, on a ventilator and a kidney dialysis machine. She was also receiving regular intravenous drips to increase her blood pressure. Despite her serious condition, other nurses had noted that Peggy Lou grew worse when Nurse Shook was in charge of her care. It seemed strange that the woman who had been stable for almost a month when not under the loving care of Tony Shook had expired so shortly after the one shift he spent with her.

Hospital authorities, already suspicious about Tony's performance, felt the entire matter should be turned over to the police. Local police requested the assistance of the State Bureau of Investigation. An exhaustive eleven-month investigation ensued, resulting in the arrest of Tony Shook. He was charged with the murder of Peggy Lou Epley.

At his trial, Tony's fellow nurses all testified that he had put in a special request to care for Peggy Lou during the eight-hour shift preceding her death. At 8:30 A.M., Tony finished his shift and left the hospital. Without warning, Peggy Lou's blood pressure dropped alarmingly. Increased dosages of what doctors thought was levophed, a drug used to increase blood pressure, were administered. When results weren't forthcoming, doctors administered what they thought was epinephrine, a drug used when blood pressure does not respond to levophed. Nothing helped. At 10:15 A.M., Peggy Lou died. Both drugs are clear in colour. Doctors and nurses assumed they were giving Mrs. Epley the proper drugs. They were wrong. In place of the drugs, someone had substituted plain sugar water. Tony Shook had prepared the blood pressure medications before he went off his shift.

Dr. John Butts, North Carolina's chief medical officer, stated from the witness stand, "In my opinion, the immediate cause of death was the removal of pharmacological support to her blood pressure."

The nurses who had looked after Peggy Lou before Tony had come on duty had checked her blood pressure every fifteen minutes. They had checked her medication as well. They testified that they had detected no change in her condition. When Tony took over, it was noted that he, too, had checked Peggy Lou's blood pressure every quarter hour. The prosecuting attorney pointed out that Tony's concern may have been motivated by the fact that he was endeavouring to appear above suspicion when the worst happened.

Several doctors testified that there was no question that their patient's long-term chance of recovery was extremely slim, but the same doctors expressed the opinion that the cause of Mrs. Epley's death was the removal of appropriate medication. Four nurses testified that Tony had often voiced special interest in Peggy Lou and wondered why they were putting her through such a lingering and agonizing death.

In his defence, Tony's lawyers theorized that he could have made an error in preparing the medication. While this is always a possibility, Tony himself shot down his own defence by testifying that he recalled preparing the solutions. He swore that he had prepared them correctly just before going off his shift. He stated that in his opinion Peggy Lou had died because she was too ill to respond to the drugs. Tony also insinuated that doctors and nurses at the hospital were blaming the death on him to cover up the substandard brand of medicine practised at the hospital.

Investigators testified that when Mrs. Epley's intravenous-feeding solution was tested immediately after her death, levophed and epinephrine were not present. In their opinion, the drugs had been deliberately removed and sugar water substituted.

There was a great deal of sympathy in the courtroom for Nurse Tony Shook. Despite his irksome personality trait of exuding superiority, his colleagues all agreed that he was a competent nurse. It was also felt that Tony cared for his patient and was not a calculating killer in the strict sense of the word. However, he was a nurse and his sole duty was to care for and sustain life, not to terminate it. The North Carolina jury found Tony guilty of murder. He was sentenced to life imprisonment, a term he is now serving.

Since Tony Shook's conviction, officials have found that a number of untimely deaths occurred at Baptist Hospital while Tony was on duty or shortly thereafter. Deaths at other hospitals where Tony was employed are also being investigated.

Ruth Snyder

(Picture Wire)

Ruth Brown was one unhappy woman. She dreamed of life in the fast lane. One day she would be released from the constraints of living with her frugal parents in their plain home in New York City. Marriage—that would be her ticket to big cars, luxury liners and a loving, worshipping husband.

Shapely, good-looking Ruth caught on as a switchboard operator with the New York Telephone Co. It wasn't a glamorous job and didn't give her much of a chance to meet her Prince Charming, but it was a start, a move away from her strict Scandinavian parents. In time, Ruth met Albert Snyder, an art editor with *Motor Boating* magazine. Nineteen-year-old Ruth thought Albert was the answer to all her prayers. True, he was thirteen years older than her, but so what—he took her out to dinner often, didn't he? Moreover, Ruth was a virgin and Albert respected her rather unique status.

In 1915, Ruth married steady Albert Snyder. As far as Ruth was concerned, the marriage soured within thirty days. Albert was an intellectual. He talked of literature, art and the state of the Union. Ruth longed for parties and excitement.

And so Ruth Snyder lived the life of a bored housewife, month after weary month, year after boring year. The Snyders had a daughter, Lorraine. The birth of their daughter did little to change Ruth's lifestyle.

Ten long years passed until, quite by chance, Ruth met her Sir Galahad. Judd Gray didn't dress in a suit of armour. He didn't ride down the street upon a trusty steed. He was a salesman for the Bien Jolie Corset Co. Judd was of average looks, average height and slightly below-average intelligence. He habitually wore a sporty pair of horn-rimmed glasses. Above all, Sir Galahad was well married to Isabel Gray and was the father of a 9-year-old daughter. Judd was quick to point out that Isabel was every bit as boring as Albert Snyder.

A mutual friend, Harry Folson, had introduced Ruth and Judd. The time was ripe. Ruth poured out the details of her unhappy marriage to Judd. The attentive corset salesman looked at the well-preserved Ruth. He liked what he saw. Thereafter, the two would meet regularly at Henry's Restaurant, a popular Swedish watering hole on 35th Street

About two weeks after their first meeting, Judd suggested that he fit Ruth out with a new girdle. It would be no trouble at all. The impetuous pair made their way to the Bien Jolie Corset Co. offices on 34th Street and 5th Avenue. The girdle fitting progressed into massaging Ruth's sore back. The pair alighted on a convenient sofa and had sex. Nothing like this had ever happened to Judd in his entire corset-selling career. This woman treated him with genuine affection. As for Ruth, she now had a man who wasn't afraid to take a slug of bootleg whisky, a man who would jump at her beck and call. Right from the beginning, Ruth was the dominant personality.

For the next two years, Ruth and Judd engaged in a delicious affair. They met at Henry's and had sex at every opportunity. Sometimes, when her husband and daughter could be hustled away from the Snyders' clapboard house in Queens, Ruth had Judd over for fun and games. He called her Mommy; she called him Lover Boy. No one knows who first brought up the subject of killing Albert Snyder. It is of little concern, because both agreed that it was the greatest idea since bathtub gin. To add a bonus to the enterprise, Ruth took out three insurance policies on Albert's life, in the amounts of $1,000, $5,000 and $45,000. Each contained a double-indemnity accident clause—a neat little package totalling $102,000.

In February 1927, it was decided that Albert Snyder had to go. To get the show on the road, Ruth gave Judd a list of materials needed to do the job. Let's see now, there was chloroform, a heavy sash weight and picture wire. On March 20, by prearrangement with Ruth, Judd let himself in through a side door of the Snyders' home in Queens. It was a little after midnight. Ruth, Albert and Lorraine were attending a bridge party at the home of a neighbour, Mrs. Milton Fidgeon. Judd hid in an upstairs spare bedroom. He had brought along an Italian newspaper as a false clue to leave at the scene of the crime. To pass the time and to gain courage to perform the task at hand, he sipped from a bottle of whisky.

At a little after 2 A.M., the Snyders arrived home. Albert had had a bit too much to drink at the bridge party. He lurched upstairs and went directly to bed. Ruth put Lorraine to bed in her own room. All was in readiness. Ruth visited Judd in his hiding place. Did he have the chloroform, sash weight and wire? You bet he did. Ruth, ever the cautious one, slipped back between the sheets with hubby. She stayed there until about 3 A.M., when Albert's deep snoring was evidence that he was sound asleep. Then she rejoined Judd. After a few slugs from the whisky bottle, Ruth told her lover it was time.

Together, they made their way into the master bedroom. For the first time, Judd Gray laid eyes on Albert Snyder. Their acquaintance wasn't of a lengthy duration. Judd brought the sash weight down on Albert's head. It stunned Albert, but the blow didn't kill him. He attempted to rise. Judd brought the sash weight down a second time. Once again, Albert struggled for his life. This time, he managed to get ahold of Judd's necktie. The sash weight fell to the floor.

Ruth came to the rescue. She picked up the sash weight and brought it down for the third time on her husband's head. Albert thrashed around on the bed. Ruth climbed on top of him and stuffed chloroform-soaked cotton in his mouth and nostrils. Ruth kept busy. She tied Albert's hands and feet and then wound the picture wire around her helpless husband's neck. At last, Albert was dead.

During the struggle, Albert had bled profusely. There was blood all over the room, on the bedclothes and on Ruth's nightie. The two killers spent the next hour washing up. Then, according to plan, they hid the sash weight in the cellar and stuffed Ruth's jewellery under a mattress. Judd even had the gall to borrow one of Albert's clean white shirts. This would appear to be a murder committed during the commission of a robbery.

Silently, so as not to awaken Lorraine, the conspirators overturned chairs and other furniture in the living room. Instructing her lover in whispers, Ruth had Judd tie her up in the spare bedroom. He carefully placed cheesecloth over her mouth. Before leaving the house, he tossed the Italian newspaper into the bedroom to cleverly throw police off the trail.

The sun came up that morning of March 20, 1927. Little Lorraine Snyder was tired. She had been up much later than usual the night before. What was that tapping on her bedroom door? She yelled out for her dog. He didn't respond. She yelled out for her mother. No answer, other than the continued rhythmic tapping.

Lorraine got out of bed, opened the door and staggered back in terror. There was her mother, tied, gagged, lying on the floor.

Lorraine undid the cheesecloth gag. Ruth told her daughter to get help. In moments, neighbours Harriet and Louis Mulhauser were at Ruth's side. Hysterically, she blurted out that robbers were responsible. They had taken her jewels. She prayed that Albert was not harmed. Mulhauser opened the door to the master bedroom. He didn't need a medical degree to figure out that Albert was indeed very dead.

Police were summoned. Dr. Harry Hansen examined the body. He also examined Ruth for signs of injury and found none. Ruth kept talking about a 35-year-old big guy who looked Italian. In all, sixty police officers descended on the Snyder home. Not one of them believed Ruth's story. Her nightie was new and showed no signs of her supposed ordeal. The chairs and tables overturned downstairs didn't make sense. Jewel thieves don't usually turn over furniture where jewels would not be hidden.

When detectives found Ruth's jewellery stuffed under a mattress, the jig was up. But there was more. They discovered Judd Gray's name in an address book. Detectives guessed that no woman had rained blows on Albert's head all by herself. They guessed right. Investigating officers told Ruth a little white lie. They informed her that her boyfriend had confessed and had blamed the whole thing on her. Ruth was furious. She confessed that she and Judd Gray had planned the murder but that Judd had actually killed Albert. Ruth claimed that she had attempted to stop Judd at the last moment but had failed.

Could things get worse for Ruth and Judd? Well, yes, definitely. The sash weight was located in the cellar. Judd was located in Syracuse, doing what he did best, peddling corsets. After he was taken into custody, he spilled more beans than Libby's sells in a year.

By the time the murderous pair stood trial on April 18, 1927, the details of their diabolical plot had made headlines around the world. Ruth was called "The Granite Woman." Judd was known as "The Putty Man." Both were found guilty of murder and sentenced to death.

All appeals failed. On January 12, 1928, Ruth Snyder and Judd Gray were put to death in Sing Sing's electric chair.

Lewis Staunton

(STARVATION)

IT HAS BEEN SAID that all killers are despicable, but even in the murder business there are degrees. Today's nasties rank right up there with the most reprehensible of all time. The curtain of our horror story rises on the not-so-happy occasion of the marriage of 24-year-old Lewis Staunton to 36-year-old Harriet Butterfield. The nuptials took place on June 16, 1875, in London, England.

Lewis was small, cunning and totally bored with his occupation of clerk in an auctioneer's office. Harriet was a dumpy, ugly creature who, in the language of the day, was considered an imbecile. A year before her marriage, her mother had attempted in vain to have her certified as a lunatic. One might wonder why Lewis Staunton would marry such an unappealing woman. The answer was cold hard cash. Harriet came complete with £4,000, a veritable fortune in those long-ago days.

The unlikely pair set up housekeeping in Loughborough Road, Brixton. Right from the start, things didn't go well. A few weeks into the marriage, Mrs. Butterfield visited her daughter. She was coolly received by Lewis and left quite disturbed that all was not right with Harriet and her husband. Next day, she received a letter from Lewis, accompanied by one from Harriet. Both missives contained the same message. She was told in no uncertain terms that she wasn't welcome in the Staunton home and never to call again. I suppose mothers-in-law are accustomed to such treatment, but it still must have been hard to take.

Lewis retired from the clerking business and invested his newfound wealth. He also took up with a former girlfriend, Alice Rhodes. Alice was everything Harriet was not. Besides, she was sort of family, being the sister of his brother Patrick's wife, Elizabeth.

In March 1876, Harriet gave birth to a boy, Tommy. Rather than being pleased, Lewis found the child almost as obnoxious as he found Harriet. He had Alice Rhodes move into his house, ostensibly to look after his wife and his new son. Alice didn't do any of those things. She looked after Lewis.

Two months after Harriet gave birth, Lewis wrote to his brother relating how repulsive Harriet was and how she didn't take care of her personal hygiene. Patrick responded by suggesting that Harriet might find it pleasant to spend some time at his home, The Woodlands, in Cudham, Kent. The country air would do her good.

Lewis shipped Harriet and Tommy to his brother's home, where mother and child were given a room upstairs in the attic. Initially, Harriet took her meals with Patrick and Elizabeth, but it wasn't long before her meals were delivered to her in her room. Gradually, Harriet and her son were ignored and neglected. The one window in the room was boarded up. Harriet, who hadn't washed herself in the best of times, now totally neglected to clean herself or Tommy.

In October, Lewis and Alice Rhodes took up residence about a twenty-minute walk from The Woodlands. Alice posed as Lewis's wife. No one had the vaguest idea that a few miles down the road his real wife and son were virtual prisoners, slowly starving to death. Tommy grew so weak from lack of nourishment that Patrick took him to Guy's Hospital, where the boy died the following day. The death did not arouse any undue suspicion. When Lewis was notified of his son's death, he was somewhat less than distraught. He told hospital authorities his name was Harris and that the little boy was the son of one of his farm employees. He passed over 25 shillings for the child's burial. In Lewis's warped mind, that was the end of the matter.

By this time, Harriet was being fed leftover scraps from the Stauntons' table. When there were no leftovers, she wasn't fed at all. She had no washing facilities and grew so filthy that the other members of the family avoided the odour when they passed by her door. Because she had no shoes, crusts formed on the soles of her feet. In time, she lost the power of speech and made only guttural, animal-like sounds.

As the months passed, Harriet was something that lived upstairs. She didn't exist to the outside world and was almost nonexistent to the Staunton clan. No great plan was hatched, but individually all three Stauntons and Alice Rhodes were waiting for Harriet to die.

Two things happened. Alice became pregnant and Lewis came to believe there might be an investigation if Harriet died at home. The four schemers decided to move Harriet out of Patrick's house. Lewis located a bedroom and sitting-room arrangement at 15 shillings a week, operated by a Mrs. Chalkins in Penge, London. Harriet was in terrible shape. After all, she had not left her room all winter. The Stauntons knew they had to come up with a story for Mrs. Chalkins. They told her that the facilities were for Lewis's mother, who was basically healthy but refused to eat. The concerned Stauntons asked Mrs. Chalkins for the name of a doctor. She recommended a Dr. Longrigg.

Harriet arrived at the rooming house on Forbes Road. Lewis and Patrick assisted her into the house. Mrs. Chalkins was shocked at her new roomer's appearance. Harriet reeked of neglect. That night, Alice and Elizabeth stayed with Harriet. The two men took rooms at a nearby hotel.

Next morning, a Friday, the two women informed Mrs. Chalkins that Harriet had spent a difficult night and appeared to be very ill. Dr. Longrigg was summoned. He examined Harriet and told all concerned that she would be dead within twenty-four hours. She was placed in a nurse's care. The nurse was startled at the emaciated condition of her patient. At one-thirty that afternoon, Harriet died in her bedroom while the Stauntons relaxed in the sitting room. No one shed a tear.

Within the hour, Lewis had an undertaker in the house. Dr. Longrigg signed the death certificate and left instructions with the nurse to lay out the body. Lewis attempted to have the burial take place that day, but the undertaker couldn't do the job until Monday. The Stauntons returned to Patrick's farm. On Monday, the annoying Harriet would be nothing but a memory. They would take the boards off the window and give her attic room a thorough cleaning.

Had the Stauntons displayed some emotion at Harriet's death, there is little doubt they would have gotten away with murder. Their callousness caused the nurse at Penge to wonder about the emaciated woman who must have been so neglected in life. She told the undertaker of her suspicions. He in turn spoke to a friend, who happened to be acquainted with Mrs. Butterfield. The acquaintance thought the dead woman might be Harriet. When Mrs. Butterfield learned of the death, she notified police. As a result of her complaint, the funeral was delayed and a post-mortem conducted. Dr. Longrigg immediately withdrew the death certificate.

The post-mortem indicated protracted undernourishment and neglect. At the time of her death. Harriet weighed seventy pounds A coroner's inquest was conducted. As a result, all four conspirators were arrested and charged with Harriet's murder. Their trial was closely followed throughout England. Rarely have defendants been more despised by the British public. All four were found guilty of murder and sentenced to death.

Three days before the sentences were to be carried out, Alice Rhodes was given a free pardon. The sentences of Lewis, Patrick and Elizabeth Staunton were commuted to life imprisonment.

Joel Steinberg

(Fists)

CERTAIN CRIMES HAVE held cities and nations in a state of siege. Who can forget Peter Sutcliffe, England's Yorkshire Ripper, who murdered prostitutes year after year, or Los Angeles's Hillside Stranglers Buono and Bianchi, whose torture killings held the City of Angels in a viselike grip of fear?

Mass murderers and serial killers, by their ferocity and number of victims, boggle the imagination. It is a much rarer phenomenon when the death of one individual shocks an entire country. The abuse and death of 6-year-old Lisa Steinberg was such a case. Her fate riveted the nation's attention on the lifestyle of Joel Steinberg, Hedda Nussbaum and 16-month-old Mitchell Steinberg.

Joel Steinberg had a privileged childhood. The only son of a New York attorney, he was brought up in a garden apartment in Yonkers. Always a good student, Joel won a scholarship to Fordham University. After receiving a degree in political science, he pursued a law degree at New York University. Law school proved to be Joel's first setback. He had trouble in his second year and was forced to drop out. With nothing better to do, he enlisted in the air force and served in Vietnam as an intelligence officer. Back on civvie street in 1968, Joel again entered New York University to obtain his law degree. This time, he was successful, graduating in 1970.

Joel lived in an apartment on West 10th Street and was one of the thousands of smart, young professionals sipping red wine in the Village each evening. He even bought a Great Dane to complete what some would call the "in" picture. Joel's law practice consisted of dope peddlers and assorted hoods. He also specialized in illegal adoptions. While his ability as a lawyer has always been suspect, there is no question that he prospered. By the mid-seventies he was a millionaire. His fees were astronomical. He often charged drug kingpins $200,000 for their defence. Adoptions brought $10,000 to $25,000 each. To Joel Steinberg's way of thinking, he had everything—everything except a wife and children. But that would soon be remedied.

Hedda Nussbaum was born on August 8, 1942, in New York City. Her Polish immigrant parents were strict disciplinarians. Hedda grew up to be a shy, introverted girl with a deep sense of worthlessness. Despite this drawback, she was a bright student who sailed through George Washington High School and later obtained a degree in English from Hunter College.

Hedda accepted a position as a grade-three teacher in Manhattan, but left the profession to take a job as editor of juvenile books at a division of Random House. She was well liked by superiors and fellow employees. When she moved to her new position, she was a five-foot-five, 130-pound, attractive young woman. Socially, Hedda didn't mix much with other members of Random House, nor did she have outside interests. Shy Hedda kept to herself. Then she met Joel Steinberg.

Hedda had been coerced into attending a house party on Long Island. It was here she met bombastic, confident Joel. She was immediately overwhelmed by the attention he showered on her. No one had ever treated her in quite the same manner. His conversation was far different from that of the other young men she knew. Joel was on a first-name basis with Mafia kingpins, notorious men whose exploits could be read in the newspapers each day. He was bright, articulate and even of the same faith. Truly, Hedda figured, God had smiled down upon her. At Random House she talked of little else but her Joel.

There was one thing. Joel insisted that Hedda improve herself. Psychiatric consultations might help. Then there was her hair. At Joel's insistence, she changed hairstyles. Joel thought that, at 130 pounds, Hedda was a bit heavy. She went on a diet. By 1975, Joel and Hedda were talking marriage. In January 1976, she moved into Joel's apartment, number 3W at 14 West 10th Street.

Once ensconced in the apartment, it seemed as if nothing Hedda did pleased Joel. One day, in a temper tantrum, he let her know that it was he who had improved her appearance, he who had brought her out of her shell. For two years, Hedda endured what amounted to psychological abuse. Then, in the winter of 1978, for the first time, Joel punched Hedda in the face. The force of the blow affected Hedda's eyesight. It was necessary for her to see a doctor. When she showed up at Random House with a black eye, she told co-workers she had been mugged.

A couple of weeks later, Hedda again showed up with bruises around her eyes. This time she told friends she had walked into a door. There followed a long string of inventive excuses for bruises to her body. She wasn't fooling anyone. Her colleagues knew she was being abused. Summer and winter, Hedda wore sunglasses. Neighbours grew accustomed to her screams.

To ease her pain, Hedda tried cocaine. It wasn't hard to come by. After all, the drug was the stock-in-trade of Joel's clients. By 1980, Joel too was addicted. The pair often got high together. In fact, Joel became a freebase freak. When he was high, he punched out Hedda.

During the day, Hedda dragged her dissipated body down to Random House, where she immersed herself in her work. At night, she returned to her apartment and the living hell that she chose to endure. In the winter of 1981, Hedda received such a heavy pounding from Joel that her spleen was ruptured. She crawled out of the apartment and hailed a cab to St. Vincent's Hospital, where her spleen was removed. Joel claimed he saved her life.

When a young, unwed Catholic girl, Michele Launders, became pregnant, she was referred to an obstetrician who could take care of a discreet adoption. He knew a lawyer who would see the baby was placed with good parents. The lawyer was Joel Steinberg. When the baby was born, all documents at the hospital were falsified, with the newborn's address given as c/o Joel Steinberg. Initially, Joel had no intention of keeping the baby. He had a couple who were willing to pay $50,000, no questions asked. When the prospective parents reneged on the deal, Joel presented Hedda with a brand-new baby. She was an overnight mother. The child was never legally adopted.

Lisa, as the baby was called, was placed in a cradle in the living room. Hedda tried daycare, but it didn't work out. Most days, she took baby Lisa to work at Random House, but finally her superiors told her that this practice was too disruptive. More often than not, Hedda missed work. When she stayed away for two weeks without explanation, she was fired. At 41 years of age, grey-haired Hedda Nussbaum looked 60. The beatings didn't stop. To vent his insane anger, Joel choked Hedda, burned her legs and stomped on her knees. She developed a permanent limp.

In 1986, when Lisa was five, Joel brought home another baby, Mitchell. To those who knew her, Lisa was a happy, pleasant child. In public, her father doted on her. Inside apartment 3W, Hedda, Lisa and Mitchell lived in squalor. The baby lay in urine-soaked clothing all day. Bits of food lay scattered about the house. Joel had accumulated over a million dollars, but was constantly hounded by the superintendent for back rent.

In 1987, Lisa's condition deteriorated. She attended school in dirty clothing. A year earlier, she had been a punctual, attentive pupil. She now either came late or missed school altogether. Lisa wore long-sleeved shirts and heavy socks. She had to. Her arms were covered with bruises. By now, Joel Steinberg was abusing Lisa as well as Hedda.

On November 2, 1987, Hedda Nussbaum called police. Her daughter, Lisa, had stopped breathing. Hedda opened the door to apartment 3W and let the police inside. The officers reeled at the stench of urine. And it was cold. The wind whistled through a missing window. Rotting food lay around the apartment. Walls were blood spattered. Mitchell, 16 months old, played on the floor, tied to a playpen with a piece of rope. He sucked on a milk bottle filled with curdled milk. Lisa, weighing only forty-three pounds, was black and blue with bruises. She lay in Joel's arms, perfectly still. Paramedics detected a pulse and rushed her to St. Vincent's Hospital. Three days later, she died of her injuries.

Both Joel and Hedda were arrested and charged with the murder of their daughter. Charges against Hedda Nussbaum were dropped when it was ascertained that she was "so physically and mentally incapacitated on the night of the murder that she was not criminally responsible for Lisa's death."

Joel Steinberg was convicted of second-degree manslaughter. He was sentenced to the maximum term of eight to twenty-five years in jail.

Dr. Ken Taylor

(EXERCISE EQUIPMENT)

WHEN DR. KEN TAYLOR MARRIED for the third time, he would have to be placed in the high-risk category as far as faithful, long-lasting husbands are concerned. The successful dentist, by his own admission, had always been a ladies' man.

Ken met wife number one when he was a 21-year-old dental student at Indiana University. He entered a naval program that provided him with a scholarship for his entire education. In return, upon graduation, he was compelled to serve several years in the navy. When Mrs. Taylor became pregnant, Ken was not overjoyed. For one thing, he didn't like the responsibility of another mouth to feed. In addition, a new baby might curtail his favourite hobby, that of bedding down with anything in skirts. Ken picked a most inopportune time to leave his wife—June 1974, while she was in her ninth month.

The reason for the separation was a beautiful stewardess. In October, Ken's divorce became final. He married the stewardess in December. Fast worker, our Ken. The marriage wasn't a successful one. One night, while wife number two was asleep in bed, Ken attacked her. He jumped on her and held a chloroform sponge over her mouth. The poor woman struggled and managed to roll off the bed, but Ken again pounced on her. Then, as suddenly as the attack had started, it abruptly stopped.

Ken begged for forgiveness. When his wife suggested he

receive professional help, he agreed and placed himself in the care of a navy psychiatrist. The doctor believed that Ken was a maniac. He suggested that the police be called in to the case and that the dentist be charged with attempted murder. Mrs. Taylor took the doctor's advice and Ken was charged.

Another navy doctor attributed Ken's action to his mixing alcohol and drugs. He felt that the violent incident was an isolated one. The charge of attempted murder was dropped. Ken received counselling and the Taylors' marriage seemed to get back on the rails. In 1979, wife number two gave birth to a baby girl. Ken didn't exactly advertise the fact that he still took dope, drank excessively and slept with every dental assistant at the naval base.

In July 1980, Ken finished his navy service. He opened a dental clinic in Brooklyn, which prospered from the beginning. The practice was so lucrative that other dentists and hygienists were hired. One fine day, Teresa Benigno, a gorgeous young thing, applied for a job as a hygienist. Ken took one look at her figure, face and accessories and knew immediately that Teresa was for him. After a few months of his undivided attention, Teresa became Ken's lover.

Back home, wife number two noticed the telltale signs—the missed appointments, the lack of attention, the handkerchiefs smeared with lipstick. The marriage disintegrated and finally, in 1983, was dissolved.

On July 10, 1983, Teresa became wife number three. The happy couple honeymooned at a luxury resort in Acapulco. When Teresa's parents travelled to John F. Kennedy Airport to pick up the newlyweds at the end of their honeymoon, there was no sign of Ken or Teresa. Next day, Mr. Benigno called the Mexican resort and was amazed to learn that the Taylors had checked out three days earlier. A call to the American consular agent in

Acapulco gleaned the information that Teresa had been seriously hurt and was in hospital. Dr. Taylor was in jail as the chief suspect in his wife's beating.

Within hours, Ken called his wife's family, explaining that robbers had attacked him and Teresa in their luxurious cottage. He had not been badly hurt and had just visited Teresa in hospital. His short stint in jail had been a farce. The Mexican police had insisted on a $500 bribe before releasing him.

Mr. Benigno and another daughter, Celeste, flew to Acapulco. They found Teresa in terrible shape. She had been badly beaten about the head and her throat had been slashed. She spoke to her father and couldn't tell him much about the attack, as she had not seen her assailants. Unfortunately, Mexican authorities had found cocaine in their room. That's why Ken had been taken into custody. Ken told his father-in-law that no charges had been laid against him. Two days later, the honeymooners were back in the United States. Teresa remained in hospital for another week. Slowly, she made a complete recovery.

The months that followed were the happiest of the Taylors' married life. When Teresa informed Ken that there would be an addition to the family, he appeared to be thrilled. Ken was ecstatic at little Philip's birth. But then his urge to play the field took over and once more Ken began leading a double life. There is some evidence that Teresa took to drugs during this time. Certainly the Taylors were willing drug users at private parties. Sometimes Ken admonished Teresa for being spaced out.

On November 12, 1984, Teresa failed to drop off Philip at her mother's on her way to work at Ken's clinic. Mrs. Benigno called Teresa at home, but received no reply. At about 10:30 A.M., Ken called. He told the family that Teresa had a bad drug problem. She had decided to go away by herself for a while to kick the habit. He had driven her to the airport in Newark and was taking baby Philip to his parents in Indiana. He explained that he couldn't care for the baby himself and didn't want to impose on his mother-in-law. He realized they would be worried and was calling from the road. He didn't know where Teresa was staying, but she had told him she'd be back in a few weeks.

The family couldn't help but think of the incident in Acapulco. Was it within the realm of possibility that Dr. Ken Taylor was some kind of maniac? They went over to Teresa's house and found such items as a half-baked cake and her keys. Unusual for a meticulous housekeeper who never left the house without her keys. The Benignos reported their daughter missing to police. When Ken returned from the round trip to Indiana, he was questioned by the family and repeated the story he had told them on the phone.

Three days later, on November 15, Neil Griesemer was looking for beer cans along the highway at the bottom of Hawk Mountain in Pennsylvania when he spotted a sleeping bag beside the road. He pulled open the bag, exposing the body of a young woman. Mr. Benigno identified the body as that of his daughter, Teresa.

Dr. Ken Taylor was immediately suspected in his wife's murder. He told police of her movements on the night before she disappeared. According to Ken, Teresa had stayed up while he went to bed. He woke up at 4 A.M. Teresa was still up, spaced out on drugs. They had a long talk and she agreed that she had a drug problem. Later that same morning, at around 8 A.M., Teresa told him that she was going away to deal with her problem on her own. She preferred not to tell him where she was going. He drove her to the Newark airport and never saw or heard from his wife until her body was found.

That was Ken's story, but the police didn't believe it for a minute. When they found a bloodstained earring in the Taylors' garage that matched one found on Teresa's body, they were positive they had the right man. Faced with this incriminating evidence, Dr. Taylor broke down and confessed.

He told detectives that on the night in question he had come downstairs to find his wife strung out on drugs. But there was more. As he came down the stairs, he witnessed her sexually abusing their young son. Their eyes met. Teresa dashed into the sewing room, where the family's workout equipment was kept. Ken placed the baby in a child seat. Teresa suddenly threw a five-pound dumbbell at his head, striking him in the shoulder and sending him sprawling to the floor. She leaped on him like a wild animal. He clutched a bar and struck her on the head, at the same time pushing her off. Teresa rushed at him again. He swung the bar, striking her once more on the head. He could remember little else about the attack, but he did recall cleaning the house of blood, placing Teresa's body in the trunk of his car and dumping the body in Pennsylvania.

Dr. Taylor was arrested and charged with his wife's murder. His case was based on self-defence, but the jury didn't believe his story. Even if his story were true, Teresa was unarmed, so he couldn't have struck out in defence of his life.

Ken Taylor was found guilty of murder in the first degree and was sentenced to life imprisonment with no possibility of parole for thirty years. He is presently serving his sentence and has made four unsuccessful escape attempts since his incarceration.

Taracithio Gate wa Baragu

(GUN)

IN 1945, BRITAIN'S EAST AFRICAN ARMY SERVICE CORPS was stationed outside Nairobi, Kenya. On Friday, August 24, female army personnel gathered as usual at the McMillan Library in Nairobi for the drive back to camp. Ordinarily, an army truck, driven by a native African driver accompanied by a female sergeant, picked up the women promptly at 11 P.M. On the night in question, the African driver was Taracithio Gate wa Baragu, who had served in the army for three years. He was accompanied by Staff Sergeant Josephine Aston.

The truck never did show up at the library, and the waiting women made their way back to camp any way they could. When Jo Aston didn't return on schedule, her superiors inquired about the truck. They discovered that it too was missing. In the wee hours of the morning, authorities sought out driver Baragu.

He told military police that he had driven to Nairobi with Jo Aston the night before. A few minutes after they left camp, she asked him to pick up a male army sergeant, who jumped onto the back of the truck. This sergeant was let off at Sadler Street, at the rear of the municipal market. Baragu went on to say that he proceeded toward the McMillan Library, where he was to pick up the servicewomen. He had only gone a short distance when a male member of the RAF approached the truck. Baragu stopped. Jo Aston alighted to talk to the man. Baragu took this opportunity to make his way to the market to heed the call of nature. When he returned, he reported, he could find neither his truck nor Staff Sergeant Aston.

Baragu told the police that he didn't hear or see anything unusual. He made his way back to camp on foot, crossing the Nairobi River on stepping stones. He was let into camp by a sentry manning a side gate. Baragu sought out his African orderly sergeant to report the loss of the truck. When he found the sergeant asleep, he decided not to wake him. After all, to his way of thinking, nothing could be done until morning. Baragu took off his clothing and went to sleep. The inference taken from Baragu's story was clear. The airman and Jo Aston had taken off in the truck. Quite possibly they had met with an accident.

Bright and early that morning, someone reported seeing the truck in a ditch outside Nairobi. Military police rushed to the scene. There, in the ditch, under a foot and a half of water, about a hundred feet from the truck, they found the body of Jo Aston. She was clothed only in a necktie, brassiere and stockings. Her missing clothing was later found in a hole near a riverbank. Jo, who was engaged to be married to a serviceman in England, had been wearing an engagement ring. The ring was missing from her finger. An autopsy indicated that sexual intercourse had taken place, most probably while the victim was unconscious.

Jo Aston would have celebrated her twenty-fifth birthday the day after she was murdered. She was looking forward to her marriage. The Second World War had been over for a mere ten days. The world was Jo Aston's oyster, until those few minutes when someone had attacked her on a lonely road outside Nairobi.

Driver Baragu was immediately suspected. His clothing was confiscated and found to be damp. So was clothing found in his kit bag. His boots were soaking wet. His webbing belt was damp to the touch. Sentries with whom Baragu claimed to have spoken when he entered camp were questioned. None remembered seeing him return to camp, nor had they spoken to him. The sergeant whom Baragu claimed to have picked up and let off on Sadler Street was located. He alone corroborated the driver's story.

Less than twelve hours after the discovery of the truck and Jo Aston's body, Baragu was charged with murder.

The investigation into the murder continued. Baragu explained that he did not get his boots wet when he crossed the Nairobi River. He had washed them inside and out that night, as was his custom. He went on to state that he had washed most of the contents of his kit on the afternoon of the crime. When water was cut off at the camp, as sometimes happened, he put his half-completed wash back in his kit. This accounted for the contents of his kit being damp.

A fingerprint expert stated that he had found several indecipherable fingerprints on the steering wheel of the truck. He had also found six complete prints made by Baragu.

Dr. R.M. Dowdeswell, a pathologist, revealed that Jo's body bore multiple bruises. She was bruised on the forehead, chin, ear, hand, wrist and right shoulder blade. Death was due to drowning. She had received a severe blow under the chin, which had probably caused unconsciousness. It appeared that the woman had been attacked by someone who had been taught unarmed combat. Algae removed from the ditch matched algae taken from Baragu's clothing.

Plaster casts of footprints at the scene matched one of Jo's shoes, as well as those of the suspect. Some of the prints matched Jo's stockinged foot. It appeared from the evidence that she had lost one shoe, possibly when the truck hit the ditch. As she attempted to hobble away, her adversary caught up to her and attacked.

On October 9, Baragu stood trial for the murder of Josephine Aston. The prosecution presented much of the evidence outlined above. They claimed that after Baragu dropped off the sergeant, he had Jo at his mercy. He had sped away at great speed, making it impossible for her to jump from the vehicle. When the truck went into the ditch, she jumped out and limped away, only to be caught, knocked unconscious, sexually attacked and put in the ditch to die.

Baragu took the witness stand in his own defence. He claimed to know absolutely nothing about the murder. The missing truck had not been reported because he saw no point in doing so until morning. He had filled the radiator of the truck with water and had splashed water on his clothing. The dampness of his boots had not been caused by walking through the ditch water, nor from crossing the Nairobi River, but simply because he washed his boots each night. He had only half completed his wash, as he had previously stated, when he placed his clothing in his kit bag. Unfortunately, no other soldiers had seen him wash his clothing, but it was confirmed that water had been turned off on the day of the murder, as Baragu claimed.

Baragu didn't have a chance. He was found guilty of murder. Before being sentenced, he was allowed to make a last statement. He pointed out that, as an African, he had never received unarmed training. Certainly, anyone driving his truck after him could have obliterated their fingerprints, while leaving his intact on the steering wheel. Baragu asked the court, if he had driven away and raped the deceased, why was he not scratched? While algae taken from the ditch matched algae on his clothing, the same algae could be found in many other locations.

Baragu pointed out that if he had killed the woman, why had he hidden her clothing and made no attempt to hide or destroy his own? If he had robbed the victim of her ring, why was it not found in his kit bag with his other belongings? Why was no semen found on his clothing if he had committed rape?

After listening patiently, the presiding judge sentenced Baragu to death. On February 15, 1946, Baragu's appeal was dismissed. He was hanged on April 24. Baragu never deviated from the story he told when he was first awakened a few hours after his truck was reported missing.

Up to the present day, there are those who believe an innocent man was executed. Was there really an RAF officer who jumped into Baragu's truck and drove away to rape and murder Jo Aston? Was the murderer someone she knew well, someone who may have been jealous of her engagement, someone who struck out in a frenzy?

Can anyone restrain a woman from jumping from a moving army truck while driving? It has been suggested that someone with a gun could do the job. What happened to Jo's engagement ring? Did Baragu hide it on the way back to camp with the idea of retrieving it later?

It is these little unsolved mysteries that make truth stranger than fiction.

Doug Worth

(Hands)

THIS IS THE STORY of two losers. One, abused in prison as a teenager, turned out to be a sexual sadist, pedophile and murderer. The other, a tragedy of our times, was his 12-year-old victim.

Douglas Robert Worth was born on January 7, 1952, in New Glasgow, Nova Scotia, just down the road from his parents' home in Stellarton. Times could be tough in that part of Nova Scotia when the coal mines were down or the Trenton Steel Works was operating part-time.

Doug, one of ten Worth children, got into trouble at age 16 when he stole a car and received a two-year jail sentence. A month before his sentence was up, while out on a day pass, he stole a car and raped a girl in New Glasgow. He received two years for breach of prison regulations, two years for stealing a car and two years for rape. Doug Worth was well on his way to a lifetime of crime.

In 1974, Worth was released from prison on mandatory supervision. Now a bitter young man who claimed that he had been sexually abused while incarcerated, he left the Atlantic provinces to roam the rest of Canada. Worth made his way to Oakville, Ontario. In August 1975, he assaulted a police officer. For this offence he was jailed for thirty days. Upon release, Worth travelled to Kenora, Ontario, where he tried his luck at breaking and entering. His luck was out to lunch, as it had been all his life. He was convicted of two counts of B 'n' E and found himself once more behind bars, this time for ninety days.

Once he'd served his sentence, the displaced Maritimer made his way to Edmonton, Alberta. It didn't take long. In 1979, he was convicted of raping a 19-year-old girl and was sentenced to eight years in jail.

While serving time in a Fort Saskatchewan, Alberta, prison, Worth met Mary Kelly, who was visiting a relative in the pen. When Worth received a day pass, he spent it with Mary. He didn't return on schedule and was transferred to a maximum-security prison in Edmonton and later to Kingston Penitentiary.

Doug Worth spent every day of his eight-year sentence in prison. He was released on June 11, 1987, exactly eight years to the day he was sentenced. Kingston penal authorities placed him on a plane to Edmonton and told Edmonton officials that one bad apple was headed their way. In Edmonton, Worth moved in with his old flame, Mary Kelly, a divorced mother of three. Her daughter and son, both in their twenties, moved out when Worth moved in. The third Kelly offspring, a boy of 14, stayed with his mother.

Worth obtained work as a roofer, although he had taken a meat-cutting course while in prison. Kelly worked in a restaurant. At home, she was physically abused by her common-law husband. Worth beat her at the least provocation. Sometimes he choked her. But she never left her man, nor did she report the abuse to authorities.

In September 1987, Worth and Kelly quit their jobs, sold their belongings and, together with Mary's teenage son, moved to Orangeville, Ontario, where Kelly's adult daughter lived. The very next night, a Friday, Kelly and her daughter went to a bingo game. They won $600. Worth was elated. He confiscated the winnings, as well as $800 they had received for their belongings back in Edmonton, and took off to visit his family in Nova Scotia. A month later, he returned to Orangeville minus the $1,400.

Worth tried his hand as a labourer with a construction crew. A month after returning from Nova Scotia, he decided to leave Kelly and move into a rooming house at 244 Main Street North in Brampton. Mary Kelly, despite the beatings, was very upset at Worth moving out. She and her son moved back to Edmonton.

Trina Campbell stood four-foot-eleven and weighed eighty-five pounds at the time of her death. If ever a youngster was born to a life of hard knocks, it was Trina. Born in Melford, Saskatchewan, to an alcoholic mother and father, she and her two brothers were taken by child welfare workers when her parents parted company. Trina was 9 years old when her mother was killed jumping from a truck while intoxicated. In 1984, the Campbell family of Streetsville, Ontario, adopted all three children. Trina was enrolled in school and did well enough, but she was a troubled youngster. She often stole things from her home. When confronted, she ran away. In short, she was a problem child.

It was decided that Trina would function best in a group home located in Brampton. She often ran away from the group home as well. In the wee hours of the morning of December 11, 1987, she was found in a local doughnut shop and was taken back to the group home by Peel Regional Police. That day, it was decided that Trina would attend school as usual. She was picked up by bus and returned at around five in the afternoon. There is some evidence that Trina spent the next few days in a dilapidated house often frequented by vagrants and runaways. The 12-year-old was reported missing to police.

A few days later, a man who had spent time in prison with Doug Worth spotted him on the street in Brampton. Worth had a young girl in tow. He was leading her by the arm. It appeared to the man that the girl was being coerced by his old prison buddy.

Later, he and Worth met in a tavern and had a few beers. The friend noted that Worth had blood on his hands and shirt. When he inquired, Worth said he'd been in a fist fight. The friend asked, "What about the girl I saw you with earlier?" Worth replied ominously, "She got everything she deserved."

What had happened to Trina Campbell? According to later testimony, Worth told Dr. Robert Woodhill, a psychiatrist, that he had met Trina in a store and figured from her actions that she was a runaway. He befriended her, took her to his rooming house, where he sexually attacked then killed her. On December 14, 1987, Doug Worth took the body of Trina Campbell out of his room to a field behind the house. He covered the body as best he could with bushes. That same day, he sought a new place to stay. A few days later, he found a room in a private home. Worth moved in, then took off for Stellarton, Nova Scotia, to spend Christmas with his family. During the holidays, Worth drank more than usual and was notably depressed. He was a man with a problem and that problem lay in a field behind a rooming house in Brampton, Ontario. Worth had to tell someone.

Worth's sister Sharon was married to Wayne Lewis. Worth confided in his brother-in-law, but he didn't tell the exact truth. He told Lewis that he'd been in a fight with a man he had met in a bar. He had been forced to kill the man, a drifter with no family. Something within Worth's psyche wouldn't let him admit that he had murdered a child. Worth went on to tell his brother-in-law that he had been seen with this man and if the body were discovered, he would be apprehended. He planned to return to Brampton to bury the body.

On January 2, Worth returned to Brampton. Two weeks later, Mary Kelly returned from out West and moved into her own accommodations. She started seeing Worth again, but he hadn't changed. He still beat her. The pair rented a car to visit relatives in St. Catharines. During the visit, Worth attacked Mary and tossed her out of the car. This time, Mary reported the beating. Worth was picked up but soon released. He patched up his difficulties with Mary.

By mid-February, Worth had fed Mary a string of lies to cover his latest plan. He told her, "I've done something really bad. Don't get the wrong idea. It's not a body, it's not a woman, it's not a man. I just stole some guns." He went on to explain that he had to move the guns from their hiding place because there was a witness who knew where he had stashed the weapons. But there were no guns, only the tiny nude body of Trina Campbell, which had been lying behind his rooming house under some bushes for over two months.

On March 4, 1988, Doug instructed Mary Kelly to rent a Dodge Colt from Budget Rent-A-Car in Brampton. They would move those guns he was always talking about. Instead of acting immediately, the urge to return to his birthplace overcame him. He and Mary made a quick trip to Nova Scotia and returned March 11.

Two days later, Mary drove Doug to the field behind his old rooming house. He left the car carrying an empty hockey bag. Mary waited in the parked vehicle. About a half an hour later, Doug returned with a bulging hockey bag and placed it in the trunk. He was perspiring and appeared to be nervous and pale. All the while, Peel Regional Police were trying to locate the missing Trina Campbell. Ten thousand flyers describing Trina were distributed throughout the country.

Doug and Mary made their way to the Orangeville area with their macabre cargo. It had been a hard night's work. Doug was tired. He and Mary parked and soon fell asleep in the car. One can only imagine what went through Doug Worth's mind when he was awakened by an Orangeville police officer. The officer, who had no idea that he had stumbled upon one of the most bizarre killers in Ontario's history, advised the occupants to move on. Doug mumbled to Mary, "We're all right, long as he doesn't look in the trunk."

The Dodge Colt made its way to Terra Nova, where Doug told Mary to park until daylight. When dawn broke, they were noticed. A customer walked into the Terra Nova general store at 7:50 for coffee. He told Mr. Bernier, the owner, that there was a suspicious-looking couple parked down the road. Mr. Bernier called the Ontario Provincial Police detachment at Shelburne, but when he was placed on hold he grew impatient and hung up. Only months later did the folks of Terra Nova learn they had had a murderer among them that morning. It was time. Doug took the hockey bag out of the trunk and lugged it into a nearby field. Mary observed what she thought was blood oozing out of the bag. When she mentioned this to Doug, he told her it was transmission fluid.

Police believe Doug visited the body behind his rooming house many times. When he discovered it wouldn't fit into his hockey bag, he systematically dissected the body with a hacksaw. Doug had taken a meat-cutting course while in prison and so knew something about what he was doing.

Now divested of the body, the pair made their way back to Brampton. Realizing that blood had dripped out of the bag, staining the trunk, Doug had Mary's young son and another lad wash out the trunk. They noticed bloodstains and they too were told the stains had been caused by transmission fluid. The boys couldn't remove the stains from the rug. Next day, Doug asked Mary to cut out the stained portion of the rug. She told him she had done as he'd instructed, but in reality she hadn't bothered. The vehicle was returned to the car-rental agency.

On March 30, 1988, Doug, Mary and her young son left both their rooms in Brampton, stealing anything of value. They made off with jewellery, towels, cigarettes and loose change. Once again, Doug Worth was going back to Nova Scotia in a rented car. Doug discussed his most pressing problem with his sister and brother-in-law. He told Sharon and Wayne that he had dismembered a body and moved it from behind his old rooming house. Doug was curious about how long it would take a body to decompose. He also told his sister he thought teeth were the only way police could identify a decomposed body. Without funds, it was impossible for Doug to get back to Ontario to dispose of his victim's head. He thought it would be a good idea to bring it back to Nova Scotia and bury it deep in the woods.

Usually, Doug referred to his victim as a man, but a few times in relating his story he slipped up and called his victim a girl. Somewhere along the line, he saw a poster of Trina Campbell. Doug almost flipped out, not for what he had done, but from the urgency to dispose of his victim's head.

Doug and Mary moved from Stellarton to their own apartment in Pictou. On April 22, a teenage lad overheard Doug, Mary and the Lewises discussing a murder and the moving of a body. He related the story to his guidance counsellor, who took the tale seriously and contacted the RCMP in Pictou. They, in turn, contacted Peel Regional Police. Was there anyone who had been reported missing around December 14 of the previous year? There was only one outstanding missing person: 12-year-old Trina Campbell.

Under the direction of Inspector Rod Piukkala of the Peel Regional Police, an investigation into Doug Worth's background was conducted. It was soon discovered that Doug had a long police record that included rape. Then police located the vehicle used to transport the body at Budget in Brampton. Inside the trunk were the telltale bloodstains. Laboratory analyses of the most sophisticated nature were conducted at the Forensic Sciences Centre, which determined that the stains had been made by decomposed human blood. Everything fit: the missing Trina, the bloodstains and the youngster's story in Pictou. Still, police had no body, no confession and no real proof that a murder had been committed.

Piukkala dispatched Detective-Sergeant Edward Toye and Detective-Sergeant Len Favreau to Nova Scotia. With the help of the RCMP, they would learn more about Doug Worth without revealing to friends and relatives that he was the prime suspect in what they felt certain was a murder case. The undercover officers learned of Doug's hatred of women and his reputation in the area, but as no new developments took place, it was decided that the RCMP would keep tabs on Doug while the Ontario officers returned home.

Toye and Favreau were scheduled to fly back to Toronto on the night of May 6, 1988. Unexpectedly, at 10 A.M. that same day, Wayne Lewis walked into the local police station and told the whole story. He revealed that Worth wanted to return to Ontario to retrieve the head of a person he had murdered and dissected. Doug hadn't left because he was broke. Toye and Favreau cancelled their flights. When Wayne Lewis's wife, Sharon, was informed that her husband had told what he knew, she corroborated his statement.

The Lewises agreed to co-operate with investigating officers. Outfitted with recording equipment, they engaged Doug in a conversation in which he gave what amounted to a confession. Police rented an old car and gave Wayne $300. Wayne, under instructions, gave the car and the money to Doug so he could return to Ontario to complete the task of disposing of the victim's head. Doug thanked the Lewises profusely. He inquired if they had a spare shovel. They didn't.

Within forty-five minutes, Doug and Mary were on their way to Ontario. With Piukkala acting as anchor man, the pair was tailed all the way to Quebec City, where fresh surveillance officers were put on the job of following them. In Port Hope, Doug unsuccessfully attempted to purchase a shovel. In Brampton, he scoured a few construction sites, obviously looking for a shovel.

The man with the gruesome mission made his way north and parked close to the spot where he had placed the body. He was waiting for daylight, unaware he was under surveillance. He left the car carrying a gym bag while Mary waited. He wasn't long returning with the bag, which was placed on the back seat. Doug stopped at a Shell station to dispose of a pair of gloves, which were immediately picked up by the trailing officers. Down Highway 10 he and Mary proceeded. Ironically, they drove past Peel Regional Police headquarters before being pulled over. Inside the gym bag was the decomposed head of Trina Campbell.

During his trial, it was revealed that Doug had often bragged in prison that after his release he would "go to a public school in Kingston with an axe and chop as many children as he could." He once told prison psychologist Sharon Williams he would "wreak havoc on society" as revenge for his years in prison. On another occasion, he stated he would "make serial killer Clifford Olson look like a choirboy."

Doug pleaded innocent by reason of insanity. He was judged to be sane and guilty of second-degree murder. Later on, the charge of being an accessory after the fact of murder against Mary Kelly was dropped.

Doug Worth was sentenced to life imprisonment with no possibility of parole for twenty-three years. Before being sentenced, he yelled from the prisoner's box, "First of all, I'm not a cold-hearted son of a bitch. You're all saying I'm a monster. I've got feelings. I feel for people. I've got to get this out before I kill somebody up at the detention centre with my pent-up emotions."

Dr. Thomas Young

(SOMMONOFORM)

IT IS DIFFICULT to apprehend a murderer when no crime is known to have been committed.

Grace Hunt hailed from a well-known California family. When she met and married Patrick Grogan in 1909, her happiness seemed assured. After all, Grogan had made a fortune in the olive trade and was a bona fide millionaire. Grace and Pat had one son, Charles.

As the years drifted by, Grace and her husband agreed to disagree. When Charles was 10, she and Patrick were divorced. The divorce was a civilized affair. Grace was given custody of Charles and a cool half-million dollars to soothe any hurts and to keep the wolf from the door. There were wolves of a far different kind at Grace's door. She was an attractive young woman with oodles of cash, just waiting for the right swain to come a-calling.

Two years later, when Patrick died, leaving the balance of his estate to his son, with Grace sole administratrix, she became an extremely attractive catch indeed. After Patrick had been duly planted, Grace became a regular in Los Angeles's social circles. Many a young stud with one eye on Grace's figure and the other on the figures in her bank book courted the widow with a vengeance. One such suitor emerged with the prize.

Dr. Thomas Young was a newly turned-out dentist who had decided to establish his practice among the socially prominent of Los Angeles. He homed in on Grace like the lead hound pursuing the fox. Initially, Grace rejected the dentist, but eventually his persistence paid off. In the winter of 1923, Grace became Mrs. Thomas Young. For two years, Dr. Young's practice flourished, as did his marriage to Grace. The attractive couple were seen in the best restaurants and were asked to the most prestigious parties. The Youngs were definitely leading the good life in Lotus Land.

And then it happened. On February 22, 1925, Dr. Young contacted Los Angeles police, informing them that his wife, Grace, had disappeared. The dentist told his story. Twenty-four hours earlier, he and Grace had left their Beverley Glen cottage for dinner in Venice. They had a few drinks, enjoyed dinner and were about to leave the restaurant when they happened to bump into a woman he knew. It was nothing more than a chance meeting, but afterwards Grace flew into a jealous rage. According to Young, this was not an isolated incident. Grace, he told police, was insanely jealous. Embarrassed, he hustled his wife out to their car.

While driving back to Los Angeles, Grace was beside herself with rage. During the trip, she took a swing at her husband and broke his glasses. Eventually, she quieted down and even apologized for causing a scene. The Youngs made up and decided to drop into Los Angeles's Hotel Biltmore to dance and have a few drinks.

Grace excused herself in the lobby of the hotel and made her way to the powder room. As far as her husband knew, no one had seen her since that moment. Dr. Young added that Grace was carrying $150,000 in negotiable securities and all her jewellery. In total, Grace was lugging around a quarter of a million dollars on her person. Young's statement begged the question—why would a woman carry a fortune in her purse? Dr. Young told police he thought his wife may have been afraid that their cottage in Beverley Glen was susceptible to burglary.

The unusual disappearance made front-page headlines. It's not often that a socially prominent woman disappears carrying a fortune in her purse. A few weeks after the disappearance, Grace's friends began to receive letters, apparently in Grace's handwriting. The letters were postmarked from towns and cities within five hundred miles of Los Angeles. In these letters, Grace informed friends that she was tired of the incessant arguments with her husband. She planned to get away from it all for a while in Europe.

It all seemed so perfect, except for one thing. Anyone who knew Grace realized that she would write or contact her son, Charles, if she were leaving her home for any prolonged period of time. Grace's father, Earl R. Hunt, was not satisfied with the way the investigation was being conducted. He hired the famed Burns Detective Agency to find out what had happened to his daughter. Dr. Young hired another detective agency to locate his wife. In all, there were now three different organizations searching for Grace Young.

Months passed. The investigation wound down. Dr. Young and Charles spent a lot of time together at their cottage. Since his mother's disappearance, Charles Grogan had changed his will, which had previously left everything to his mother. His new will made his stepfather sole beneficiary. Gradually, Young started to live a normal life again. He even threw a few parties for friends.

Early that summer, the Burns Detective Agency came up with the disconcerting information that Dr. Young's secretary had been seen wearing one of Grace's rings. When questioned, the secretary said Young had shown up at work one day with the ring. She had worn it for a day or so and had returned it to him. For the first time, it was discovered that Dr. Young had lied. He had told police that his wife had taken all her jewellery with her. Witnesses were located who swore Grace had been carrying a tiny purse on the night she disappeared. It could not possibly have held all her jewellery as well as negotiable securities. The Burns boys shared their information with the authorities.

A meeting was held. It was decided that the various organizations conducting inquiries into Grace Young's disappearance share their information. It seems everyone had found out something that incriminated Dr. Young.

The Burns Agency had unearthed the hitherto unknown fact that Young had been married twice before.

Police were successful in obtaining a search warrant to go over the Beverley Glen cottage during Young's absence. They found a three-carat diamond ring. Dr. Young was questioned. When he was shown the ring, he was as cool as a cucumber, claiming that Grace often placed various pieces of her jewellery in the side pockets of their automobile. He had found the ring in the car and had placed it with his personal papers in the cottage. Dr. Young apologized for not informing police that he had found it.

Everyone concerned was now sure that Young was lying, but they had absolutely no proof that he had committed any crime. In fact, they had no positive proof that any crime had been committed at all.

On June 14, 1925, Young was brought to police headquarters for another round of questioning. Worn to a frazzle by the constant harassment, he broke down and revealed what had happened to Grace. He blurted out that she had accidentally struck her head and had fallen into a cistern at their cottage.

Police rushed out to the cottage. In the cistern, under a thin layer of concrete, they uncovered the body of Grace Young. A piece of rubber tubing was in her mouth. Dr. Young changed his story. He now told police that after an argument in the hotel, he had taken his wife to his office, where he had given her enough scotch to render her unconscious. He then drove to the cottage and put her to bed. He administered a gas called sommonoform (used by dentists during that era) through a rubber tube until Grace was dead. Then he threw her body into the cistern.

The very next day, he had Charles mix the cement that was to cover Grace's body. Young told police, "I had covered the body with newspapers and I thought it would be a great joke on the boy to have him unknowingly cover his mother's body with cement." Dr. Young went on to state that he had killed Grace to get rid of her and obtain her fortune. He revealed that he was planning to kill his stepson, Charles, and place him in the cistern as well.

Dr. Young's murder trial was in its tenth day when he was found dead in his cell. He had managed to strangle himself with a piece of wire.